GAME THEORY AT WORK

How to Use Game Theory to Outthink
and Outmaneuver Your Competition

GAME THEORY AT WORK

How to Use Game Theory to Outthink
and Outmaneuver Your Competition

James D. Miller

McGraw-Hill
New York   Chicago   San Francisco   Lisbon   London
Madrid   Mexico City   Milan   New Delhi
San Juan   Seoul   Singapore
Sydney   Toronto

McGraw-Hill

A Division of The McGraw·Hill Companies

4 5 6 7 8 9 0   DOC/DOC   0 9 8 7 6 5 4

ISBN 0-07-140020-6

McGraw-Hill books are available at special discounts to use as premiums and sales promotions, or for use in corporate training programs. For more information, please write to the Director of Special Sales, Professional Publishing, McGraw-Hill, Two Penn Plaza, New York, NY 10121-2298. Or contact your local bookstore.

Library of Congress Cataloging-in-Publication Data

Miller, James D.
    Game theory at work : how to use game theory to outthink and
outmaneuver your competition / by James D. Miller.
        p. cm.
    ISBN 0-07-140020-6 (hardcover : alk. paper)
    1. Management games. I. Title: How to use game theory to outthink and
outmaneuver your competition. II. Title.
  HD30.26 .M54 2003
  658.4'0353—dc21   2002013681

 This book is printed on recycled, acid-free paper
containing a minimum of 50% recycled, de-inked paper.

CONTENTS

ACKNOWLEDGMENTS

I'm extremely grateful to my wife Debbie for her stylistic assistance and proofreading, to my editor Kelli Christiansen for her patiently shepherding a first-time author, to my parents and grandfather for their embedding in me a love of learning, and to the students of Smith College for teaching me how to explain economics.

GAME THEORY AT WORK

How to Use Game Theory to Outthink
and Outmaneuver Your Competition

1

INTRODUCTION

"Honour and profit lie not in one sack."

Proverb[1]

Y OUR LIFE CONSISTS OF GAMES, situations in which you compete for a high score. Game theory studies how smart, ruthless people should act and interact in strategic settings. This book will teach you to solve games. In some games you will negotiate for a raise; in others you will strive to ensure that an employee works as hard as possible. Sometimes you will know everything, while in other games you will have to guess at what others know that you don't. Occasionally competitors will have to work together to survive, while in other situations cooperation will be impossible since the winner will take all. Many of the games will seemingly have nothing to do with business, but will be presented to give you insights into strategy. Since the games that businesspeople play are both complicated and diverse, this book will provide you with the intellectual tools necessary to recognize what kind of game you're playing, and, more important, to maximize your payoff in any game you're in.

In the world of game theory there exists no mercy or compassion, only self-interest. Most people care solely about

1

themselves and everyone knows and accepts this. In game theory land your employer would never give you a raise because it "would be a nice thing to do." You get the raise only if you convince your employer that it serves his interests to give you more money. Game theory land resembles the hypercompetitive all-against-all environment that often characterizes business in the capitalist world. But, as this book will show, even when everyone acts totally ruthlessly and extremely competitively, the logic of game theory often dictates that selfish people cooperate and even treat each other with loyalty and respect.

This book is fluff free! *Game Theory at Work* won't teach you about power-chants, discuss the importance of balancing work and family, or inspire you to become a more caring leader. This book will instead help you to outstrategize, or at least keep up with, competitors inside and outside your company.

Economists have devoted much thought to how you should play games of strategy, and these ideas, which constitute game theory, influence the thinking of businesspeople, military strategists, and even biologists. They also infiltrate everyday life, whether you recognize it or not. Almost all MBA students and undergraduate economics majors will formally encounter game theory in the classroom. Not understanding game theory puts you at a tactical disadvantage when playing against those who do.

You will find game theory ideally suited for solitary study because it's *interesting*. Sure, accounting is at least as important to business as game theory, but do you really want to spend your free time memorizing the rules of what constitutes a debit? Perhaps the most interesting thing that human beings do is compete. Game theory, the study of conflict, illuminates how rational, self-interested people struggle against each other for supremacy.

In game theory players often base their moves on what they think other people might do. But if your move is based on what your opponents might do, and their moves are based on what they think you are going to do, then your move will in fact be somewhat based on what you think your opponents think that you will do! Game theory can get complicated, but then so can business.

Ideally, you would learn game theory by reading a textbook. Actually, this isn't true. Your time is valuable, and textbooks are designed to be studied over several months. So ideally you should learn game theory by reading a relatively short, accessible book such as this. *Game Theory at Work* is more accessible than a textbook, but perhaps more challenging to read than the typical mass-market book. To master game theory you must engage in active learning: you need to struggle with puzzles and (obviously) games. The Appendix contains study questions to many chapters. Although you could follow the entire book even if you skip all these questions, struggling with them will make you a stronger player.

This book will challenge your intellect by showing how strange and seemingly paradoxical results manifest themselves when humans compete. Among this book's lessons are the following:

- Never hire someone too eager to work for you.
- Have less trust in smokers.
- Many people in business exhibit honesty not because they are moral but because they are greedy.
- Eliminating choices can increase your payoff.
- Burning money can increase your wealth.
- Stock prices respond quickly to new information.
- Day-traders still need to worry about their stock's long-term prospects.
- Exposing yourself to potential humiliation can increase your negotiating strength when seeking a raise.
- Inmates in mental institutions have a few negotiating advantages over their somewhat more sane corporate counterparts.
- Learning about Odysseus' recruitment into the Trojan War provides insight into why stores issue coupons.

You might ask, "Will reading this book help me make money?" A true game-theoretic answer might be that since you have probably already bought this book, I don't really care what benefit you would receive from reading it, so why should I bother answering the question? In fact, you likely only purchased this book after reading the jacket, the table of contents and maybe the first paragraph of the introduction. Perhaps I should only bother putting a lot of effort into these very small parts of the book and just ramble on for the rest of it to fill up space. For the rest of the book I could just ramble on and on by being very, very, very verbose as I repeat myself over and over again by just rambling on to fill up the space that I have to fill up for you to think that this book is thick enough to be worth the book's purchase price. After all, I have more important things to do in my life than write for the pleasure of people I have never even met. Of course, I like money, and the more copies of this book that sell, the more money I'll get. If you do like this book, you might suggest to a friend that she buy a copy. Also, if I choose to write another book, you will be more likely to buy it if you enjoy this one, so probably for purely selfish reasons I should make some attempt to provide you with useful information. Furthermore, as of this writing my publisher, McGraw-Hill, still has the contractual right to reject this manuscript. Since McGraw-Hill is a long-term player in the publishing game, they would be harmed by fooling book buyers into purchasing nicely wrapped crap. Alas, this means that if I manifestly fail to put anything of value in this book my publisher will demand the return of my advance. Beware, however, if you end up enjoying this book, it's not because I wrote it for the purpose of making you happy. I wrote it to maximize my own payoff. I don't care, in any way, about your welfare. It's just that the capitalist system under which books are produced in the United States creates incentives for me to seriously attempt to write a book that customers will enjoy and perhaps even benefit from reading.

WHAT EXACTLY IS GAME THEORY?

There are three parts to any game:

- A set of players
- Moves the players can make
- Payoffs the players might receive

The players choose their moves to maximize their payoff. Each player always assumes that other players are also trying to maximize their score.

Game theory gets interesting, however, only when there is tactical interaction, that is, when everyone tries to figure out their rivals' strategy before they move. Football (American or European) could be analyzed using game theory because the players try to determine their opponents' strategy before making their move. Bowling and golf are not interesting to game theorists because although players compete in these sports, they mostly ignore their competitors when formulating their moves because they have no control over how their competitor might play.

Mathematics dominates much of formal game theory. In an attempt to maximize this author's book royalties, however, *Game Theory at Work* keeps the math to a minimum. Fortunately, you can learn most of the practical applications of game theory without using any math more complicated than addition and subtraction. This book does, however, contain many figures and diagrams, and if you skip them you will learn little.

In game theory land people always act in their own self-interest, and consequently everyone lies whenever lying serves their interests. So, how can you make your threat or promise believable when your word is worthless? Chapter 2 considers the credibility of threats and promises.

THREATS, PROMISES, AND SEQUENTIAL GAMES

"A prince never lacks legitimate reasons to break his promise."

Machiavelli[1]

ONE SUMMER WHILE IN COLLEGE I had a job teaching simple computer programming to fourth graders. As an inexperienced teacher I made the mistake of acting like the children's friend, not their instructor. I told the students to call me Jim rather than Mr. Miller. Alas, my informality caused the students to have absolutely no fear of me. I found it difficult to maintain order and discipline in class until I determined how to threaten my students.

The children's parents were all going to attend the last day of class. Whereas the students might not have considered me a real teacher, they knew that their parents would. I discovered that although my students had no direct fear of me, they were afraid of what I might tell their parents, and I used this fear to control the children. If I merely told two students to stop hitting each other, they ignored me. If, however, I told the children that I would describe their behavior to their parents, then the hitting would immediately cease.

The children should not have believed my threat, however. After the summer ended, I would never see my students again, so I had absolutely nothing to gain by telling the parents that their children were not perfect angels. It was definitely not in my interest to say anything bad about my students since

- It would have upset their parents.
- I realized that their bad behavior was mostly my fault because I had not been acting like a real teacher.
- The people running this for-profit program would have been furious with me for angering their customers.

Since they were only fourth graders, it was understandable that my students (who were all very smart) didn't grasp that my threat was noncredible. When making threats in the business world, however, don't assume that your fellow game players have the trusting nature of fourth graders.

Let's model the game I played with my students. Figure 1 presents a game tree. The game starts at decision node A. At node A, a child decides whether or not to behave, and if he behaves, the game ends. If he doesn't behave, then the game moves to decision node B; and at B I have to decide whether to tell the parents that their child has misbehaved. In the actual game the children all believed that at B I would tell their parents. As a consequence the children chose to behave at A. Since it was not in my interest to inform the parents of any misbehavior, however, my only logical response at B would be to not tell their parents. If the children had a better understanding of game theory they would have anticipated my move at B and thus misbehaved at A. My students' irrational trust caused them to believe my noncredible threat.

CONTROLLING A WILD DAUGHTER

Parents, as well as teachers, often try to control their children's behavior with threats. Imagine that two parents fear their wild teenage

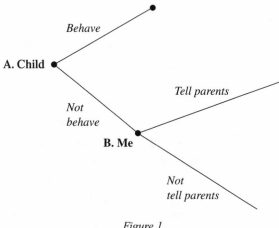

Figure 1

daughter will become pregnant. First, they try reason and urge her to be more careful. But when reason fails, the parents resort to threatening to disown their daughter and kick her out of the house if she becomes pregnant. Should the daughter believe her parents' threat? Not if she knows that her parents love her.

If the daughter trusts in her parents' love, then she will believe that the threat was made to improve her welfare. If the daughter became pregnant, she would need her parents more than ever. The daughter should thus realize that her caring parents would devote even more resources to her if she got pregnant. An intelligent but still wild daughter should ignore her parents' threat as lacking credibility. Sure, loving parents might threaten their daughter to dissuade her from having sex. If she gets pregnant, however, it would not be in the interest of caring parents to actually carry out the threat. The manifest love of the parents weakens their negotiating strength. Interestingly, if the daughter suspected that her parents didn't love her, then she might believe their threat, and all three of them would be better off.

Circumstances in life and business often arise where you would gain from making a believable threat. Unfortunately, game theory shows that many threats can and should be ignored, since a man is never as good as his word in game theory land. Game theory, fortunately, provides many means of making credible threats.

ELIMINATING OPTIONS

Normally, you benefit from choices. We usually think that the more options we have, the more ways we might profit. The existence of some choices, however, increases the difficulty of issuing credible threats. Consequently, eliminating options can increase your payoff.

Imagine that you're a medieval military commander seeking to capture the castle depicted in Figure 2. Your troops have just sailed over on boats to the castle's island. Everybody knows that if you were determined to fight to the end, then your army would ultimately be victorious. Unfortunately, the battle would be long and bloody. You would lose much of your army in a full-blown battle for the castle, so you desperately pray for your enemy's surrender. Since the enemy knows that it would lose the battle, one might think that it indeed should surrender.

Unfortunately, your enemy has heard of your compassion. You don't care at all about the welfare of the enemy, but you do worry about the lives of your own soldiers (perhaps for selfish reasons). The enemy correctly suspects that if it holds out long enough, you will be sickened by your losses and retreat, for although you desire the castle, you wouldn't decimate your army to obtain it.

Your opponents would immediately capitulate if they believed you would fight to the end, so if you could make a believable threat to fight until victory, they would give up and you would not have to risk your troops. Unfortunately, a mere threat to fight to the finish lacks credibility, so what should you do? You should burn your own boats!

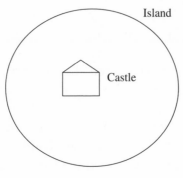

Figure 2

Imagine that if your boats were burned, it would take many months for your allies to bring new boats to the island to rescue your army. Meanwhile, you would perish if you did not occupy the castle. Losing your boats would compel you to fight on until victory. More important, your enemy would believe that with your boats burned you would never retreat. Surrender is the optimal response of the enemy to the burning of your boats. By destroying your boats, you limit your choices. You can no longer take the easy way out of the battle by retreating. Eliminating the option of retreating makes your threat credible and allows you to win a bloodless victory.

Cortez, conqueror of the Aztecs, employed this boat-burning tactic.[2] Shortly after landing in Mexico, Cortez destroyed his ships, thus showing his potential enemies and allies that he would not be quickly driven back to Europe. Consider the effect this tactic had on local tribes that were considering allying with Cortez against the powerful Aztecs. No tribe would want to ally with Cortez if it thought that he might someday abandon his fight against the Aztecs and return to Europe, for then the tribe would be left to the mercy of their mighty human-sacrificing neighbors. Cortez would likely have promised local tribes that regardless of how poorly he did in his fight against the Aztecs he would not leave until they were vanquished. Such a promise, by itself, was not believable. If Cortez had not burned his ships, his potential allies would have thought that Cortez would run away if he suffered an early defeat. By burning his ships and eliminating the option of quickly retreating to Europe, Cortez guaranteed that he wouldn't leave his allies. As we shall see, eliminating options can be a useful strategy in business as well as military negotiations.

ASKING FOR A RAISE

You desperately desire a $20,000 per year raise. The company you work for likes money as much as you do, however, so you will get the raise only if you can convince your boss that it is in her interest to give it to you. But why should your boss give you a raise? Why is it in her interest to be "nice" to you? If you have any chance at getting a raise, you contribute to your company, which would be worse off without your labors. Your best chance of obtaining a raise, therefore, lies in convincing your boss that you will leave if you don't get the money.

If you simply tell your boss that you will quit if you don't get the raise, she might not believe your threat. For your boss to take your threat to quit seriously, she must think that it would be in your self-interest to walk away if you're not given the money. The best way to make your threat credible would be to prove to the boss that another company would pay you $20,000 a year more. (Of course, if you've found another firm that's willing to give you the raise, then you don't need to read a book on game theory to learn how to get the extra $20,000.)

Another way to get the raise would be to tell everyone in the firm that you will definitely quit if you don't obtain it. Ideally, you should put yourself in a position where you would suffer complete humiliation if you were denied the money and still stayed in your job. Your goal should be to make it as painful as possible for you to stay if you weren't given the salary increase. This tactic is the equivalent of reducing your options. By effectively eliminating your choice to stay, your boss will find it in her self-interest to give you the money because she knows you will have to leave if you don't get the raise.

Figure 3 presents the game tree for this raise negotiation game. The game starts at *A* where you ask for a raise. Then at *B* your boss has the option of giving it to you or not. If she does not give you the raise, the game moves to *C*, where you either stay at your job or quit. There are thus three possible outcomes to the game, and Figure 3 shows what your boss gets at each outcome. Obviously, your boss would consider giving you the raise only if she knew that at *C* you would quit. So, you need to make your threat to quit credible. You do this either by getting a high payoff if you quit or a low payoff if you stay, given that your raise request was rejected. Interestingly, if you got your raise, then the game would never get to *C*. Your boss's perception of what you would have done at *C*, however, was still the cause of your triumph. Often, what might have happened, but never did, determines the outcome of the game.

RELINQUISHING CONTROL

Giving up control of events can also strengthen your negotiating position. Imagine that you're now a manager trying to resist wage increases. Your employees are extremely valuable to you, but unfortu-

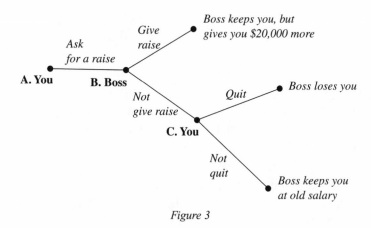

Figure 3

nately your workers are aware of their importance and know that you would be reluctant to lose them. You consequently have a weak nego-tiating position, for if your employees could ever convince you that they would leave if not given a raise, then you would give in to their salary demands. Giving up control of salary decisions could free you from this dilemma. Relinquishing control allows you to credibly claim that you can't increase wages.

Of course, your precious employees could play their games with the people who now make the salary decisions. But these new salary setters might not care if an employee left. For example, the loss of an efficient secretary who understands your routine would be devastating. If the secretary grasps his importance, he has a very strong negotiat-ing position if you have the power to grant him a raise. A manager in human resources, however, might not care if your efficient secretary quit. If your secretary had to negotiate with this indifferent manager, then his position would be weakened because the HR manager would be more willing to allow your secretary to leave the company than you would.

Telling others that you have given up control is a common negoti-ating tactic. When lawyers try to settle lawsuits, they often claim that their client has authorized them to go only to a certain amount. If this limitation on the lawyer's authority is believed, then the lawyer's prom-ise to never accept a higher offer is credible. Broadcasting your lack of decision-making authority makes it easier to turn down unwanted requests.

An ancient English law punished communities that paid tribute to pirates.[3] Had a coastal community merely told pirates that they would never pay tribute, the pirates would probably not have believed them. The ancient law, however, made their statement more credible by effectively eliminating the option of paying tribute.

Smith College, where I teach, has a similar antitribute law that protects professors from students. At Smith College professors are not permitted to grant students extensions beyond the last day of finals, so students must go to their deans for such extensions. One might think this policy signals that Smith professors are administratively weak relative to deans. In fact, professors dislike dealing with students asking for extensions, so Smith professors are consequently made better off by a rule that circumscribes their extension-granting abilities. Managers can similarly benefit from limitations on their authority. Many managers, like professors, desire popularity and consequently dislike having to turn down their peoples' requests. It's much easier to say no when everyone understands that you lack the ability to say yes.

CUTTING OFF COMMUNICATIONS

Giving up control by cutting off communications would also help you capture our hypothetical castle. Recall that in the battle for the castle your enemies will surrender only if they believe you will fight until victory. To credibly commit to never retreating, you could first order your troops to fight to the death, then leave your troops behind on the island. If your enemies see you leave and believe that no one else on the island has the ability to call off the attack, then they will think that your troops will fight to the end.

Cutting off communications can be useful in business negotiations as well. For example, imagine facing a buyer who won't accept your current offer because she believes you will soon make a better one. To credibly convince this buyer that you won't lower your price, you could make one final offer, walk away from the negotiations, and then not return the buyer's calls, faxes, or e-mails. Refusing contact can enhance credibility.

In a 1965 prison riot a warden refused to listen to prisoner demands until they released the guard hostages.[4] By refusing to even listen to the prisoners, the warden made credible his implicit promise never to give in.[5] Likewise, if an employee constantly pesters you for a salary increase, refusing to even listen to her demands credibly signals that she has no chance of prevailing.

KIDNAPPING, BLACKMAIL, AND HONESTY

Securing a reputation for honesty also increases your credibility. Outside of game theory land, nice people strive to be honest because it's "the right thing to do." In the hypercompetitive business world, however, honest behavior arises more from self-interest than morality. Consider, for example, why kidnappers and blackmailers profit from being thought honest.

A kidnapper demands ransom, but the victim's family should comply only if paying the ransom increases the chance that the victim will be released. It's challenging for a kidnapper to satisfy this condition. Imagine that you're a kidnapper who has just been paid a ransom. Should you release your victim? It won't earn you any more money, and releasing the victim will provide police with clues as to your identity and whereabouts.

There are advantages, however, to not killing your hostage. First, the police won't work as hard to catch you if you're guilty of just kidnapping rather than kidnapping and murder. Second, you will get a far lighter sentence, if caught, if you didn't kill. Both of these advantages apply, however, regardless of whether you get the ransom.

If the victim's family thinks that you will release their loved one because you fear a murder conviction, then they should believe that you will fear this conviction regardless of whether they meet your ransom demands. Remember, the victim's family will pay a ransom only if they believe it increases the chance of your freeing the victim. Only a professional kidnapper could meet this condition.

A kidnapper planning on plying his trade in the future would benefit from having a reputation for honesty. A repeat kidnapper wants his victim's families to know that in the past he has released his victims if, but only if, his demands were met. Consequently, a victim's family should perhaps only pay off a kidnapper who intends to kidnap again.

Blackmailers, as well as kidnappers, face substantial credibility problems. A blackmailer promises to disclose embarrassing information about his victim if the victim doesn't pay. For example, a treacherous mistress might threaten to reveal her married boyfriend's adulterous activities if he does not give her $30,000. Would this disclosure threat be credible, however?

Before you ever pay off a blackmailer, you should examine her incentives to disclose the embarrassing information. If your blackmailer hated you and would enjoy seeing you suffer, then she would disclose the information regardless of whether you pay her off.

Blackmail is illegal, even if the blackmailer has the complete legal right to reveal the embarrassing information. If your blackmailer reveals her information, it increases the chance of her getting jailed, if for no other reason than you are now more likely to file charges. The criminality of blackmail provides an incentive for the blackmailer not to disclose, but this incentive exists with equal force whether or not you pay her off. A rational one-time blackmailer, therefore, should be just as likely to disclose regardless of whether you pay her.

Furthermore, even if you met your blackmailer's demands, why wouldn't she continue to demand money? When you pay off a blackmailer, she gets your money, but all you get is her word not to disclose. A professional blackmailer would not want future victims to believe that she has betrayed past customers. A one-time blackmailer, however, would have a strong incentive to make further demands of her victim. After all, if a victim were willing to pay $30,000 last month not to have the information released, then surely he would be willing to pay a few thousand more this month to avoid humiliation. The best way to deal with a one-time blackmailer, then, is probably either to take your chances and not pay her off or to agree to pay her small sums for the rest of your life. If the blackmailer expects to get a continuous stream of income, then she would be made considerably worse off by disclosing the information. By paying the blackmailer throughout her life, you turn her into a professional and consequently make it in her interest to be honest.

If your blackmailer plans on playing her games again, then, as with kidnappers, she has an incentive to develop a reputation for honesty. A professional blackmailer would want people to know that in the past she disclosed her information if, but only if, her extortion demands were not met.

What does blackmail and kidnapping have to do with business? Blackmailers and kidnappers can hope to profit from their trade only if they can get people to trust them. Since these criminals can't rely upon others believing in their honor or morality, they must devise mechanisms whereby people will trust them because honesty serves their interests. Many businesses, too, can profit only if others trust in their honesty.

WHEN BUSINESSES SHOULD BE HONEST

Like kidnappers and blackmailers, businesses have a greater incentive to treat their customers fairly if they plan on playing their game again. Consider Figure 4. The customer first decides at A whether to take his business to Acme. If the customer goes to Acme, then at B Acme can either exploit the customer or treat him fairly. If Acme takes advantage of the customer, it gets a profit of $1,000; if it treats the customer fairly, it earns only $100. If Acme intended on playing this game only once, it would always take advantage of the customer at B. In a one-shot game, the customer should never believe Acme's promise to treat him fairly because Acme would always benefit from cheating. Knowing this, the customer at A would not go to Acme. Interestingly, if the business could guarantee its honesty, it would make a $100 profit. Since the customer knows Acme is self-interested, however, the customer won't trust Acme, and so Acme will get nothing.

One might ask, "since Acme suffers from its own dishonesty, wouldn't Acme really benefit from treating the customer fairly at B?" If the customer at A did go to Acme, Acme would maximize its profit by cheating the customer. Unless the customer has a time machine, Acme's decision to cheat the customer at B can't influence the customer's decision at A because B takes place after A. Consequently, no matter how much Acme promises to be nice, the customer should never believe Acme because Acme's promise lacks credibility. Yes, this result makes everyone worse off, but game theory land is often an unpleasant place.

Games like the one depicted in Figure 4 are commonplace, and often the business *won't* exploit its customers. Fear of lawsuits keeps

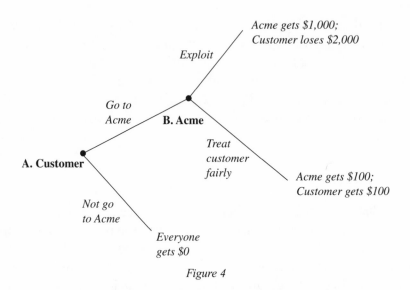

Figure 4

a few businesses honest. The expense of lawsuits makes it impractical for most consumers to sue, however, so implicit legal threats don't deter many businesses from cheating consumers. The true catalyst of business honesty is *repeated play.*

If Acme plans to play the game in Figure 4 over and over again, then Acme probably shouldn't take advantage of a customer. If Acme were to cheat a customer at *B*, it would do better for that one game. In future games, however, customers would abandon a dishonest Acme. Consequently, a completely selfish and greedy Acme would profit from treating its customers fairly and honestly.

Repeated play doesn't guarantee honesty, though. A firm that could make enough through cheating today should be willing to sacrifice its reputation. For example, imagine that your company considers placing a massive order with a supplier that has always treated you fairly in the past. If the supplier could benefit enough by cheating you this one time, then it should sacrifice its reputation in favor of short-term prof-its. Also, if a firm develops a short-term time horizon because, say, it's about to face bankruptcy, then it might cheat you today even though it has always been honest in previous dealings.

In our personal relations we usually assume that someone is either "good" or "bad." If someone has always been nice to us, we generally believe that her type is "good," so she will continue to treat us fairly. In business, however, companies don't have types so much as interests.

A firm might have treated you honestly in the past because being honest had served its interests. If these interests change, however, then you should not use the company's past behavior to predict its future actions.

You should always consider what a firm would lose if it took advantage of you. The firm would probably lose your future business, but would this be significant enough to matter? It might suffer a loss in reputation, but will it be around long enough to care?

Companies invest in brand names to prove their trustworthiness. A company that spends millions of dollars promoting its brand name obviously cares about its long-term reputation and won't decimate its brand-name's worth through the short-term exploiting of customers. An expensive brand name is a hostage to honesty—a hostage that dies if customer trust is lost.

DEADLINE DIFFICULTIES

Credibility problems make deadlines difficult to impose. For example, imagine that your business just made an employment offer to Sue. Your company would like to hire someone quickly and would prefer that Sue accept or decline your job offer within one week. You know that Sue, however, has another job interview scheduled in two weeks. While Sue would prefer this other job, she has only a tiny chance of obtaining it. If you could force Sue to decide within one week, you're confident she would accept your offer rather than take a chance on her long-shot dream job. Unfortunately, you messed up in the job interview and signaled to Sue that you really wanted to hire her. If you told her that she had to decide within a week, she would ignore your deadline, confident that you would grant an extension.

What if you told Sue that you promised another candidate the job if Sue didn't accept within a week? Again, since you already revealed your true inclinations, Sue would have no reason to believe this promise, because it would be in your interests to break it. What if you tried gaining credibility by giving up control of the situation? Perhaps you could go on vacation for a few weeks and instruct your human resource manager to give Sue one week and then offer the job to another candidate. This vacation strategy is flawed because Sue would never believe that you would really implement it. It would always be in your interests to tell Sue she has only a week, but then tell your HR manager to give Sue an extension if she ignored your deadline.

CRIMINAL COMPENSATION

Should we let criminals purchase clemency? Say that a captured criminal offers to compensate his victim in return for the victim dropping all charges. If the victim agrees, should the government go along?

Actually, game theory shows that individuals can be too forgiving. Imagine that you have just been mugged. Trauma causes mugging victims to lose far more than just their stolen property, so assume that although the mugger got $30 from you, he caused you $9,000 worth of mental anguish. Fortunately, the mugger was caught and faces one year in jail. He offers you everything he has, say, $3,000, to drop the charges. Should you accept? Why not? If the mugger escapes his jail sentence, you are extremely unlikely to become one of his future victims. Sure, the mugger did $9,030 of damage to you, and he is offering only $3,000. If he goes to jail, however, you get nothing, so you're better off accepting the mugger's offer.

Unfortunately, being able to pay off victims will embolden muggers. Consequently, all decent citizens would probably be better off if we were prohibited from offering muggers compensated clemency.

Consider the game illustrated in Figure 5, where the mugger first decides whether to mug you at A. If he mugs, then nature moves at B. Nature represents the random forces of the universe that determine whether the mugger gets caught. The mugger perceives that there is a 1 percent chance that he will get caught at B. If the mugger is caught at B, then you decide at C whether to send the mugger to jail or get paid $3,000. Let's make the likely assumption that the mugger would prefer paying $3,000 to going to jail. Thus, from the point of view of the mugger, it is more beneficial to mug you if at C you would accept the $3,000 because in the 1 percent of the time the mugger gets caught he won't go to jail. True, if the mugger gets caught and pays you $3,000, he is worse off for having mugged you. Reducing the harm to the mugger of getting caught, however, makes the mugger more likely to strike.

At C you are probably better off accepting the $3,000. Since you have already been harmed, sending the mugger to jail won't erase the trauma. Of course, ideally you wouldn't get mugged at A.

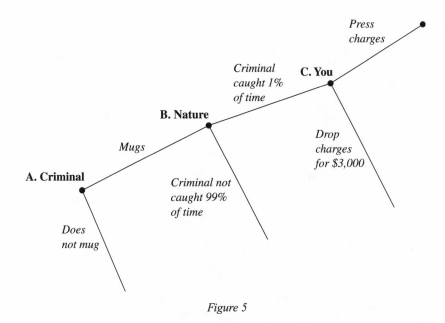

Figure 5

The mugger might have attacked only because he knew it would be in your interest at *C* to accept the money. Thus, you might have been better off if in the beginning of the game you could credibly promise to send the mugger to jail if the game ever reached *C*. In the Figure 5 game this promise not to accept the mugger's money lacks credibility. Consequently, you would benefit from a law that forbids you to drop charges in return for a monetary payment from the mugger. Players often have insufficient incentives to punish those who have done them wrong.

FORGIVENESS

Once someone has harmed you, it is often impossible to reverse the damage. If you would profit from continuing your relationship with the transgressor, however, it would be in your interest to forgive. Unfortunately, people are more likely to harm you if they expect to receive your future forgiveness.

Consider a game in which Acme regularly receives scheduled shipments from its supplier. Unfortunately, one-time difficulties make it extremely costly for the supplier to deliver the goods when promised. If the supplier believed that Acme would never use it again if its shipment was late, then the supplier would incur extra costs to deliver the

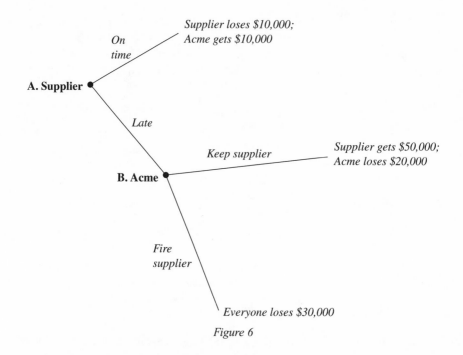

Figure 6

goods on time. If, however, the supplier believed that Acme would for-give its tardiness, then it would not deliver the goods when promised.

Figure 6 models this game. The supplier moves first at *A*. If the supplier chooses to be late, then at *B* Acme can either keep or fire the supplier.

Acme benefits at *B* from forgiving a late supplier. One might argue that it isn't really in Acme's interest to forgive since the supplier will take this generosity into account and be late at *A*. The supplier does not know what Acme will do, however, until after the supplier has decided whether to deliver its product on time. If the supplier chooses to be late, then Acme might as well forgive the tardiness since it will lose even more by firing the supplier. True, Acme could promise that it will fire a late supplier, but such a threat lacks credibility.

Acme could win this game by developing a reputation for being strict with suppliers. If the game in Figure 6 were played only once, then Acme would always be better off not punishing its supplier. To avoid future exploitation, however, Acme shouldn't forgive. Acme could also win by convincing the supplier that it was a little irrational and just couldn't stand being taken advantage of. If the supplier believed that Acme would always fire them at *B* just to get revenge, then it would always deliver its goods on time.

CORPORATE TAKEOVERS AND POISON PILLS

It's hardest to forgive those who have misused your money. Corporate executives entrusted with their shareholders' capital sometimes squander this wealth on lavish salaries and lackluster investments. Shareholders can theoretically fire corporate executives who prove unworthy of their trust. Incompetent executives, however, often use poison pills to protect their power.

A poison pill gives its owner the ability to destroy shareholder assets. Having the ability to destroy, however, also gives one the capacity to protect. For example, after Internet stocks started to decline, many dot.com companies like Yahoo adopted poison pill defenses to protect their managers from ouster.[6] Before considering poison pills and their relationship to game theory, I will first provide some background on shareholder democracy.

When you buy a share of stock, you acquire an ownership interest in a company. Corporations are democracies in which you usually get one vote for every share you own, and companies are supposed to be run for the benefit of the stockholders, because they are the true owners. Just as elected government officials don't always serve the best interests of their country, however, corporate executives don't always run their companies in the best interests of their shareholders, as has been seen in recent years with Enron and Tyco. Shareholders, theoretically, have the right to replace poorly performing corporate executives. Unfortunately, most shareholders don't follow closely what happens in their companies. If you own stock in 100 firms, it's probably not worth your time to determine which ones are well run, so most shareholders don't really value their stock's voting rights and almost never attempt to unseat incompetent executives.

Corporate raiders, however, sometimes use hostile takeovers to expel incompetent management teams. Here's how it can work: Imagine there are 10,000,000 shares of Acme outstanding, so having one share gives you 1/10,000,000 ownership of Acme. Let's say that a share of Acme currently sells for $10 and thus the total market value of Acme is $100 million. A corporate raider believes that shares of Acme are selling for only $10 each because Acme's executives are fools. This corporate raider feels that if people she picked ran Acme, its share value would increase to $15. At its current price the raider could buy 50 percent of the shares in Acme for $50 million. After acquiring half of the shares, the raider could fire the current management and put in her own people. If the raider could then increase the value of Acme's stock to $15 a share, she could then sell her 5,000,000 shares of Acme for a $25 million profit.

Raider's Plan

Buy 5,000,000 shares of Acme at $10 each taking control of 50 percent of company.

Replace management and raise share price of Acme to $15.

Sell all 5,000,000 shares earning a profit of $25 million.

The preceding scenario could take place only if the original executives were hyperpassive. No one enjoys being fired, and in the United States a highly paid employee about to lose his job instinctively turns to lawyers for help.

Wall Street lawyers devised poison pills to protect incumbent executives from corporate raiders. A poison pill gives executives the ability to reduce their company's stock value. For example, a poison pill could force the incumbent management to give all employees a $50,000 bonus if any outside investor acquires more than 20 percent of its company's stock. If some investor went above this 20 percent threshold, management would have the right, but not the obligation, to swallow the poison pill. While such bonuses would benefit workers, they would, of course, harm stockholders.

Now, imagine that you are a raider thinking of taking control of the company that has such a bonus poison pill. You wouldn't want the company if the pill was going to be swallowed. But should you believe that the board of directors would ever decimate its own company? Is the executive's threat to use the poison pill credible?

People aware of their impending termination tend to get angry. If the incumbent managers knew that they were going to be terminated, then they might use the bonus poison pill to take revenge on their tormentor, the corporate raider. Of course, the executives probably own stock in their company. Eating the poison pill would hurt them as well as the raider.

In his game with the company, the raider moves first. The raider initially decides whether to cross the 20 percent threshold, and then the executives determine whether to swallow the pill. If activating the poison pill would stop the raider and protect the managers' jobs, then perhaps the managers would use their pill. Giving large bonuses to all employees, however, should not stop the raider from taking over the company if he already owns 20 percent of it. The poison pill reduces the value of the company and harms the raider. It also, however, lowers the company's stock price and so makes it easier for the raider to acquire the additional shares he needs to take control of the company.

Furthermore, once the poison pill harms the raider, the raider cannot mitigate the pill's harm by backing down. The poison pill inflicts a sunk cost upon the raider. Once incurred, sunk costs should be ignored because you can't do anything about them. Figure 7 shows why, once the poison pill has been activated, the raider should ignore its effects. This figure assumes that taking over the company gives the raider $25 million, while the poison pill costs him $30 million. If the pill is consumed, the raider can't retract the bonuses. Taking over the company gives the raider $25 million, netting him a loss of only $5 million. Once the poison pill is used, therefore, the raider might as well continue replacing the incumbent management.

Of course, if the raider knows at the beginning of the game in Figure 7 that the managers will activate the poison pill, then the raider should leave the company alone. While the poison pill won't stop a raider who has already acquired 20 percent of Acme, it would stop the raider from even attempting to take over Acme if the raider believes that the pill would be implemented. The pill deters the raider, however, only if he believes that it will be used. Unfortunately for the incumbent executives, other than the joy they get from revenge, they receive no additional benefit from destroying the value of their company. Indeed, since they almost certainly own shares in their company, eating their poison pill will actually make them worse off, so their threat to use the poison pill lacks credibility.

To protect their jobs, managers need a more credible device such as a dilution poison pill. If a corporate raider acquired more than 20 percent of a company's stock, a dilution poison pill could result in

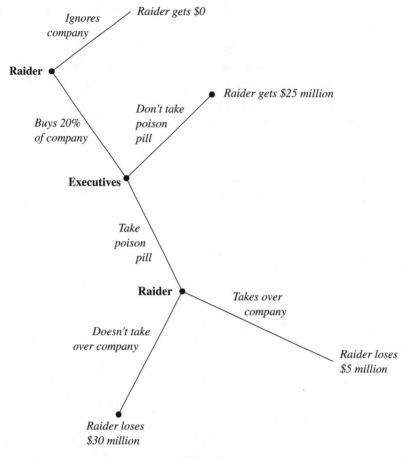

Ignores company

Raider gets $0

Raider

Buys 20% of company

Don't take poison pill

Raider gets $25 million

Executives

Take poison pill

Raider

Takes over company

Doesn't take over company

Raider loses $5 million

Raider loses $30 million

Figure 7

every shareholder except the raider receiving an additional share for each one he owns. This would dilute the raider's interests and help the other shareholders. Consequently, the incumbent management would be willing to use this poison pill since that would cause its ownership interest in the firm to increase. A corporate raider facing a company that had a dilution poison pill would therefore be extremely reluctant to initiate a hostile takeover.

Dilution poison pills protect incompetent managements and so usually harm shareholder interests. Indeed, Fidelity Investments, an extremely large institutional investor, has a policy of withholding support from corporate managers who enact new poison pills.[7] Theoretically, though, ordinary shareholders could benefit from a dilution poison pill. Such a poison pill would force any potential corporate raider to get permission from the board of directors before acquiring the company. If the board of directors were really concerned with the interests of its shareholders, the board could use the poison pill to negotiate a better deal for the takeover and force the raider to pay more for the company. Recall in our example that Acme's stock originally sells for $10 a share, and the raider believes that if he were in control, he could increase its value to $15 a share. The raider's plan is to try to buy half or more of the stock of Acme for $10 a share. If the raider has to negotiate with the board before getting more than 20 percent of the company, the board could force the raider to pay, say, $13 a share rather than just $10.

This poison pill tale illustrates the essential nature of credible threats. Let's say I want to credibly threaten to hurt you in July if you do something I don't like today. My threat is credible only if it would actually be in my self-interest to hurt you in July if you harm me today. Consequently, when making a threat, ensure that it's a threat you will want to carry out.

GAMES GOVERNMENTS PLAY WITH THE PHARMACEUTICAL INDUSTRY

The only player who can do more harm to a company than an incompetent management team is a confiscating government. Would you be willing to work long hours generating wealth if the government was just going to expropriate the fruits of your labor? Governments have varying degrees of capacity to seize the wealth of companies. The high sunk costs of the pharmaceutical industry make it especially vulnerable to governmental takings.

Governments sometimes force companies to cut prices in shallow attempts to placate voters. The marketplace normally puts a reasonable limit on the government's ability to mandate low prices. For example, imagine that it costs companies $100 to make a widget that they sell for $110. If the government forces widget makers to sell their product for only $50, disaster would result because the widget makers would go bankrupt. Politicians receive no political payoff from mandating suicide prices.

Now imagine, however, that a widget that sells for $110 costs only $1 to manufacture. If the government forced widget makers to sell their product for $50, the companies would comply and the politicians would become more popular for having lowered consumer prices.

Pharmaceutical products are often sold at prices far above manufacturing costs because of the high sunk costs associated with the pharmaceutical industry. It costs millions to make the first copy of a drug but sometimes only pennies to make the second. Massive sunk costs permit the government to impose low prices on pharmaceutical companies. To understand this, assume that

$99 million = the cost to design the drug or make the first copy.

$1 = the cost of making the second and subsequent copies of the drug.

1 million = the total number of people who want to buy the drug.

If the pharmaceutical company sells one million of these drugs, its costs will be the $99 million sunk costs to make the first copy plus the $1 million variable costs to manufacture a million copies, so the total cost of producing 1 million copies of this drug is $100 million, or on average, $100 per drug. Let's imagine that this company charges a price of $110, but the government complains, claiming that since the company pays only $1 to make each new drug, it's unfair to charge $110. What if the government told the pharmaceutical company that it could charge no more than $50 a unit? Since the drug costs the pharmaceutical company on average $100 a unit, should they be willing to sell their product for merely $50? Yes, because of the drug's high sunk costs. If the pharmaceutical company sells one more drug for $50, it obviously gets an additional $50 but only pays an extra $1 in manufacturing costs. Therefore, once the pharmaceutical company has incurred the $99 million sunk cost, it is better off selling a drug so long as it gets more than $1 for it.

It takes more than a decade to develop and test a new drug. Consequently, pharmaceutical companies must try to predict what future restrictions on price the government will impose. Governments have strong political incentives to limit pharmaceutical prices. When the government lowers drug prices it reduces research and development for not-yet-developed drugs but lowers prices for today's consumers. The benefits of price restrictions are felt immediately, while the cost, which is a reduced number of future drugs, takes at least a decade to manifest itself.

The pharmaceutical companies fear they are playing a game like Figure 8. In this game the pharmaceutical company first decides whether to incur the sunk costs to develop the new drug. If they make the investment, the government decides whether to impose price controls. The game assumes that the government cares mostly about the present and so benefits from imposing price controls on developed drugs. Of course, if the company knows that the government will impose price controls, it won't develop the product; this would be the worst case for the government. The government would benefit from credibly promising not to impose price controls. Pharmaceutical companies would probably not believe such a promise, however, because of the political payoffs politicians receive from lowering drug prices. The only solution to this credibility problem is for the government to develop a long-term perspective and genuinely come to believe that the damage done by price controls exceeds their short-term political benefits.

Many AIDS activists seem ignorant of pharmaceutical economics. AIDS activists continually pressure pharmaceutical companies to lower prices. They also argue that the low cost of making additional copies of AIDS drugs means that pharmaceutical companies should give their drugs away for free to poor countries. Tragically, the AIDS

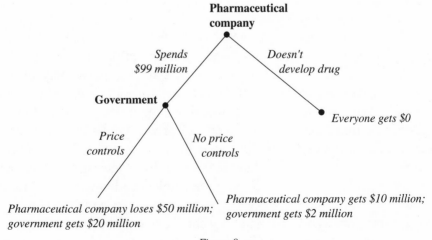

Figure 8

activists' complaints signal that if someone ever does find a cure for AIDS, then the activists will do their best to ensure that the cure is sold for a very low price. The activists are effectively promising to reduce the future profits of anyone who finds a cure or vaccine for AIDS. Indeed, I predict that if a for-profit organization does find a cure or vaccine for AIDS, then AIDS activists will loudly condemn this organization for not selling the wonder treatment at a lower cost. Obviously, the pharmaceutical companies take these potential profit objections into account when deciding how much to spend on AIDS research.

FRIGHTENING MANY WITH ONE THREAT[8]

So far we have assumed that a player threatens only one person or organization.

Sometimes, however, you need to threaten many. Interestingly, game theory demonstrates how many can be induced to comply even if you can carry out your threat against only one. To see this, assume that you have 10 employees.

Each employee gets the following payoff:

Employee's Payoff

Work Hard	$5,000
Slack Off	$10,000
Get Fired	0

You want all your employees to work hard. If an employee knew that she wouldn't get fired, however, she would prefer to slack off. An employee is worse off working hard than slacking off because of the mental anguish caused by effort. To get them to work hard, you need to threaten your employees with termination. An obvious solution to this game is for you to declare that an employee will get fired if she slacks off. If the employees all believe your threat, they will all work hard. Let's make the game somewhat challenging by assuming that you can fire, at most, one employee, and your employees know this. Perhaps your company couldn't survive if you fired more then one person.

If your strategy was to randomly choose one of the employees who slacked off and fire her then there would be two possible outcomes. In the good outcome, everyone would work hard. If all the other employees worked hard, each one would also want to, or else she would get fired. If the employees worked together, however, they should all agree to slack off. In this outcome you could fire only one employee. Therefore if an employee was lazy, then 90 percent of the time she would get a payoff of $10,000 and 10 percent of the time she would get 0. This outcome is probably better for an employee than always working hard and getting a payoff of $5,000.

How could you motivate all employees with just one threat? First, put the employees in some arbitrary but announced order. You tell employee 1 that if she doesn't work hard, you will fire her. This would obviously cause employee 1 to work hard. Next, you tell employee 2 that if employee 1 does work hard, you will fire 2 if she doesn't work hard. Since employee 2 expects employee 1 to work hard, this will cause employee 2 to work hard. Next, you tell employee 3 that if employees 1 and 2 work hard, you will fire 3 if she slacks off. Again, since employee 3 expects 1 and 2 to work hard, she will expect to get fired if she is lazy. You continue this process until all the employees have an incentive to work. Your employees can't circumvent your system by colluding to be lazy because employee 1 would never agree to slack off since it would result in his termination.

Another application of this game would be if you had 10 errant suppliers, but your production demands meant that you could fire at most one. Even if the suppliers knew of your limitations, you could still effectively threaten them all by first threatening one, then the next, and so forth.

The key lesson from this game is that when you assign responsibility randomly, all might accept the chance of getting punished and choose not to work. It's much better to have a clear chain of punishment. You choose one person most responsible and then go down the line. Unless your employees are crazy, your threat will induce them to comply with your demands.

THE BENEFITS OF INSANITY

Insanity has its privileges. Inmates of mental institutions sometimes "deliberately or instinctively [cultivate] value systems that make them less susceptible to disciplinary threats."[9]An inmate could gain some freedom from staff coercion by, for example, becoming self-destructive whenever the mental institution tried to discipline him. If a rational person told his boss that he would cut his own vein if demoted, the boss would likely not believe the threat. An inmate in a mental institution, however, could credibly use a threat of self-mutilation to, say, get permission to watch Seinfeld reruns.

I have attempted to extort $20 each from my students by threatening suicide. I first ask my students to raise their hands if they would spend $20 to save my life. (Some, *but not all,* raise their hands.) Next, I tell my students that if those who have raised their hands don't each give me $20 I will kill myself. Of course, the students don't pay because they don't believe my threat. If they had believed me to be (more) crazy, however, I might have gotten some money.

Exhibiting insanity can enhance your threat's credibility. In many of the games presented in this chapter, your threat could easily become believable if your opponent thought it was more important for you to "win" than to maximize your payoff.

The purpose of business is to make as much money as possible. Any firm that sacrifices profit maximization to further other goals is considered irrational by economists. Interestingly, however, an irrational person might actually make more money than someone who cares only for money. Consider the game in Figure 9. Your competitor moves first. He can be either nice or mean. If he is nice, both of you get $1,000 and the game ends. If he is mean, then you get to move and choose whether to be nice or mean. If you are mean, both of you get zero. If you are nice, you get $100 and he gets $2,000.

If you care only about money, then if the game gets to *B,* you should be nice. True, this would cause your competitor to make more than you. Recall that the goal of business, however, is to make as much money as possible, not to make more than your competition does. (Would you rather own the most profitable restaurant in a small town but make only $50,000 a year or the third most profitable one in a large city and make $1,000,000 a year? Would anyone ever want to invest with someone who would prefer the $50,000 option?) Consequently, a rational businessperson would choose to be nice at *B* especially if the game is played only once. Unfortunately, if your competitor believes you will choose to be nice, he will choose to be mean, and you will get only $100. In contrast, if your competitor believes you would seek revenge on him for being mean and would choose to be mean yourself,

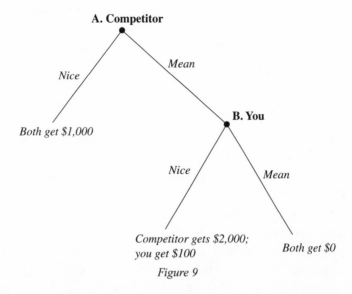

Figure 9

he will be nice and you will get $1,000. This situation seems paradoxical, for how could a person who cares only about money make less than someone who has more diverse goals?

You wouldn't suffer in this game from being rational per se; you would suffer for being perceived as rational. Your competitor would make her decision not based upon whether you were actually interested in revenge, but on whether she *thought* you were interested in revenge. This game provides an important business lesson. This chapter has shown how, in many situations, it might not be in your interest to carry out a threat. Others might realize this and not take your threat seriously. A way around this credibility problem is to convince others that you are somewhat "crazy" and would carry out a threat even if doing so was costly. For example, when asking for a raise, it might be beneficial if your boss thought that if he turned you down you would get mad and quit, even if quitting would not be in your own best interest. Of course, this does not mean you should ever strive to become crazy; rather, it means that you should sometimes strive to convince others that profit maximization is not your only goal.

Another lesson from this game is that others may have an incentive to convince you that they are crazy when they really aren't. You should suspect anyone who acts insane in a way that "coincidentally" strengthens his negotiating position.

Interestingly, evolution might have made humans irrational precisely because of the benefits of insanity. Consider the emotion of revenge. At its core, revenge means hurting someone else who has harmed you, even if you would be better off leaving him alone. Revenge is an irrational desire to harm others who have injured our loved ones or us.

To see the benefit of being known as vengeful, consider a small community living in prehistoric times. Imagine that a group of raiders stole food from this community. A rational community would hunt down the raiders only if the cost of doing so was not too high. A vengeance-endowed community would hunt down the raiders regard-less of the cost. Since the raiders would rather go after the rational community, being perceived as vengeful provides you with protection and therefore confers an evolutionary advantage.

A reputation for vengeance could benefit a person in the business community, too. While few businesspeople outside of the drug cartels hunt down and kill those who have done them wrong, businesspeople often seek vengeance through lawyers. Lawyers are very expensive, though. Therefore, once someone has already harmed you, it is often better to forget the incident than to pursue legal recourse. If, however, people believe that you irrationally lust for legal revenge, then they will avoid giving you a cause of action. The optimal strategy to adopt with respect to legal vengeance is to convince people that you are insanely attached to vengeance when, if someone did violate your legal rights, you would really rationally evaluate whether to sue.

ENTRY DETERRENCE

Competition benefits everyone but the competitors. More competition means lower prices and reduced profits. Businessmen would like to come to agreements not to compete, but alas, antitrust laws make such agreements illegal.

Imagine that you run Beta Brothers, which has a highly profitable local monopoly on "bbogs." In fact, you are probably making a little too much money for your own long-term good. A potential competitor is eyeing your business and figures your huge monopoly profits should be shared. You desperately want to keep the competitor out, but your antitrust lawyer won't let you bribe it to stay away and you lack the criminal contacts necessary to make physical threats. How can you protect your bbog monopoly?

Would cutting prices to suicide levels deter your rival from challenging you? You could set prices below costs so that neither you nor anyone who tried to enter the market could make money. When your potential competitor abandons its plans to enter your market, you can raise prices to their previous level. By setting suicide prices you make an implied threat that if your rival enters you will keep your low prices and your rival will lose money. Unfortunately, credibility problems make suicide prices an ineffective way of deterring entry.

Your potential competition doesn't care per se about what price you charge before it enters. If it believed you would maintain suicide prices after its entry, then it would stay away. Unfortunately, your implied threat to maintain suicide prices is devoid of credibility. If the competition enters your market, it would be fairly stupid for you to bankrupt your own business just to spite it. Once the competition starts selling bbogs, it would be in your interest to set a price that maximized your profit given that you have competition. This price is unlikely to be one where everyone in the industry (including you!) suffers permanent losses. Consequently, charging extremely low prices today does not credibly signal to the competition that you will continue to set low prices if they enter your market.

Consider the game in Figure 10. The game starts by assuming that you have set suicide prices. The competition then decides whether to enter the market. If it enters, you decide whether to keep low prices or raise them. If you keep low prices, you lose money (as does the competition). If you raise prices, then you make a small profit. If the potential competition thought that you would keep low prices, then it would not enter. Unfortunately, once it enters, you should raise prices since you are now stuck with the competition. Your rival should predict your actions and enter your bbog market. As a result, setting suicide prices before entry does not keep away the competition.

So, threatening to charge suicide prices isn't credible. But, what about threatening to set a price that's low, but not so low that it would cause you to lose money? For example, imagine that it costs you $10 to make each bbog, but bbog production costs your rival $12 per unit.

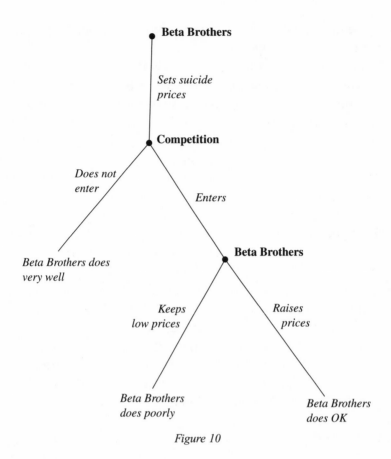

Figure 10

$10 /unit = your costs

$12 /unit = the potential competition's costs

We have shown that charging $9 per unit wouldn't keep out the competition because it would not believe you would keep losing money if it entered. What about charging $11 per unit, however? At $11 per unit you could still make money, but the competition couldn't, so is $11 your optimal price? To consider this, let's assume that if the other firm enters, $15 would be the price that earns you the highest profit. If, before the other firm enters, you set a price lower than $15, then the competition should believe that if it enters, you would raise the price to $15. Once you have competition, if there is nothing you can do about it, then you might as well set the price that maximizes your profit. There is no point in setting a very low price to deter the potential competition from entering because the potential competition should believe that it will always be in your interest to raise this price once you know you are stuck with it. Remember, your potential competition probably doesn't have a time machine, so punishing it after it has entered can't stop it from initially entering.

Changing prices is easy. In judging what price you would set in the future, the potential competition should not look at what price you are currently setting, but rather at what price it would be in your interest to set if it entered your market.

CHAIN STORE PARADOX

What if you're trying to keep competition out of multiple markets? Imagine that Acme operates in 10 markets, and, while it currently has no competition, rivals are considering moving into each of its areas. The rival enters a market by building a store or factory, so once a rival enters a market, it won't leave.

Could Acme use limited-range suicide pricing as a warning shot to prove its willingness to fight? If a competitor entered one area, Acme could set extremely low prices for just that one market. True, it would lose money with that store, but might it not scare away the competition from other markets? If for some reason the competition didn't take the hint and entered two markets, then Acme could use suicide prices for the stores in both of these markets. Would not such a strategy keep at least some of Acme's stores safe from competition? Does repeated play add credibility to Acme's suicide pricing threat?

Interestingly, even if Acme operates in multiple markets, it couldn't effectively use suicide pricing to deter entry. Game theorists refer to this counterintuitive result as the chain store paradox. To understand the chain store paradox, consider why Acme might want to impose suicide pricing in market #1. By setting suicide prices in market #1, Acme says to rivals:

> I set suicide prices in market #1 after you entered, so you should believe that I would set suicide prices in any other market you enter. Since you can never make money in any market where I charge extremely low prices, you should never enter any of my other markets.

While this statement seems logical, consider what would happen if the competition has already entered 9 markets and considers entering a tenth. Say that the competition would enter the tenth market if and only if Acme did not set suicide prices for this market. Would Acme ever charge suicide prices in its tenth market? No! The only reason Acme would ever set suicide prices would be to deter future entry, since setting suicide prices in a given market means you lose money in that market. If the competition had already invaded all of Acme's markets, there would be absolutely no point in Acme trying to deter future entry. Consequently, all competitors know that Acme would never set suicide prices in the tenth market if its other 9 markets had already been invaded.

Now consider this: should Acme ever set suicide prices in the 9th market? Again, the only point of setting extremely low prices is to deter entry in future markets. The supposed purpose of suicide prices is to send a signal to the competition it had better not enter future markets because if it did, then you would set suicide prices in these markets, too. We have already established, however, that Acme would never set suicide prices in market 10. Thus, there would be no point in setting suicide prices in market 9 because doing so would not send a signal about what you would do if the competition entered all 10 of your markets. Everybody already knows that in market 10 you will set "reasonable" prices regardless of whether the competition enters.

Given that Acme will never use suicide prices in the ninth and tenth invaded markets, should it ever bother using them in market 8? Again, the only possible purpose of setting low prices is to signal what you would do if the competition entered even more markets. Setting suicide prices in market 8 constitutes a threat to the competition that if it entered markets 9 or 10, you would set suicide prices there, too. No one, however, should believe this threat, since it would never be in your self-interest to set extremely low prices in markets 9 and 10. Consequently, you shouldn't ever bother setting them in market 8.

Obviously, this chain of logic continues, and you shouldn't set suicide prices in market 7, 6, 5, and so on. This reasoning applies all the way back to market 1. Acme, consequently, can never use suicide prices to deter entry.

ENTRY DETERRENCE THROUGH INSANITY

Feigning insanity might deter rivals. Since sane businesspeople always try to maximize profit, threatening to maintain suicide prices isn't usually credible because it's not profit maximizing. If others perceive you as having objectives other then profit maximization, however, they might believe your threat to keep low prices. For example, imagine that others believed that you were irrationally committed to being king of your little hill, and that you would set whatever prices it took to be the dominant (and perhaps only) firm in your industry. Following through on such a strategy would obliterate your profits. Fortunately, if others believed that you would be silly enough to keep suicide prices, then they would never bother competing with you, so you would never actually have to kill your business with low prices.

SANE METHODS OF ENTRY DETERRENCE

While threatening to set low prices won't deter rivals from entering your market if they believe you to be rational, game theory provides other ways of keeping out the competition. Because you can so easily change prices, threats to maintain low prices lack credibility. Thus, to convince the competition that it would lose money if it entered your market, you need to employ a more permanent mechanism than price setting.

You could, for example, contractually agree to charge your customers low prices for a long period. Since your customers could sue if you violated such an agreement, your rivals would believe a threat to keep low prices if these prices were guaranteed by contract. Of course, if the potential competition decided not to enter, you would still be stuck with these low, contractually mandated prices.

An ideal mechanism to deter entry would be to contractually promise lower prices to customers only if the competition enters your market. Such a contingent contract would deter rivals from entering, but if they didn't enter, you could continue to enjoy high prices. Unfortunately, such an agreement would almost certainly be declared illegal under antitrust laws. The paramount objective of antitrust law is to promote competition, so if a plan's clear and obvious purpose were to restrict competition, then it would probably be found illegal. (Of course, no sane person should rely on a game theory book for legal advice.)

Increasing factory production could also credibly deter entry. If you build an extra factory, you will have a lot of new products to sell so you will have to lower prices regardless of whether your competition increases. Building extra production capacity credibly signals to the potential competition that you will maintain low prices. Once you have built the extra capacity, your interests would actually be served by charging less.

READING PEOPLE

Most people consider themselves exceptionally good judges of human nature. Many of us are convinced that we can "read" people to figure out if they are lying to us. This chapter suggests, however, that to determine truthfulness we should often go beyond emotions to interests. When someone makes a promise or threat, sure, use your people skills to try to discern their honesty. Also, however, figure out if they would be better off in the future keeping their word. Furthermore, when competing against a rational player, remember that she might judge your truthfulness based not upon how you come across, but rather on whether you will serve your future interests by keeping your threat or promise.

THE DANGERS OF PRICE COMPETITION

This chapter has shown how credibility problems can make it challenging to use low prices as a means of deterring competition. Chapter 3 explores the dangers of competition to businesses. It illuminates why price competition inhibits profit maximization.

LESSONS LEARNED

- Fear only credible threats. Trust only credible promises.
- Being perceived as irrational can be advantageous.

- Worry about your own payoff, not your opponent's. Since profit maximization is the objective of business, you shouldn't fret about making more money than your rival.

- Unless you have a time machine, you should ignore sunk costs and not let them influence your moves because nothing you do in the future will save you from having paid the sunk costs in the past. The proverb, "It is no use crying over spilt milk," illustrates this lesson.

- Lowering your prices to deter potential competitors is an ineffective tactic because prices can be changed so easily.

3

THE DANGERS OF PRICE COMPETITION

The trouble with the rat race is that even if you win, you're still a rat.[1]

Lily Tomlin

S PECTATORS IN ANCIENT ROME most enjoyed gladiator games when the competition was fierce. The gladiators themselves, however, undoubtedly preferred days when little blood was spilled in the coliseum.

When businesses fight, they don't spill blood but something equally as precious, profits. While businesses compete along many dimensions, their competition is never as draining as when they are fighting over price. Price competition is ferocious because low prices are both visible and desirable to consumers.

Customers perceive quality differently and inexactly. Your customers might not realize that a rival is selling a superior product. If, however, the rival charges $90 and you charge $100, then even your most dimwitted customers realize that your rival's product costs less. A simple game I play with my students illustrates the destructive power of price competition.

I first tell my students that I'm going to conduct an auction, and that this is no mere class exercise; all sales are real and binding. The person who bids the most must buy the item I'm selling for the amount she bids. I auction a twenty-dollar bill. I start the bidding at one penny and ask how many would be willing to pay this price for my merchandise. Almost everyone raises a hand. I then slowly increase the bid amount, and as long as I'm asking for less than $20, virtually everyone offers to pay what I ask. The bidding continues until the price reaches $20. I then ask if any student is willing to pay more than $20, but none ever does. (Too bad, it would have been an easy way for someone to get an A.) After the bidding stops, I collect my $20 from the winning student and hand her the twenty-dollar bill.

After the auction I chastise my students for throwing away money. I had been willing to sell a twenty-dollar bill for a mere one penny, yet their greed cost them this profitable opportunity. Because they kept competing against each other, the bid price went up to the point where the winner took no profit from me. They were like gladiators who, competing for the emperor's favor, fought so viciously that they all lost limbs. (OK, it wasn't that bad, but $20 can mean a lot to some undergrads.)

Game theory, of course, doomed the students to bid the price up to $20. As long as the bid price was below $20, each student wanted to bid slightly more than the rest of her classmates. Competition raised the bids to $20. If enough of the students are self-interested, they will necessarily outbid each other and drive the price to the value of the good being sold.

Wireless companies have recently behaved like my students. Many western governments have raised astronomical sums through telephone spectrum auctions. Normally, firms dislike giving money to governments. When governments forced telecommunication companies to compete on price for limited spectrum space, however, these companies continually outbid each other, raising the amounts they eventually had to pay the government.

Competition does the most harm to companies when it forces them to set low product prices. Pretend that two firms sell identical goods. Say it costs each business $30 to produce the good, but fortunately a lot of customers are willing to pay up to $100 for the item. Since both firms sell the same product, customers will buy from the firm that offers the lowest price. In the previous example, if my students had worked together, they would have bid only one penny. If the firms in this example cooperate, they would obviously each charge $100 and split the customers. What happens, however, if the firms compete on price? If the other firm is charging $100, your firm could charge $100 and get about one-half of the customers, or charge a little less and get nearly all of them. Clearly, it would be beneficial to slightly undercut the other firm's price if it drastically increases your firm's sales. Alas, this same game theoretic logic applies to your competitor.

If both firms continually try to undercut each other, then prices will be driven down to cost. (Once your rival's price equals your cost, you won't lower prices because you would rather lose all of your customers than sell each good at a loss.) How can firms prevent destructive price competition from draining all of the profits? If antitrust laws didn't exist, the easiest way would be for the firms to make an explicit agreement to charge the same price. Alas, under antitrust laws such an agreement could land you in prison.

STOPPING PRICE WARS WITH CREDIBLE THREATS

During much of the Cold War, the Soviet Empire had both the desire and the ability to destroy the United States, but fear of retaliation kept the peace. The evil empire believed that attacking the U.S. with nuclear weaponry would cause America to respond in kind. A similar type of retaliation can keep firms in your market from lowering prices.

While credibly threatening to use atomic weapons against a price-cutting rival would be an effective means to limit price competition, acquiring the necessary fissionable materials could be challenging. An easier method is to threaten to match any price cut. If your rival considers cutting prices to steal your customers, then his justification for a price cut would be obliterated if he believes that you would meet any price challenge.

For retaliation to be effective it must be both swift and assured. If your rival suspects that you might not respond to a price cut, he might lower his price to see how you act. Furthermore, if he believes that it would take you a few months to respond, he might lower prices to steal some of your customers. In the time it takes you to act he could get a short-term boost in sales that might more than make up for starting a minor price war.

Threats of retaliation won't always be enough to suppress price competition, though. When I auctioned off the twenty-dollar bill, why couldn't my students come to an agreement not to bid against each other? One of the most challenging endeavors in life is getting a large group of friends to agree on which movie they should rent and then collectively watch. This challenge becomes an impossibility when everyone in the group has veto rights. The reason that my students could not come to an agreement to limit their bidding was because there were too many of them. After all, it would have taken just one student to break an agreement. If, for example, all but one had agreed to bid only one penny and split the profits among themselves then the student left out of the agreement could bid two cents and make herself a $19.98 profit.

When there are many firms selling the same product it can be nearly impossible for them to limit price competition. If the prevailing price is above the cost of production, each firm will have an incentive to slightly undercut its rivals to gain much of the market. Unfortunately, when everyone does this, prices are driven down to cost, and profits disappear. In a market with only two firms, each may well believe that if it cuts its price the competition will do likewise. When a market consists of 50 firms, however, then one single small firm is unlikely to believe that if it lowers prices then everyone else will immediately follow. As a result, all the firms will believe that they can get away with reducing prices without suffering massive retaliation. If all the firms believe this, of course, then all the firms will lower their prices until all the profits have dissipated. Game theory thus shows that firms should avoid entering markets where (1) there are a large number of competing firms and (2) they sell near-identical products. Internet retailing is an industry where long-term high profits probably can't ever be maintained because these two conditions are so readily met.

INTERNET PRICE COMPETITION

Amazon.com was one of the brightest stars of the tech boom, yet its stock market success baffled many economists. The Internet multiplies competition, and nearly anyone can sell books on-line, so Amazon was destined to compete for consumers based on price alone. While a firm fighting with prices can survive, it shouldn't prosper.

Imagine two neighboring bookstores in a mall. If a customer found a book in one store that he liked, it would be easy for him to check whether it was being sold for a lower price in the other store. If one of these stores had consistently higher prices than the other, therefore, it would generate little business. Each store would face enormous pressure to charge lower prices than its neighbor. Now imagine instead that these two bookstores are in opposite sides of a large mall. It would be much more challenging for customers to compare prices. A store now could afford to maintain higher prices because its customers (1) might not realize its prices were higher and (2) might not be willing to walk to the other store just to save a few cents. The closer the stores, the more likely the stores are to compete on price because price will have a greater influence on sales.

On the Internet all stores are next to each other. It's easy to compare prices at different Internet retailers. This is especially true if you use intelligent searching agents to seek out low-cost providers. Consequently, web consumers are especially price-sensitive and Internet retailers have large incentives to undercut rivals because the firm that charges the lowest price is likely to get most of the business. Of course, if everyone tries to charge the lowest price, then prices plunge and profits disappear.

Not only do Internet retailers compete mostly on price, but they also face more competition than their brick-and-mortar cousins do. If there were, say, 10,000 brick-and-mortar widget retailers spread across the United States, but only 20 on-line sellers of widgets, then Internet retailers might actually face more competition. Two stores in the real world compete only if a customer is willing to shop at either of them. Consequently, in the real world two bookstores should consider themselves rivals only if they are within, say, 15 miles of each other. Any connected person can visit any virtual retail store, regardless of where the store is really located. The actual number of competitors an Internet retailer faces will thus usually be much higher than the number faced by real-world stores. Since more rivals means more price competition, Internet retailers will never achieve sustained high profitability unless, perhaps, they use complex pricing.

USING COMPLICATION TO REDUCE PRICE COMPETITION[2]

You're offered a choice between two long-distance services. One plan charges you ten cents a minute and the other nine. Obviously, you go with the cheaper plan. Long-distance providers, however, rarely provide such a stark choice. They offer you complicated pricing plans that make it difficult to compare long-distance packages.[3]

Complications reduce the damage of price competition. When firms compete directly on price, it's easy for customers to compare. Consequently, there is a massive benefit for every firm to undercut its rivals. When everyone uses complicated pricing schemes, however, the benefits to undercutting your rival diminish since customers will be challenged to find the low-cost provider.

Airlines achieve complicated pricing through frequent-flyer programs.[4] Frequent-flyer miles effectively change the price of airline tickets and make it difficult to determine which airline offers the lowest price and consequently reduce the benefit to firms of undercutting their rivals.

RETAIL PRICE MAINTENANCE

Can retail price competition ever harm manufacturers? Imagine you are a producer of high-end tennis rackets. You had been selling rackets for $150 each to retail stores, which in turn sold them to customers for $300 each. Retail customers bought your expensive rackets only after handling them and consulting with knowledgeable salespeople. Consequently, the retailers needed a high markup to cover store expenses.

Imagine that an Internet sports business starts up that sells your rackets for only $240 each. This net store still pays you $150 per racket. Should you have any objections to their reduced price? Normally, manufacturers benefit when independent retailers set low prices for their goods, since low prices result in higher sales.

This Internet retailer, however, wouldn't offer services to customers. It certainly couldn't give customers the opportunity to touch your rackets. A rational customer might therefore go to a brick-and-mortar store to try out your racket, and then if he likes it, buy the good over the Internet. Obviously, if enough customers adopt this strategy, physical stores will stop stocking your rackets, so the discount virtual store could actually reduce your total sales.

When retailers compete on price, service suffers. This is especially true when customers can enjoy the services at high-end stores and buy your product at the discount outlets. To reduce price competition, many retailers try to impose minimum prices on their goods. When retailers can't compete on price, they might compete on service. Consequently, when deciding if you should encourage deep Internet discounts you need to ask, which do my customers value more, low prices or high levels of service?

Price Competition

Compete on quality, service, brand names, or product color but always strive to avoid price competition. When firms compete on price, high profits become unsustainable. Try to reach implicit agreements with your rivals to limit pricing wars, but remember even if these agreements are successful, they might simply attract new rivals who won't play by the rules. If you must compete on price, adopt confusing pricing plans so customers can't directly compare.

SIMULTANEOUS GAMES

Timing matters. In pricing games, for example, it might be very significant whether one firm picks its price first and then its rival moves, or if both firms pick their prices simultaneously. The previous chapter examined games where the players moved one at a time. The next chapter explores games where the players move simultaneously.

LESSONS LEARNED

- Firms have trouble profiting when they compete on price because price is very visible to consumers.
- To stop your rival from undercutting your price, your rival needs to believe that you will quickly respond to any price reduction.
- It's almost impossible to restrict price competition among many firms that sell near identical goods.
- Internet retailers necessarily face massive competition because every other store that sells similar products is a rival.
- Complex pricing can reduce price competition by making it difficult for customers to comparison shop.

4

SIMULTANEOUS GAMES

Interest will not lie.

17th-century proverb[1]

SOFTENING SALES CAUSE BOTH FORD AND GM to reconsider their pricing.[2] If both move at the same time, then they are playing a simultaneous-move game. Figure 11 presents an example of a simultaneous-move game. It's important that you understand how to interpret games like this one, so please read this paragraph very carefully. In this game Player One chooses A or B, while at the same time Player Two chooses X or Y. Each player moves without knowing what the other person is going to do. The players' combined moves determine their payoffs. For example, if Player One chooses A, and Player Two chooses X, then we are in the top left corner. Player One scores the first number, 10, as his payoff, and Player Two scores the second number, 5, as her payoff. If Player One chooses A, and Player Two chooses Y, then we would be in the top right box, and Player One scores 3 while Player Two scores 0. In all simultaneous-move games Player One will always be on the left, and Player Two will always be on top. The first number in the box will usually be Player One's payoff and the second will be Player Two's payoff. The players always know what

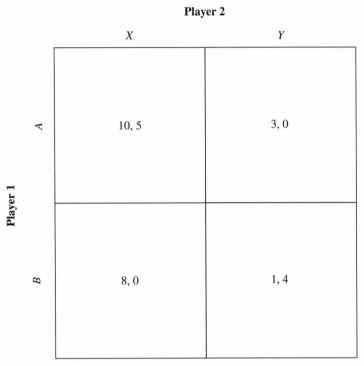

Figure 11

score they will receive if they end up in any given box. The players, therefore, see Figure 11 before they move. Each player knows everything except what his opponent is going to do.

As with sequential games, in simultaneous games a player's only goal is to maximize his payoff. The players are not trying to win by getting a higher score than their opponents. Consequently, Player Two would rather be in the top left box (where Player One gets 10, and Player Two gets 5) than the bottom right box (where Player One gets 1, and Player Two gets 4).

What should the players do in a simultaneous game? The best way to solve a simultaneous-move game is to look for a dominant strategy. A dominant strategy is one that you should play, regardless of what the other player does. In Figure 11, strategy A is dominant for Player One. If Player Two chooses X, then Player One gets 10 if he picks A, and 8 if he picks B. Thus, Player One would be better off playing A if he knows that Player Two will play X. Also, if Player Two plays Y, then Player One gets 3 if he plays A and 1 if he plays B. Consequently, Player One is also better off playing A if Player Two plays Y. Thus, regardless of what Player Two does, Player One gets a higher payoff playing A than B. Strategy A is therefore a dominant strategy and should be played by Player One no matter what.

A dominant strategy is a strategy that gives you a higher payoff than all of your other strategies, regardless of what your opponent does.

Player Two does not have a dominant strategy in this game. If Player Two believes that Player One will play A, then Player Two should play X. If, for some strange reason, Player Two believes that her opponent will play B, then she should play Y. Thus, while Player One should always play A no matter what, Player Two's optimal strategy is determined by what she thinks Player One will do.

A dominant strategy is a powerful solution concept because you should play it even if you think your opponent is insane, is trying to help you, or is trying to destroy you. Playing a dominant strategy, by definition, maximizes your payoff.

To test your understanding of dominant strategies, consider this: Is stopping at a red light and going on a green light a dominant strategy when driving? Actually, no, it isn't. You only want to go on green lights and stop on red lights if other drivers do the same. If you happened to drive through a town where everyone else went on red and stopped on green, you would be best off following their custom. In contrast, if everyone in this strange place were intent on electrocuting herself, you would be best served by not following the crowd. Avoiding electrocution is a dominant strategy; you should do it regardless of what other people do. In contrast, driving on the right side of the road is not a dominant strategy; you should do it only if other people also do it.

Let's return to Ford and GM's pricing game. Figures 12 and 13 present possible models for the auto pricing game. In these games Ford is Player One while GM is Player Two. In response to weakening sales, both firms can either offer a discount or not offer a discount. Please look at these two figures and determine how the firms' optimal strategies differ in these two games.

In Figure 12, offering a discount is a dominant strategy for both firms since offering a discount always yields a greater profit. Perhaps in this game, consumers will purchase cars only if given discounts. Figure 13 lacks dominant strategies. If your opponent offers a discount, you are better off giving one too. If, however, your opponent doesn't lower his prices, then neither should you. Perhaps in this game consumers are willing to forgo discounts only as long as no one offers

General Motors

	Discount	No discount
Discount	*Low profits, Medium profits*	*High profits, Low profits*
No discount	*Zero profits, High profits*	*Zero profits, Low profits*

Ford is labeled on the vertical axis.

Figure 12

them. Of course, if you can maintain the same sales, you are always better off not lowering prices. This doesn't mean that neither firm in Figure 13 should offer a discount. Not offering a discount is not a dominant strategy. Rather, each firm must try to guess its opponent's strategy before formulating its own move.

The opposite of a dominant strategy is a strictly stupid strategy.[3] A strictly stupid strategy always gives you a lower payoff than some other strategy, regardless of what your opponent does. In Figure 12, not offering a discount is a strictly stupid strategy for both firms, since it always results in their getting zero profits. In a game where you have only two strategies, if one is dominant, then the other must be strictly stupid.

A strictly stupid strategy is a strategy that gives you a lower payoff than at least one of your other strategies, regardless of what your opponent does.

Knowing that your opponent will never play a strictly stupid strategy can help you formulate your optimal move. Consider the game in

General Motors

		Discount	No discount

Figure 13

Figure 14 in which two competitors each pick what price they should charge. Player Two can choose to charge either a high, medium, or low price, while for some reason Player One can charge only a high or low price. As you should be able to see from Figure 14, if Player One knows that Player Two will choose high or medium prices, than Player One will be better off with high prices. If, however, Player Two goes with low prices, then Player One would also want low prices. The following chart shows Player One's optimal move for all three strategies that Player Two could employ:

Table 1

Player Two's Strategy	Player One's Best Strategy*
High	High
Medium	High
Low	Low

*If he knows what Player Two is going to do.

Player 2

	High	Medium	Low
High	50, 7	30, 5	0, 0
Low	40, 1	25, 60	10, 0

Player 1

Figure 14

When Player One moves, he doesn't know how Player Two will move. Player One, however, could try to figure out what Player Two will do. Indeed, to solve most simultaneous games, a player must make some guess as to what strategies the other players will employ. In this game, at least, it's easy to figure out what Player Two won't do because Player Two always gets a payoff of zero if she plays low. (Remember, the second number in each box is Player Two's payoff.) Playing high or medium always gives Player Two a positive payoff. Consequently, for Player Two, low is a strictly stupid strategy and should never be played. Once Player One knows that Player Two will never play low, Player One should play high. When Player Two realizes that Player One will play high, she will also play high since Player Two gets a payoff of 7 if both play high and gets a payoff of only 5 if she plays medium while Player One plays high.

Player Two will play high because Player One also will play high. Player One, however, only plays high because Player One believes that Player Two will not play low. Player Two's strategy is thus determined by what she thinks Player One thinks that Player Two will do. Before you can move in game theory land, you must often predict what other people guess you will do.

A BILLIONAIRE'S POLITICAL STRATEGY

Warren Buffett once proposed using dominant and strictly stupid strategies to get both the Republicans and Democrats to support campaign finance reform.[4] He suggested that some eccentric billionaire (not himself) propose a campaign finance bill. The billionaire promises that if the bill doesn't get enacted into law, then he will give $1 billion to whichever party did the most to support it. Figure 15 presents this game where each party can either support or not support the bill. Assume that the bill doesn't pass unless both parties support it. The boxes show the outcome rather than each party's score.

In the game that Buffett proposed, supporting the bill is a dominant strategy, and not supporting it is strictly stupid. If the other party supports the bill then you have to as well or else they get $1 billion. Similarly, if they don't support the reform, you should support the bill, and then use your billion dollars to crush them in the next election. Buf-

Democrats

	Support	*Not support*
Support	Bill passes	Bill fails but Republicans get $1 billion
Not support	Bill fails but Democrats get $1 billion	Bill fails

Republicans

Figure 15

fet's plan would likely work, and not even cost the billionaire anything, because both parties would always play their dominant strategy.

MORE CHALLENGING SIMULTANEOUS GAMES

Games involving dominant or strictly stupid strategies are usually easy to solve, so we will now consider more challenging games.

Coordination Games

How would you play the game in Figure 16? Obviously you should try to guess your opponent's move. If you're Player One you want to play A if your opponent plays X and play B if she plays Y. Fortunately, Player Two would be willing to work with you to achieve this goal so, for example, if she knows you are going to play A she will play X. In games like the one in Figure 16 the players benefit from cooperation. It would be silly for either player to hide her move or lie about what she planned on doing. In these types of games the players need to coordinate their actions.

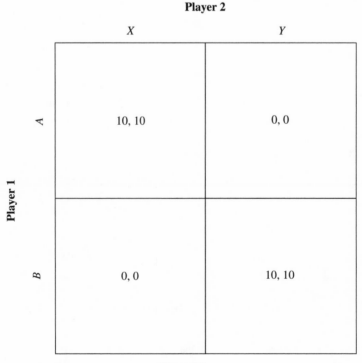

Figure 16

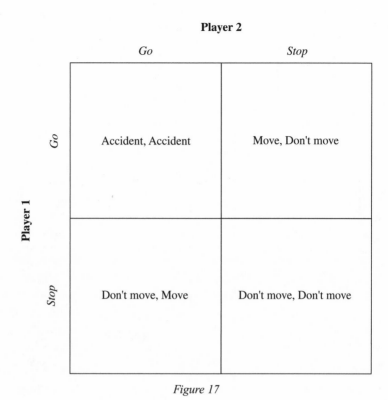

Figure 17

Traffic lights are a real-life coordination mechanism. Consider Figure 17. It illustrates a game that all drivers play. Two drivers approach each other at an intersection. Each driver can go or stop. While both drivers would prefer to not stop, if they both go they have a problem.

Coordination games also manifest when you are arranging to meet someone, and you both obviously want to end up at the same location, or where you're trying to match your production schedule with a supplier's deliveries. Figure 18 shows a coordination game that two movie studios play, in which they each plan to release a big budget film over one of the next three weeks. Each studio would prefer not to release its film when its rival does. The obvious strategy for the studios to follow is for at least one of them to announce when its film will be released. The other can choose a different week to premiere its film, so that both can reap high sales.

Technology companies play coordination games when they try to implement common standards. For example, several companies are

Player 2

	Release week 1	Release week 2	Release week 3
Release week 1	Low sales, Low sales	High sales, High sales	High sales, High sales
Release week 2	High sales, High sales	Low sales, Low sales	High sales, High sales
Release week 3	High sales, High sales	High sales, High sales	Low sales, Low sales

Figure 18

currently attempting to adopt a high-capacity blue-laser–based replacement for DVD players. Consumers are more likely to buy a DVD replacement if there is one standard that will run most software, rather than if they must get separate machines for each movie format. Consequently, companies have incentives to work together to design and market one standard.

In game theory land you do not trust someone because she is honorable or smiles sweetly when conversing with you. You trust someone only when it serves her interest to be honest. In traffic games a rational person would rarely try to fake someone out by pretending to stop at a red light only to quickly speed through the traffic signal. Since coordination leads to victory (avoiding accidents) in traffic games, you should trust your fellow drivers. In all coordination games your fellow player wants you to know her move and her benefits from keeping her promises about what moves she will make. The key to succeeding in coordination games is to be open, honest, and trusting.

Trust Games

Trust games are like coordination games except that you have a safe course to take if you're not sure whether your coordination efforts will succeed. Figure 19 illustrates a trust game. In this game, both players would be willing to play A if each knew that the other would play A as well. If, however, either player doubts that the other will play A, then he or she will play B. Playing B is the safe strategy because you get the same moderate payoff regardless of what your opponent does. Playing A is more risky; if your opponent also plays A, you do fairly well. Playing A when your opponent plays B, however, gives you an extremely low payoff.

Figure 20 illustrates a trust game where both you and a coworker demand a raise. In this game your boss could and would be willing to

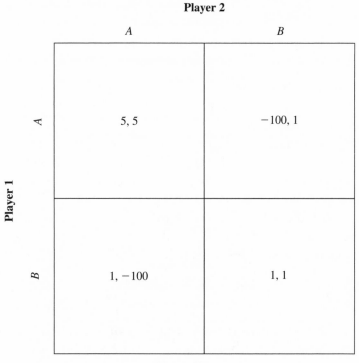

Figure 19

Player 2

	Demand raise	*Do nothing*
Demand raise	Get raise, Get raise	Get fired, Nothing
Do nothing	Nothing, Get fired	Nothing, Nothing

Figure 20

fire one of you, but couldn't afford to lose you both. If you jointly demand a raise, you both get it. Alas, if only one tries to get more money, he gets terminated.

In any trust game there is a safe course where you get a guaranteed payoff, and there is a risky strategy that gives you a high payoff if your fellow player does what he is supposed to. A simple example of a trust game is where two companies work together on a research project and both must complete their research for the project to succeed. The safe course for each company to take would be not to do any research, and thereby ensure that neither company has anything to lose in a joint venture. If your company does invest in the project, it receives a high payoff if the other firm fulfills its obligations. If, however, the other firm does not complete its research, then your firm loses its investment.

Let's consider a trust game played by criminals. When two individuals hope to profit from an illegal insider-trading scheme, they enter a trust game. Imagine you work at a law firm. Through your job you learn that Acme Corporation intends to buy Beta Company. You and only a few others know of Acme's plans. When Acme's takeover plans become public in a few days, you're sure that the value of Beta stock will rise. Obviously, you would like to buy lots of Beta stock before its price increases, but unfortunately, if you did buy Beta stock you would be guilty of insider trading and might face a prison term. Of course, you go to prison for insider trading only if you get caught, and the way not to get caught is to have someone else buy the stock based upon your information. You first consider suggesting to your father that he buy Beta stock. You realize the stupidity of this plan because if the SEC (the stock market police) found out that your father bought the stock, they might become suspicious. You need to get someone with whom you do not have a strong connection to buy the stock. You therefore propose to a friend you haven't seen since high school that he buy lots of Beta stock and split the profits with you. You and your friend have now entered into a trust game. Of course, the safe course of action would be not to engage in the illegal insider-trading scheme at all. If you engage in the insider-trading scheme you have very little chance of getting caught if neither of you does something stupid like brag about your exploits to a friend. If, however, the two of you carry out your plan, you each could suffer a massive loss if your fellow player proves untrustworthy.

Workers who go on strike are also often engaged in trust games. Frequently, if all the workers show solidarity and remain on strike until their demands are met, then management usually will have to give in, and the workers will be better off. Going on strike is risky, though, for you will be hurt if your fellow workers abandon the strike before management submits to the demands.

The obvious solution to any trust game might be for all parties simply to embark on the risky course. A small amount of doubt, however, might make the risk unbearable.

Doubts within Doubts: A Confusing Recursive Discourse
Doubts are deadly in trust games. Indeed, even doubts about doubts can cause trouble. For example, assume that both you and your friend have the temperament to successfully execute an insider-trading scheme. Your friend, however, falsely believes that you are a blabbermouth who would discuss your schemes with casual friends. Your

friend would consequently not engage in insider trading with you even though you both are trustworthy.

Figure 21 shows the mayhem unleashed by doubts within doubts. Obviously, in the game in Figure 21 the best outcome would occur if both people played A. Small doubts, however, could make this outcome impossible to achieve. To see this, imagine that there are two kinds of people, sane and crazy. Assume that a crazy person in the game in Figure 21 will always play B. A rational person will play whatever strategy gives him the highest payoff. Let's assume (perhaps unrealistically) that you are sane. If you think your opponent is crazy, then obviously you will play B and not get the high payoff. Let's assume, however, that you know your opponent is rational, but you also know that he mistakenly believes you to be crazy. If he thinks you are crazy, he will play B and thus you should too. Even if you are rational and your opponent is also rational, the only reasonable outcome, if your opponent thinks you are crazy, is for both of you to play B. Even though both parties are rational and believe the other person too is rational, if you doubt that they know you are rational, you should play B. This, of course, means that if your opponent believes that you believe that your opponent believes that you're crazy, then he should play B and consequently so should you. Thus, to achieve the ideal outcome in a trust game it's not sufficient for both people to trust each other. There must also be an infinite chain of trust where you trust that they trust that you trust that . . . that you're trustworthy.

Outguessing Games

The opposite of a coordination game is an outguessing game, the classic example of which is the matching pennies game shown in Figure 22. In the matching pennies game two players simultaneously choose either heads or tails. Each separately writes down his choice. If both players make the same choice, then Player One wins, while if they choose different sides, then Player Two wins.

Imagine that before both players write down their choice they talk to each other about strategy. If you're Player Two you obviously want to lie to Player One. Player One wins by matching your choice. Thus, if you intend to play heads, you should tell him you would play tails so he will try and match by playing tails, and you then win. Actually, this

Player 2

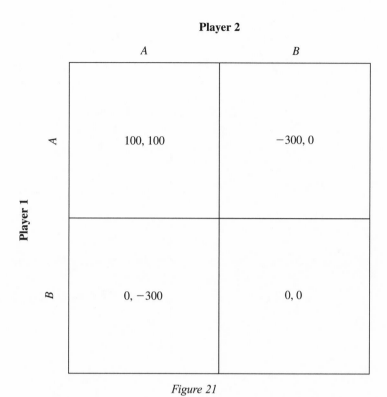

Figure 21

might not work since the other player knows you have an incentive to lie. If you are known always to lie, then people will acquire valuable information from your statements. For example, if I always lie and told you I was going to play tails, you would know that I really was about to pick heads. The matching pennies game, thus, shows that to truly deceive people (or at least provide them with no useful information) you must occasionally tell the truth. Perhaps this is why it is claimed that the Devil mixes the truth with his lies. If Satan always lied, we could achieve salvation by doing the opposite of what he says. Of course, if we always followed the strategy of doing the reverse of what Satan asked, he could take advantage of our poor gamesmanship and bring about our damnation (which results in one getting a very low payoff) by telling the truth. In contrast, if you're in a coordinating game with God, then it would be a reasonable strategy on God's part always to tell the truth because both God and you want to achieve the same outcome. Consequently, God is honest while Satan is deceptive,

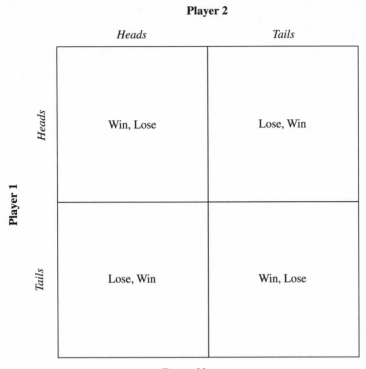

Figure 22

not merely because God is good while Satan is evil, but because the different games they are playing necessitate different strategies.

Armies often play outguessing games with each other. During World War II, the Germans knew that the Allies would try invading Nazi-occupied Europe from Britain. The Nazis didn't know, however, exactly where the Allies would land. Had the Nazis learned the landing locations, they would undoubtedly have deployed a massive number of troops at these points and probably repelled the invasion. The Allies, consequently, desperately tried to keep the invasion plans secret. Indeed, the Allies did more than this and spread false information to the Nazis. The invasion of Nazi-occupied Europe was successful because the Nazis thought the Allies were going to play tails when the Allies were really intending on playing heads.

In baseball, pitchers and batters play outguessing games. Batters try to predict what kind of ball the pitcher will throw, and pitchers try to hide their strategies. Pitchers always vary their throws to keep batters off balance and ensure that they never know what to expect. There would obviously be no advantage to a pitcher and batter negotiating over what kind of ball the pitcher should throw, since these players have conflicting goals. Pitchers and catchers usually signal to each other what kind of pitch will be thrown. The batter would be greatly helped if his team could decode these signals and transmit them to the batter. In outguessing games you can always gain by successfully spying on your opponent.

An outguessing game manifests when a company tries to catch a pilfering employee, as illustrated in Figure 23. The boxes are marked a little differently in this figure because the outcome, not the individual payoffs, is written in each box. Let's imagine that the company can secretly watch the supply room to see if someone is stealing stuff. It's too expensive for the company to monitor the room all the time, so they only occasionally have someone watch it. The company's strategy is either to monitor or not monitor. The employee enjoys stealing but only if he doesn't get caught. The employee's strategy is to steal or not steal. Obviously, the employee wants to steal only when the company isn't watching. Conversely, the company wants to watch only when the employee steals. Remember, in simultaneous games both sides move at the same time and must make their move while still ignorant of what their opponent will do. Thus, each side must predict what the other side is up to.

Randomness manifests in all outguessing games. To see this in our stealing game, assume, falsely, that there is no randomness and the outcome of the game is for the employee never to steal. In this case the company would never bother watching. Of course, if the company never watched, the employee would always steal. It is therefore unreasonable to assume that the employee will never steal. Furthermore, if the employee always steals, then the company will always watch, which of course will lead to the employee never stealing, which in turn will cause the company never to watch, which will . . . which will . . . The only stable outcome in this game is for the employee to sometimes steal and for the company to sometimes watch.

American taxpayers play an outguessing game with the IRS. People who cheat on their taxes and get caught pay fines and sometimes go to jail. People who cheat on their taxes and don't get caught,

Player 2 (Employee)

	Steal	*Not steal*
Monitor	*Employee caught*	*Company wastes resources watching*
Not monitor	*Supplies stolen*	*Nothing*

Player 1 (Company)

Figure 23

well, they just pay lower taxes. When a rational taxpayer decides whether to cheat on his taxes he thus must try to guess the likelihood of the IRS auditing him.[5] It's costly for the IRS to audit taxpayers. They only bother to do it to catch tax cheats and punish personal enemies. Thus, taxpayers and the IRS are in an outguessing game. You want to cheat only if you're not going to get audited, and the IRS wants to audit only if you're going to cheat. The only reasonable outcome involves randomness, where sometimes people cheat, and sometimes people get audited. As with all outguessing games, there is no point in trying to communicate your move to the IRS. Writing them a letter explaining that they shouldn't audit you because you have properly filled out your taxes is probably not going to reduce the chances of their coming after you. Similarly, while the IRS would probably believe a self-made claim that you had cheated on your taxes, issuing such a pronouncement is probably not an optimal strategy. In outguessing games you want to hide your moves.

When approaching an intersection at night, it would be a very bad idea to turn off your lights to keep the other drivers from guessing your intentions. In outguessing games, however, you always want to turn your lights off. This is because while in coordination games you are better off if your opponent knows your move, in outguessing games you want to hide your actions from your opponent. Or even better, you want to spread false information. Negotiations are pointless in outguessing games since both players have strong incentives to lie. The key to winning outguessing games is to hide, never trust, and always strive to deceive.

Games of Chicken

In the classic game of chicken, shown in Figure 24, two cars drive straight toward each other. The first driver who turns loses. Of course, if neither car swerves then both drivers lose even more. The best outcome for a player results when he goes straight and his opponent turns. In this situation the winning driver will be known as *macho* while the other driver will be considered *wimpy*. The worst outcome for either player manifests when an accident is caused by both drivers going straight. Consequently, a rational player will turn if he believes that his opponent is going to drive straight.

In a chicken game, therefore, you win by convincing your rival that you will never turn.[6] Consequently, perception is reality in the game of chicken. Chicken is not just a game about who is more macho, but also about who more exudes an air of machismo. Each player wants the other to believe that he is so macho that he would rather die than give in. If you can convince your opponent that you are indeed macho, you will win the game and thus be proven macho.

Insane players have a massive edge in the classic chicken game, for would you ever want to prove that you are more willing to risk death than a crazy person is? What if you suffer from the handicap of being considered sensible, however? Would anyone believe that a sensible person would ever adopt a strategy of never turning? Yes, having a strategy of never turning is rational if your opponent will always turn. If Player Two believes that Player One will always drive straight, then Player Two should always turn. Furthermore, if Player One

Player 2

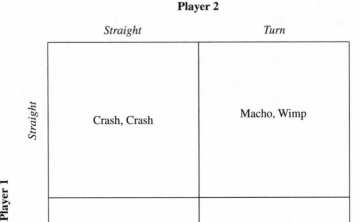

Figure 24

knows that Player Two believes that Player One will never turn, then Player One should indeed not turn. The players' beliefs about what they think will happen are self-reinforcing. If everyone thinks that one of the players will never turn, then that player's best strategy will indeed be never to turn. Again we see that in game theory land players often adopt strategies based upon what other people think they are going to do.

Excite@Home's Chicken Attempt[7]

Most negotiations don't lead to chicken games. Imagine that I own a good that you want to buy. If we fail to reach an agreement, we lose the benefit of the trade but don't necessarily destroy anything of value. A chicken game can exist only when the players might get into an accident, and an accident necessarily entails destruction.

When Excite@Home fell victim to the tech crash, its bondholders attempted to play a chicken game by creating the possibility of an accident. AT&T used Excite@Home to help provide Internet service to many AT&T customers. When Excite@Home faced bankruptcy, AT&T started negotiations to buy Excite@Home's assets. Excite@Home's creditors were unhappy with AT&T's offer, however, so they started playing chicken.

The creditors got legal permission to close down their Internet services and strand many AT&T subscribers. The creditors believed that AT&T would suffer if many of AT&T's Internet subscribers' web access was terminated. By threatening to shut down, Excite@Home attempted to increase the value of their assets to AT&T. Figure 25 illustrates this chicken game. Each party can be either a tough or soft negotiator. Had Excite@Home not been able to quickly cut off services, then AT&T's payoff if both parties were macho (top left box) would have simply been no deal. Excite@Home made this a game of chicken by causing AT&T to suffer in the event of the parties not reaching an agreement.

Imagine that I own a good worth $100 to you, so $100 is the most you would normally ever pay for it. Let's further assume, however, that

Excite@home

	Tough negotiations	Soft negotiations
AT&T Tough negotiations	Customer cut off, Assets wasted	Does well, Does poorly
AT&T Soft negotiations	Does poorly, Does well	Does OK, Does OK

Figure 25

I have the ability to cause you $30 worth of damage, and I threaten to inflict this damage if you don't buy my good for $125. As Excite@Home's bondholders understood, having the capacity to inflict pain can increase bargaining strength.

Unfortunately for Excite@Home, they overestimated their ability to harm AT&T. AT&T was able to move their Internet customers quickly to other networks, thus greatly limiting the damage from an accident. After moving their customers, AT&T withdrew their previous offer for Excite@Home's assets.

AT&T had what they thought was a long-term relationship with Excite@Home. In long-term business relationships you don't generally try to increase your profit by threatening to inflict pain on your partner. Since Excite@Home was going bankrupt, however, its time horizon shortened, so it tried to maximize its short-term payoff, rightly ignoring any long-term reputation loss. As this example shows, you can trust your business partners not to exploit you only so long as your partner still cares about his reputation.

Free Rider and Chicken Games[8]
Free rider problems can cause chicken games to manifest. In free rider games players try to be lazy and benefit from the efforts of others. Consider the game in Figure 26. Imagine that this game came about because a boss assigned two employees to complete a task. Each employee can either work at the task or evade the job. If both people work, the task will be completed, and each employee will earn a payoff of 10. If both employees shirk, the job won't get done, and both workers will be fired. To make this a free rider and chicken game, however, assume that if one employee works and the other shirks, the lazy employee who shirks gets a payoff of 15, while the stupid hardworking one gets only 0 (but doesn't get fired.) Both employees want the other to do the work, but if either believes that the other will not work, she will work to avoid getting fired.

Both players would have an incentive to tell each other that they will definitely not do the work. If I can convince you that I won't work, you definitely will so I can safely slack. Of course, you have the same incentive to convince me that you are going to slack. Consequently, neither of us should completely believe the other when we say we

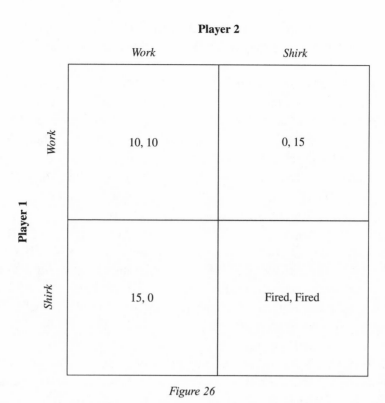

Figure 26

won't work. It is therefore possible that neither party will work because each believes that the other might.

In both coordination and chicken games the players could coordinate their actions to avoid an accident. As you recall, in coordination games you always should believe the other party so avoiding bad outcomes is relatively easy. For example, assume that you're a pedestrian at a crosswalk, and a driver signals for you to cross the street in front of his car. At this moment you and the driver are in a coordination game where the worst outcome would be if you both attempted to simultaneously cross the street. When the driver signals for you to go she is in effect telling you that he will stay put. Since the driver would have no sane reason for deceiving you about her intentions you should probably believe him and walk across the street, confident that you will avoid an accident. In chicken games, however, your fellow player has an incentive to exaggerate his commitment to going straight. Since both of you should always suspect the other might lie, an accident can occur because the two of you could not rely upon communication to avoid disaster.

I recall one real-life game of chicken I played with my sister when we were both young teenagers in which there was an "accident." Our mother told us she was going out to the yard but was expecting an important call. She told us to be sure to answer the phone when it rang. (This game took place in primitive times before answering machines had invaded middle-class homes.) When the phone did ring, both my sister and I insisted that the other get the phone. This exchange continued until the phone stopped ringing. Our mother heard the phone but was unable to reach it before the caller hung up. She expressed anger and disappointment at my sister and me. This was clearly unfair, however, as she had created the game of chicken and should have anticipated the possibility of an accident. Had our mother clearly assigned responsibility for picking up the phone to only one of us, I'm sure it would have been answered.

Assigning clear responsibility can avoid accidents in free rider/ chicken games. Let's reconsider the game in Figure 26, in which both employees want the other to do the work. Recall that there is some chance that neither player will do the work because each expects the other to complete the task. Now imagine a simpler game in which the employer splits the task in two. The boss pronounces that an employee who doesn't complete his task gets fired. Now each employee will play a game where he gets, say, 10 if he works and gets fired if he doesn't. Both employees should now work. Of course, since it's often essential for people to work in teams in business, managers can't always split responsibilities.

Chicken games also occur between firms rather than just within them. Imagine that two firms are considering entering a local market in which there is room for only one firm to operate profitably. In this example, each firm would want to convince the other that it was completely committed to staying in the market, but would also want to have plans to leave the market if the competition stayed in. Interestingly, each firm might welcome attempts by the other firm to spy on them.

Spying in Chicken Games
As you recall, in outguessing games you want to stop your opponent from spying on you. In outguessing games, if your opponent figures out

your strategy, he always wins. In chicken games, however, if your opponent knows your strategy, and that strategy is one of machismo, then you will triumph. Thus, if you believe that you could put up a brave front, you should welcome your opponent's attempts to spy on you.

Indeed, disaster would result if you tried to rebuff spying attempts. Imagine that you have told your opponent that you are definitely going to enter this small market. You hope he will believe you and not try to enter himself. But further imagine that your opponent sends a spy to your business to see if you are really planning to enter. If you turn away this spy, what should he believe? Obviously, if you know that his spy would report that you were indeed planning on entering the market, you would welcome him. Since you are rebuffing the spying attempt, however, your opponent should suspect that you have something to hide. The only thing that you would have to hide is your lack of commitment to entry. Not welcoming spies signals that you could be a wimp. Since perception is everything in chicken games, being perceived as a wimp will indeed make you wimpy. It is therefore vital in games of chicken never to openly stop your opponent from watching your actions.

The difference between counter-spying strategies in chicken and outguessing games comes about because in outguessing games a party always has something to hide. Regardless of what move a player plans to make in an outguessing game, she doesn't want her opponent to become aware of her actions. Attempts at concealment in outguessing games tell your opponent nothing, since everyone would always try to hide everything in these games. In chicken games, however, a party wants to hide something only when she has a weak commitment to adopting the macho strategy. Thus, you can't completely hide your actions from a spy in a chicken game because the very act of concealment signals your actions. Not allowing the spy in tells the spy everything she wants to know.

Chicken Treasure Hunts

A chicken game can result when multiple players seek a treasure. Imagine that a recently uncovered pirate's diary indicates the existence of buried treasure somewhere on a small island. Let's say the treasure would be worth $100,000 if found. Unfortunately, it would cost $70,000 to search the island and find the treasure. Since it would obviously be worth spending $70,000 to get a $100,000 treasure it would seem to be a good idea to search for the treasure. What happens, however, if two people know of the treasure's existence? If they teamed up, they could split both the costs and the benefits. What if one party, however, wanted the whole treasure for herself? If both players spent $70,000 searching for the treasure, at most only one of them would find it. Spending $70,000 for a 50 percent chance of getting $100,000 is a terrible investment; even Las Vegas (but not government-run lotteries) would give you better odds. Consequently, if one party is genuinely known to be committed to searching for the treasure, the other party should not even try looking for it. If only one party looks for the treasure, then that player will make a nice profit. Thus, this treasure hunt is also a game of chicken where each party wants to convince the other that each is committed to the macho (searching for the treasure) strategy.

When multiple firms conduct similar research, they are often on treasure hunts. Under the U.S. patent system the first company that discovers some useful invention receives all the rights to that invention. If my company makes the discovery one day before yours, I receive the patent rights, and you get to explain to your stockholders why you wasted so much money on research.

How much should a company be willing to pay for a patent worth $10 million? They should be willing to pay up to, but not quite including, $10 million. Now imagine that multiple firms are simultaneously trying to get the same patent. If they all spend close to $10 million on the venture then most will lose money. It's worth spending nearly $10 million researching the patent only if you know that your research will indeed result in your getting the patent. If multiple firms are vying for the same type of patent, your firm obviously can't be sure that its research efforts will pay off. As a result, if you know that others are going for the patent, it might be optimal for you not to try.

Of course, the other firms would very much like for you not even to try. As a result they have a strong incentive to notify you that they are seeking the patent. Normally, we assume that companies like to keep research projects secret so other firms won't steal their ideas. When playing patent chicken games, however, the optimal strategy is to broadcast your research goals loudly. As with any chicken game, firms will have an incentive to lie and exaggerate their commitment to getting the patent. If the firm sells stock, however, then securities fraud laws might prevent the firm from telling too grievous a lie about its research agenda.

For example, vaporware manifests because of chicken games. Vaporware is software that a company announces but doesn't complete. Imagine that a $10 million market arises for a new type of business software. It would cost $7 million, however, for a company to develop this software. You want to capture this market, but you don't want to develop the new software immediately. If your competition knew that you would take a year before starting to write the software, they would immediately start developing and capture the market for themselves. You could use vaporware, however, to reserve the market for future capture. You could falsely announce that your software would be ready in one year. This announcement, if credible, should scare away potential entrants.

The key to prevailing in a chicken game is to convince your opponent that you are committed to the macho course. You should welcome your opponents' attempts to spy on you. If, however, you are certain that your fellow player is herself going to be macho, then your optimal strategy is to be a wimp so as to avoid an accident.

Games of Chicken and the Cuban Missile Crisis[9]
The Cuban missile crisis of 1962 was a game of chicken. The United States discovered that the Soviet Empire placed missiles in Cuba. Fortunately, America discovered the missiles before they became operational. Because Cuba was so close to the United States, the missiles greatly enhanced the Soviets' military power. Absent these Cuban missiles, the United States could have struck the Soviet Empire with far more atomic weapons than the Soviets could hit America with. The United States had a greater capacity to strike over long distances than the Soviets did, and the United States had bases in Turkey, which bordered on the Soviet Empire. President John F. Kennedy demanded the removal of the missles and imposed a naval blockade on Cuba. Both the United States and the Soviet Empire had the choice of following a macho or wimpy strategy. For the Soviets, being macho meant not removing the nuclear missiles. For Kennedy, being macho meant invading, bombing, or blockading Cuba. If both players took the macho course, atomic armageddon might have resulted.

We now know that the Kennedy Administration gave some consideration to invading Cuba. Had the United States invaded Cuba, the Soviets might have responded by taking West Berlin, and had the United States then tried to free West Berlin, war might have broken out between the two superpowers.

It must have appeared to President Kennedy that the United States was in a much stronger position than the Soviets were because America's capacity to hurt the Soviets was far greater than the Soviet's capacity to harm America. To President Kennedy it must have appeared as if the two countries were playing the classic game of chicken, but with America driving a truck and the Soviets a small car.

Unknown to the United States, however, it appears that the Soviet agents in Cuba had operational battlefield nuclear weapons. The Soviets could not have used these weapons to strike the United States, but they could have used the weapons to attack invading American troops. An American invasion of Cuba might therefore have triggered an atomic response.

The existence of the Soviet battlefield nuclear weapons would have made it easier for the Soviets and Cubans to resist an American invasion. Had President Kennedy known of these weapons' existence, he surely would have given less consideration to invading Cuba. So, in this game of chicken, while Kennedy thought the Soviets were driving a small car, they were really driving a truck.

Recall, in games of chicken you always want to convince your opponent that you will be macho. Since the battlefield nuclear weapons clearly made it more likely that the Soviets would be macho, the Soviets made a serious mistake in not informing President Kennedy about the weapons' existence. The Soviet Empire collapsed because its rulers didn't understand economics, so I guess it's not surprising that they didn't understand elementary game theory either.

In the end the Soviets backed down, at least publicly. The Soviets removed the missiles from Cuba in return for America's pledge not to invade Cuba. Privately, America agreed to remove some missiles from Turkey. These Turkey-based missiles were obsolete and due to be removed soon anyway. The agreement between the two countries specified that if the Soviets told anyone about America's promise to remove the missiles from Turkey, then America would no longer be bound to remove them. President Kennedy clearly wanted to be perceived as

Player 2

	Macho	*Wimp*
Macho	−1000, −1000	100, 0
Wimp	0, 100	0, 0

Figure 27

macho, and he no doubt feared that this perception would be tarnished if it were known that he had given away too much to the Soviets.

Winning Chicken by Burning Money

Burning money can be profitable![10] To see the advantages of burning money, consider the chicken game in Figure 27.

Obviously in this game each player would want to convince his opponent that he is committed to being macho. If, for example, Player Two believes that Player One will be macho, then Player Two will be a wimp, giving Player One his highest possible payoff. Player One could actually signal his commitment to being macho by burning money.

Let's expand the game in Figure 27. First, Player One has the option of publicly burning $5. Second, both players simultaneously choose their strategy. Player One's strategy consists of two parts: deciding whether to burn and choosing between A or B. Player One now has four possible strategies.

If Player One elects to burn $0 and be a wimp, then his payoff is $0, regardless of whether Player Two elects to be a wimp or to be macho. On the other hand, if Player One elects to burn $5 and be a wimp, then his payoff is –$5, regardless of whether Player Two elects to be a wimp or to be macho.

Burning $5 and being a wimp is a strictly stupid strategy. If you are going to be a wimp, you are always better off not burning $5. Thus, everyone should predict that if Player One does burn $5, he would not be a wimp. Hence, if Player Two observes that Player One burns $5, then Player Two should assume that Player One will be macho. If Player Two believes that Player One will be macho, then Player Two will choose to be a wimp. By publicly burning $5, Player One credibly signals that he will be macho.

Businesses have no need to actually burn money, however; for they can publicly waste funds. The best way for you to waste your money is to send it to me. Companies can also burn money by paying for celebrity endorsements. For example, to signal your commitment to enter a new market that could only profitably support one firm you could hire an expensive celebrity to star in commercials announcing your intentions. With luck, the pricey commercials will convince rivals of your absolute commitment to enter the market so your rivals will stay away.

Fixed-Sum Games

You can characterize games by their total payoff. In a fixed-sum game, what one player gets, another loses. Mathematically, in a fixed-sum game, the sum of the players' payoff in each of the boxes adds up to the same number. Chess is a fixed-sum game in which if one player wins, the other must lose. Variable-sum games consist simply of all games that are not fixed sum. In variable-sum games the players can often benefit from working together.

In fixed-sum games cooperation is pointless because the player's interests are diametrically opposed. In negotiations you seek to get something that makes you better off. If, however, my gain is your loss, then the fact that I want something necessarily means you shouldn't give it to me.

You can consider a game to be like a pie. The players' strategies determine the size of the pie and what percentage of the pie each player gets to eat. In variable-sum games the size of the pie varies, so there is room for both cooperation and competition. The players have an incentive to cooperate to make the total pie as large as possible and to compete to maximize what percentage of the pie they each get. In fixed-sum games outside forces fix the size of the pie, and the players fight over how much of the pie each of them gets to eat. Consequently, in fixed-sum games there is no room for cooperation.

Fixed-sum games can get nasty because you always want to inflict maximum pain on your opponent. Clearly, if his loss is your gain then you want him to suffer. For example, imagine that you and a coworker are up for a promotion that only one of you can get. If the only factor relevant to both payoffs is who gets the promotion, then the game is clearly fixed sum. In this game anything you could do to make your coworker look bad would increase your chances. Similarly, anything she could do to harm you would advance his interests. Thus, you would each benefit from sabotaging each other's work and spreading degrading rumors about each other.

There are, however, very few fixed-sum games in business settings. In our promotion game we assumed that the only relevant consideration was whether you got the promotion. This assumption is clearly unrealistic, as it would be possible for you both to not get the promotion and to get fired. If both you and the coworker recognize that your promotion game was not fixed sum, then you would realize the benefits of agreeing not to make each other look bad.

Consider a market where only two firms sell widgets. These firms are almost certainly not in a fixed-sum game. It's true that if one company takes a bigger percentage of the market, then the other company must lose market share. It's possible, however, for the total market for widgets to increase or for the price each firm charges for widgets to rise.

Imagine that in an effort to reduce its rival's sales, one company falsely announces that the use of widgets causes cancer. This announcement strategy would almost certainly harm the rival firm. If this game were really fixed sum, harming its rival would always help the announcing firm. Of course, announcing that a product you produce causes cancer is unlikely to be a winning strategy because firms are never really in fixed-sum games.

Politicians, however, do play fixed-sum games. Political candidates often run negative advertisements while companies almost never do because running for elected office is a fixed-sum game where only one candidate can win. Thus, anything that hurts your political rival helps you get elected. Imagine you're running for office in a two-person race. You realize that if you run a negative ad it will make 20 percent of the voters think your rival is stupid. Of course, she will retaliate and run a negative ad that makes maybe 15 percent of the voters think you are a moron. Should you run the ad? Absolutely, it will increase your chance of winning this fixed-sum game. Now imagine that you run a company and are considering running a negative ad against a competitor. As before, if you run your ad your competitor will likewise retaliate. Should you publicly attack your rival? No! Even if you can harm your rival more than she could hurt you, you would both probably end up losing money. Running the ad would shrink the size of the pie your two firms divide.

Look to Interests

To win, you must know what you are playing. Different games require different strategies. The game you're in is determined by the alignment of the player's interests, so when starting a new venture ask:

- Does everyone have the same objectives?
- Would other players benefit from lying to me about their strategy?
- Is the game fixed or variable sum?
- Do I want my opponent to guess my future moves?
- Am I better off being perceived as rational or crazy?

Mass Coordination Games

In the next chapter we will look at simultaneous coordination games that are played by millions of consumers. The outcome of these games often determines the fate of high technology companies.

Lessons Learned

- A dominant strategy gives you a higher payoff than all other strategies regardless of what your opponent does.
- A strictly stupid strategy gives you a lower payoff than some other strategies regardless of what your opponent does.
- You should always play dominant strategies and never play strictly stupid strategies, and you should assume that your opponent will do the same.
- You should be open, honest, and trusting in coordination games.
- A small amount of doubt can make it impossible for two parties to trust each other.
- It's useless to negotiate in outguessing games.
- In chicken games perception is reality, so you must do everything to convince your opponent that you are committed to the macho course.

5

MASSIVE
COORDINATION GAMES

We look for opportunities with network externalities—
where there are advantages to the vast majority of consumers to share a common standard.

Bill Gates[1]

I N THE LAST CHAPTER, we discussed simultaneous games
and learned about various classifications of games. In
this chapter we will focus on coordination games with
millions of players. Recall that in coordination games
the players need to synchronize their actions.

The introduction of the first telephones created a coordination game among its potential customers. If everyone else
was going to get one then it made sense for you to get one too.
If, however, no one you knew was planning to get a phone then
it would be silly for you to buy one. Telephones are valuable
only when commonly owned since the benefits of having a
telephone are proportional to the number of your family members, friends, and associates who are also on the telephone network. Telephones exhibit network externalities because they
become more valuable when more people own them. Network
externalities give rise to mass coordination games.

Network externalities—the more people who have the product, the more valuable the product becomes.

You should buy a device that exhibits network externalities only if people you interact with also have the product or plan to buy it soon. Many products other than telephones exhibit network externalities. For example, no matter how much you might be impressed by the technology underlying fax machines, the pleasure you would receive by faxing yourself documents would probably not justify the machine's cost.

Network externalities are the dominant strategic consideration in the computer industry. Indeed, Microsoft owes its vast success to network externalities.

ATTACK OF THE CLONES: AN EXTREMELY BRIEF HISTORY OF THE PERSONAL COMPUTER INDUSTRY

Before the personal computer, there were mainframes. IBM was the primary producer of mainframe computers. Large companies, not individual consumers, bought mainframes. Apple was the first company to sell easy-to-set-up computers to consumers and its early success caused IBM to enter the desktop computer market.

IBM wanted to sell a desktop computer, but it didn't want to design all of the computer parts itself, so IBM asked Microsoft to write an operating system for its personal computer and asked Intel to manufacture its computer's microprocessor. IBM's personal computer was a huge success and far more people bought personal computers from IBM than Apple. Unfortunately for IBM, the sale of clones caused most of the profits from the personal computer industry to go to other firms.

IBM clones worked almost exactly as an IBM-manufactured computer did. Most importantly, they would run software that had been explicitly written for IBM personal computers. These IBM clones still mostly used Microsoft operating systems and Intel microprocessors. Microsoft and Intel made far more money from personal computers than did IBM or Apple. The vast majority of the personal computers in use today have Microsoft operating systems and Intel microprocessors—not necessarily because of these products' quality, but rather because of network externalities and coordination games.

SUCCESS, FAILURE, AND NETWORK EXTERNALITIES

Many people considered and still do consider Apple computer's operating system superior to Microsoft's. Alas, Microsoft's operating system dominates the market while Apple is a smaller (sometimes it seems dying) niche player. Network externalities caused by compatibility problems are the reason that most everyone buys Microsoft operating systems. Operating systems exhibit network externalities because software written for a computer with one type of operating system will not easily run on a computer with a different system. Thus, software written for Microsoft's operating system will not work on an Apple computer or an IBM-compatible computer that has a non-Microsoft operating system.

Software makers want to sell as many copies of their product as possible. Therefore, most software makers devote the majority of their resources to writing software for the type of computer that most people have. A consumer, therefore, benefits from having the same operating system as most everyone else. As a result, the more people who use the same type of operating system as you do, the more software there will be for you to use.

Microsoft's continuing popularity arises from a virtuous, network externality–driven cycle; since most everyone uses Microsoft's operating system, most everyone else wants to use Microsoft's operating system. Consumers play a coordination game with each other where most people want to use the same kind of computer as everyone else does. For whatever reason, consumers have chosen to coordinate on Microsoft-based personal computers. As the game in Figure 28 shows, even if people prefer Apples, they might end up buying Microsoft-based computers. In this game if each person expects the other to buy a Microsoft-based computer, then they are better off getting one and receiving a payoff of 9, rather than getting an Apple computer and possibly receiving a payoff of only 5. What a great situation for Microsoft: Its product stays popular because it is popular.

Apple lost a chance to take advantage of network externalities. Bill Gates, in 1985, wanted to modify Macintosh's operating system (which required Motorola processors) so it could be run on Intel processors. Apple refused to give him the necessary legal permission.[2] Had Apple's operating system been made compatible with Intel chips, then Apple would have benefited from the network externalities that

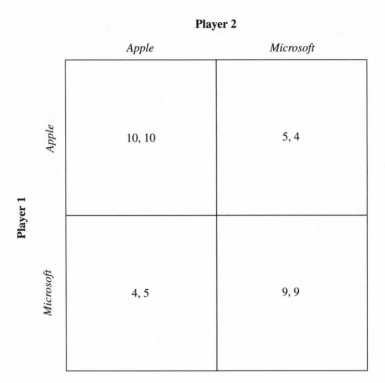

Figure 28

made Gates so rich.[3] Microsoft understood what Apple didn't: Where network externalities are concerned, size doesn't just matter, it's the dominating consideration.

Like Microsoft, Intel also benefits from network externalities. Since most computers run on Intel microprocessors, software developers make most of their products compatible with Intel microprocessors, which, of course, causes most consumers to want to buy Intel-based computers. As with Microsoft's operating system, Intel microprocessors are popular because a lot of people buy them.

COMPETING AGAINST MICROSOFT AND INTEL

How could a company compete against Intel or Microsoft? Ideally, the company would sidestep the duo's network externalities by marketing a compatible product. Absent compatibility, even if your company designed a cheaper and easier-to-use operating system than Microsoft's, consumers would still be reluctant to purchase it because most existing software would be incompatible with your operating system. If, however, your operating system could run Microsoft-compatible software, then you could imperil Microsoft's dominance.

AMD, in fact, has adopted such a strategy against the microprocessor maker Intel. AMD makes microprocessors that, from the consumer's viewpoint at least, function almost identically to Intel's. Consequently, AMD has been able to capture a small share of Intel's market.

IBM, of course, did lose its dominance to competitors' compatible products. Since many companies have made cheap IBM clones, IBM received no benefit from network externalities. When a consumer decides whether to buy an IBM or a Dell personal computer, his choice is based upon price or quality. This puts IBM and Dell on a level playing field where the edge goes to the company with the superior manufacturing skills. In contrast, network externalities protect Microsoft's market position, so even if another company made a cheaper, better product, most consumers would still buy their operating system from Microsoft.

In addition to making a compatible product, you could also compete against a company with network externalities by selling to niche markets. For example, Apple has a large share of the market for personal computers used in grade schools. Apple has the advantage when selling to grade schools because its computers have historically been easier to use than IBM-compatible computers. Furthermore, since so many grade schools use Apple computers, much grade school–specific software is written for Apple computers, and thus Apple enjoys network externalities in the grade school niche market.

For high technology products at least, perhaps the best way to attack a firm protected by network externalities is to wait until the firm's consumers decide to play another mass coordination game. High technology products quickly become obsolete. For example, most software written today wouldn't run very well on a computer bought even seven years ago because of the rapid increase in computer speed, graphics, and memory.

The quick obsolescence of computer products limits the benefits of network externalities. To understand this, consider two types of software a consumer might want: (1) old software that has already been written, and (2) new software the consumer hopes to buy in the future. Microsoft and Intel have two advantages over potential competitors. Because their products have dominated the computer market, there exists a large stock of software compatible with their products. Furthermore, because people expect most computers in the future to run on Microsoft's operating system and Intel's microprocessors, consumers expect that most future software will be compatible with these companies' products.

Now, imagine your company develops a new type of computer that won't run existing software. Unfortunately, consumers will be reluctant to buy your computer when an IBM-compatible computer (with a Microsoft operating system and an Intel microprocessor) will run far more software. You can't do anything about the existing stock of software. If you could convince software makers that your computer is going to be a big hit, however, then they should be willing to write new software that runs on your computer. The continual improvement in computer performance thus actually hurts Microsoft and Intel because it reduces the benefit of the existing stock of software that is exclusively compatible with their products.

Technological obsolescence and the challenges of achieving backward compatibility gives competitors another advantage over Microsoft and Intel. Both of these companies must continually improve their products as engineers figure out ways to make computers better, faster, and cheaper. To preserve network externalities, however, Microsoft and Intel desperately try to keep their new products compatible with old software, but it's technologically difficult to make products backward compatible. It would be easier for both Microsoft and Intel to design their products if they didn't have to worry about compatibility. If your products won't run old software anyway, your engineers won't be hindered by the limitations of backward compatibility. As a result, if your company has the same level of engineering skills as Microsoft and Intel, you should be able to make a better product. Of course, the superior quality of your product might not be sufficient to overcome the benefits of network externalities that both Microsoft and Intel enjoy.

JAVA'S THREAT TO MICROSOFT

Microsoft's Internet Explorer dominates the browser market. Although it appears that Microsoft gives Internet Explorer away for free, it is actually a tremendous source of profit for Microsoft. First, Microsoft bundles Internet Explorer with its operating system. This bundling makes the operating system more valuable to consumers and consequently raises the price that Microsoft can charge for Windows. Microsoft also profits from having special knowledge about Internet Explorer's workings.

Many types of Internet application software are written to be used by consumers running Internet Explorer. The greater knowledge a company has about how Internet Explorer works, the better they can make their application software. Since Microsoft knows more about Internet Explorer than any other company, Microsoft has an advantage when writing application software for its browser.

Java poses a threat to Internet Explorer's network externalities. Java is an Internet-friendly program that runs on top of Internet browsers and operating systems, and it was designed to work with all major types of computers. The idea behind Java is that programmers could write software specifically for it, and then these programs could run on any computer, even if the computer was not running Microsoft software. If Java, which was created by Sun Microsystems, fulfills its potential, then it, not Microsoft, will reap the benefits from network externalities. If everyone used Java, then you wouldn't need to own Internet Explorer or even a Microsoft operating system to use most Internet software applications. As of this writing, however, Java seems destined to become an important, not critical, Internet programming language and consequently network externalities will likely be a continuing source of riches for Microsoft.

EXTERNALITIES IN WORD PROCESSING PROGRAMS

Microsoft also receives massive network externality profits from Microsoft Word, its extremely popular word processing program. It's easiest to share word processing files if everyone involved uses the same program. Many businesses mandate Word, not because they like Microsoft, but rather because they like network externalities. Businesses know that it is important for their employees to use the same type of word processing program. As a result, sales of Word are kept high because of its popularity.

The Superiority of English

English is the most useful language in the world to know. English-speaking countries gain a massive advantage because of the dominance of their native language. Ambitious children in France, for example, spend years learning English because success in many professions requires mastering it. The French would benefit, therefore, if they could all magically trade their knowledge of French for knowledge of English. Of course, transitional costs would make it very difficult for the French to adopt English as their "native" language. Consequently, they try to convince people in non–French-speaking countries that learning French still has value. Because of network externalities, however, their arguments lack credibility.

Imagine a conversation between a French intellectual and a Mexican student in which the Frenchman tries to convince the student to take French rather than English as his second language. The intellectual might tout the relative beauty of French over English. The Mexican student, however, even if he believes the Frenchman's assessment, would dismiss this claim as mostly irrelevant. English's value to the Mexican student results from his being far more likely to encounter people who speak English than French, especially since most educated native speakers of French also speak English, while most native English speakers don't bother to become proficient in another language. In its massive coordination game, the educated citizens of the world have decided to learn English as either a first or second language. As with all coordination games, once everyone has decided on a strategy, everyone benefits from continuing to play along. As with Microsoft Word, English remains popular because it is widely used.

COBOL

Just as everyone benefits from speaking the same human language, programmers profit from knowing the same coding language. The U.S. government once tried to make COBOL a common computer language by announcing that it would only buy COBOL-compatible computers.[4]

The U.S. government's position as the top purchaser of computers gives it enormous power in cyber coordination games. In mass consumer coordination games everyone tries to match the decisions of other buyers. Consequently, one significant buyer can massively influence who wins the network externalities coordination sweepstakes.

WHERE WE LIVE

Mass coordination games often determine where individuals live. Many people, unfortunately, prefer to live in neighborhoods in which they are not a racial minority, and as a consequence, neighborhoods often become ethnically homogenous.

Imagine that two different ethnic groups, labeled X and Y, live in a city and assume that no one wants to live in a neighborhood in which he is a minority. Total ethnic homogeneity is the only stable outcome. If, for example, only type X lives in a certain neighborhood, then in the future no one but type X will want to move in, and so the neighborhood will remain nondiverse forever. Could a neighborhood ever be ethnically diverse, however?

Unless a neighborhood is equally divided between X and Y, then one of the groups must mathematically be in the minority, and this minority group will gradually move out. Is it stable for a neighborhood to be equally divided between Xs and Ys? Unfortunately, random shocks will always undermine ethnically balanced neighborhoods. Just by chance, in every neighborhood there will always be more of one group than another. These random shocks will be accelerated by deliberate action when one group unexpectedly finds itself in the minority and leaves the neighborhood. Consequently, the only stable outcome is for all neighborhoods to be ethnically homogenous even though both groups wouldn't object if, 40 percent of their neighbors were from a different ethnic group.

The same mass coordination games that result in neighborhoods becoming ethnically homogenous will also cause some cities to have a higher percentage of homosexuals. Most humans prioritize being able to find a sexual partner. The task of finding a mate can be more challenging for homosexuals since they make up a small percentage of the population. Consequently, when a homosexual decides where to live, the percentages of gays in different areas will rationally play a large part in his settlement decision.

When many homosexuals desire to live in a city with a large proportion of people with their sexual orientation, the consequence will be that a few cities will become known for having a large gay population. Once a city like San Francisco or Northampton, MA, gets a relatively large number of homosexuals, other gays will be attracted to the city, accelerating this effect.

The high percentage of gays in San Francisco shows the accidental nature of coordination games. There is no reason why San Francisco should have such a large gay population. Coordination games, however, often result in one city or product being extremely popular with a population group.

ONLINE BULLETIN BOARDS

English is a useful language to know because many are fluent in it. Many students at Smith College, where I teach, use the Smith dailyjolt because it too can be easily used to communicate with many people. The Smith dailyjolt is a bulletin board on which students can post anonymous comments about anything. (During course selection time they write about their professors, seemingly without taking into account that their professors have access to the dailyjolt too.) The dailyjolt provides separate bulletin boards for many different colleges. I have noticed that many other colleges' dailyjolts aren't much used. There are clearly network externalities associated with a web bulletin board. I suspect that Smith students like writing for the Smith dailyjolt because they know that many other students will read and respond to their postings. The dailyjolt at Smith is popular today because it was popular in the past. Similarly, other schools' dailyjolts are unpopular because few students have ever used them.

The popularity of the Smith dailyjolt provides a lesson for firms marketing goods with network externalities. The key to success results from getting many people to coordinate on your product. Consequently, when marketing goods with network externalities, perception becomes reality. If your new product has network externalities and many people think it will become popular then it has a good chance of actually becoming popular. Remember, people use products with network externalities because they like them, and because they think other people will use them.

www.DrudgeReport.com

The leading Internet news site belongs not to big media but to the eccentric reporter, Matt Drudge. The Drudge Report's popularity stems from its being the first to break many news stories. Indeed, Drudge was the first to tell the world about Monica Lewinsky and Bill

Clinton. I'm not exactly sure how the Drudge Report gets all of its scoops, but I suspect that coordination games create a virtuous circle for Drudge.

If you have an interesting story you want widely disseminated over the net, then the Drudge Report is an ideal venue for your story. Consequently, the circular logic that dominates coordination games benefits the Drudge Report. The Drudge Report gets the best scoops because it is popular. But the Drudge Report stays popular only because it often has the best in breaking news.

VHS VERSUS BETA

Network externalities caused Betamax's extinction. In the 1980s the Beta and VHS video formats fought for dominance. Although many people considered Beta's technology superior, VHS won the standards war.[5] Video availability determines the value of a video player. The more popular the recorder, however, the more videos will be made available for the recorder. Consequently, network externalities cause consumers to want to own the same recorder that everyone else does. Once VHS gained a large enough market share, therefore, Betamax was doomed. Will the Xbox be tomorrow's Betamax?

VIDEO GAME WARS

As of this writing, Microsoft has recently introduced its dedicated game machine, the Xbox. Should a consumer buy an Xbox? Only if he thinks that many other consumers will also buy one. The quality and quantity of games written for the Xbox will largely determine its value. Microsoft will probably write only a small percentage of Xbox software, while independent gaming companies will write the rest. These independent firms will develop Xbox games only if a lot of people own the Xbox. Thus, if most game lovers buy the Xbox, then most new games will be written for the Xbox, and most rational game lovers will buy the Xbox.

Sony's Playstation 2 is a rival for the video game network externalities Microsoft desires. Unfortunately for Microsoft, if the Playstation 2 proves more popular than the Xbox, then it's the Playstation 2 that will have the most games written for it, and it will be the Playstation 2 that most game lovers will desire. If a game written for the Xbox could be played on the Playstation 2, then consumers would not be playing a coordination game. Absent compatibility concerns, and it would be all right to be one of a very few people who own the Playstation 2 because you would still have many games to choose from. Because games are console specific, however, players want to buy the same machines that most other players buy. Consequently, if consumers purchase enough of any one game machine, sales of this machine will reach a tipping point and drive other firms from the market. After achieving this tipping point, the dominant firm's position will be self-sustaining, since gamers will buy this console because it is the dominant game machine. Coordination games among consumers tend to result in winner-take-all markets for companies. When all consumers want to coordinate on a single product, the likely outcome of competition is a monopoly. This monopoly persists until the product becomes obsolete.

Microsoft, Sony, and Nintendo (the manufacturer of another new gaming machine) are in a treasure hunt. They are spending vast amounts to win the prize of being the dominant video game manufacturer. Microsoft, for example, adopted the reasonable strategy of selling each Xbox at a loss. If Microsoft becomes the dominant video game manufacturer, then network externalities will protect its position long into the future. Therefore, Microsoft should initially sell a very cheap product to get lots of buyers. If enough people have purchased the Xbox, most new video game software will be written for the Xbox. This will increase the Xbox's value and allow Microsoft to raise its price. Of course, if the Playstation 2 becomes the dominant video game machine, then it will enjoy the benefits of network externalities, and Microsoft will never recoup the money it loses on the sale of each Xbox.

AT&T CREATES NETWORK EXTERNALITIES

AT&T has a new marketing plan whereby customers pay a flat fee to make unlimited calls to other AT&T customers.[6] Before the implementation of AT&T's plan, there were no network externalities to your choice of long-distance telephone carrier. If everyone else in the world but you used AT&T, you still had no compelling reason to switch. Under AT&T's plan, however, you would want to use them if everyone else you knew also did.

Your friends are more likely to call you if they don't have to pay for the privilege. Consequently, the more of your friends who get this plan, the greater incentive for you to adopt it as well. AT&T has thus created an artificial reason for you to go with the most popular provider (among your friends) rather than the best long-distance carrier.

What would happen if all the major long-distance companies created artificial network externalities? Would this make them all better off, or would the effects of each plan cancel out? As we have explained, price competition is terrible for companies. When all companies compete on price, they are all worse off. Long-distance phone service is pretty homogenous, with services differing only on price. Long-distance companies, consequently, should desperately try to get consumers to make choices based upon factors other than price. If all the major carriers adopted AT&T's approach, then most consumers would not make their long-distance choice based upon price, but rather on which plan most of their friends and associates have. As a result, long-distance firms would benefit by all adopting complicated pricing plans that create network externalities.

Network externalities often lead to a winner-take-all situation where only one firm prosperously survives. Government regulation, however, makes it unlikely that one carrier would ever be allowed to become a monopoly, since U.S. telephone service is heavily regulated, and regulators generally try to discourage monopolies.

HIGH-DEFINITION TV

Coordination failures prevent Americans from enjoying high-definition TV. Consumers will buy high-definition TVs only if they can use them to watch high-definition TV shows. Unfortunately, it's expensive for broadcasters to transmit high-definition signals, so they will only transmit when enough consumers have bought compatible TVs. When everyone waits for everyone else to start, however, not much happens.

The U.S. Congress tried to ensure the spread of high-definition TV by giving broadcasters the rights to billions of dollars of spectrum in return for the broadcasters promising to transmit high-definition signals. The broadcasters, however, used their political power to get out of the deal, so now they intend to use their spectrum mostly to send multiple low-definition signals rather than one high-definition transmission.

MONEY

Money acquires value through network externalities. Dollars are mere pieces of pretty paper that are useful because people value them. You can't eat, wear, or watch money. Yet most people actually prefer their employer to compensate them with money rather than with something more inherently useful like rice or books on game theory. If the entire human race save you became extinct, money would no longer hold any value to you, but rice would. Money has value because other people want it.

Because so many people want money, it's useful to have it because you can trade money for goods and services. Thus, our use of money is based upon a massive coordination game.

LOTTERIES AND SPORTS

The success of mega-jackpot state lotteries depends on network externalities. As the authors of a well-respected book on lotteries write:

> Once in place the lottery quickly becomes a commonly shared experience; like sports or weather, the lottery is something that almost everybody knows something about. Especially in the midst of the frenzy created by the occasional giant lotto jackpot, players reportedly indulge in fantasies about what could be done with the prize money. Like a snowstorm or a World Series, a multimillion-dollar jackpot creates excitement that spills over to become a social event.[7]

When many play lotteries, they become more exciting and consequently attract more players.

The 2002 World Cup soccer tournament was extremely popular for every participating country except the United States. Given the monotony of soccer play, people in other countries must have found the World Cup interesting because of network externalities. Following a sport is more interesting when the people you know also are interested in it. Consequently, sporting fans in a country effectively play a massive coordination game where they all choose the popular sports, and then it's in everyone else's interest to go along. So, if most people in your country watch soccer, then so should you. Since few Americans are interested in soccer, American soccer doesn't receive any benefit from network externalities, and so it remains unpopular.

COORDINATION

When deciding what candy bar to consume, you don't much care about the type of sweets other people buy. For many decisions in life, however, it's vital for you to coordinate your actions with others. When purchasing products with network externalities, you should buy the good that most other people plan to get. Companies need to take consumers' reactions to network externalities into account by convincing consumers not just that their product is good, but also that it will be popular.

NASH EQUILIBRIUM

This chapter did not really prove any of its results related to mass coordination games, for the book, so far, has mostly taken an intuitive approach to game theory. In the next chapter we adopt a more rigorous approach to solving games by studying a specific solution concept: the Nash equilibrium.

LESSONS LEARNED

- Massive coordination games are often winner-take-all affairs.
- To win a massive coordination game, it's often more important to be perceived as popular than as good.
- When playing a massive coordination game it's a sound strategy to buy early popularity by selling your product at a loss.

6

NASH EQUILIBRIA

In a Nash equilibrium, all of the players' expectations are
fulfilled and their chosen strategies are optimal.

From a 1994 press release announcing the
Nobel Prize winners in economics.[1]

JOHN NASH HAS BEEN ONE of the most important men
in developing game theory. Both the book and the
Oscar-winning movie *A Beautiful Mind* are about his
life. Nash developed a method of solving games that
is appropriately called a "Nash equilibrium," a no-
regrets outcome in which all the players are satisfied with
their strategy given what every other player has done. In a
Nash equilibrium you are not necessarily happy with the
other players' strategies; rather your strategy is an optimal
response to your opponents' moves. Players in a Nash equilibrium never cooperate and always assume that they can't
alter their opponent's actions.

Nash equilibrium: No player regrets his strategy, given
everyone else's move.

Consider a simple game with two employees, Tom and
Jim, who both want a raise. Assume that if just one employee
asks for a raise, he will get it, but if both ask for a salary
increase, then their employer will get mad and fire them

both. This game has two Nash equilibria: one where just Tom asks for a raise and one where just Jim asks for one. It can't be a Nash equilibrium for neither employee to ask for a raise because each person would regret not asking for a raise, knowing that the other didn't request one. It's also not a Nash equilibrium for both to request a raise because then each would regret getting fired.

The movie, *A Beautiful Mind,* carelessly provides a perfect example of what is *not* a Nash equilibrium. In the movie, four attractive women and one truly stunning babe enter a bar. John Nash explains to three of his male schoolmates how they should go about picking up the girls. Nash says that normally all four of the men would simultaneously hit on the babe. Nash claims, however, that following this strategy would be stupid because if all the men went after the same girl, they would get in each others' way, so *none* of them would score. Nash predicts that if the four men turned to the merely attractive women after being rejected by the babe, then the merely attractive women would be angry that they were everyone's second choice, so they, too, would spurn the men. Nash proposes that to avoid involuntary celibacy, the men should cooperate by ignoring the babe and pursuing the merely attractive women.[2] While the movie never directly states this, it's implied that Nash's proposed mating strategy relates to his Nobel-Prize-winning work in economics and thus to the idea of a Nash equilibrium.

Let's first focus on the pickup strategy that Nash rejects. The four men certainly shouldn't all pursue the babe. Obviously, if three other men are already hitting on her, and you know that if you too pursue her, you will fail, then it would be in your interest to go for one of the merely attractive women. It's consequently not a Nash equilibrium for all four men to go for the same woman, regardless of her sex appeal. Each of the four men would regret his choice of pursuing the babe if the three other men also hit on her. He could have done better following the alternative strategy of pursuing one of the merely attractive women. The outcome John Nash rejects is therefore not a Nash equilibrium.

A Beautiful Mind should be stripped of its Oscars because the outcome that John Nash proposes in the movie is also not a Nash equilibrium. Recall that he suggests that the four men should all ignore the babe. Each of the men, however, would regret a strategy of ignoring the babe if everyone else ignored her too. Sure, it might be reasonable not to pursue the best-looking woman in the bar if many other men are hitting on her. If, however, everyone else ignored this stunning babe, then obviously you (assuming you like women) should go for her.

The bar pickup game does have at least one Nash equilibrium, however. In one possible Nash equilibrium, the first, one man pursues the babe while the others go for lesser prizes. The one man going for the gold would clearly be happy with his strategy because he would have the field to himself. The three other men might also be happy with their choice. If this outcome is a Nash equilibrium, then each of the three men going for the merely attractive women would prefer to have a higher chance with one of them than a lower chance of scoring in a two-man competition for the babe. The only Nash equilibrium, however, might be for two or three of the men to go for the babe while the rest pursue the merely attractive women. This outcome would be a Nash equilibrium if the men pursuing the babe would prefer a lower chance of succeeding with her to a higher probability of making it with one of the other girls.

The power of a Nash equilibrium comes from its stability. Everyone is happy with his move, given what everyone else is doing, so no one wants to alter his strategy. Let's consider the Nash equilibria in Figure 29.

In this game, Player One choosing A and Player Two picking X is a Nash equilibrium. If Player One chooses A, then Player Two's best choice is X. Thus, given that Player One's choice is A, Player Two is happy with X. Similarly, if Player Two chooses X, Player One's optimal choice is A. Obviously, the players would rather be at B,Y than A,X. This doesn't prevent A,X, however, from being a Nash equilibrium because at A,X each player's strategy is an optimal response to his opponent's move. B,Y is also a Nash equilibrium in this game because each player would get his highest possible score at B,Y and thus would obviously be happy with his strategy. B,X is *not* a Nash equilibrium because both players would regret their choices. If, for example, Player Two chose X, Player One would regret playing B, because had he played A, he would have gotten a higher payoff.

In Figure 30, B,Y is an obvious Nash equilibrium, but there is another: A,X. If Player One chooses A, Player Two would not regret playing X because he will get zero no matter what. For similar reasons

Player 2

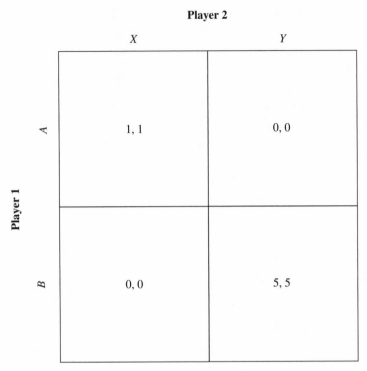

Figure 29

Player One would not regret choosing A in response to Player Two picking X. You don't regret choosing X if, given your opponent's move, you can't possibly do better than by playing X.

The outcomes in Figures 29 and 30 show multiple Nash equilibria can coexist, but one could be superior to the rest. Obviously, players in a *bad* equilibrium should try to move to a better one.

Figure 31 provides another example of a game with multiple Nash equilibria. In this game both players being nice is clearly a Nash equilibrium. If both players are nice, they each get 10. If one person is nice and the other is mean, the mean player gets only 8. It is a stable outcome for both players to be nice, because if one person were nice, the other would want to be nice too. Unfortunately, it's also a Nash equilibrium for both players to be mean. When both players are mean, they each get a payoff of zero. If, however, one player is nice and the other is mean, then the nice person loses 5. The optimal response to the other

Player 2

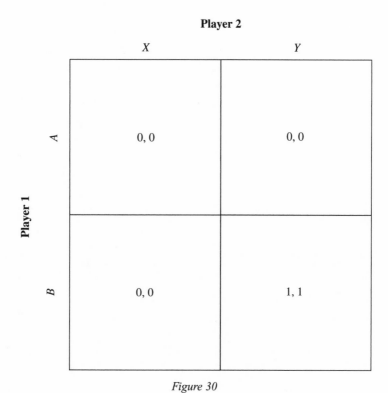

Figure 30

person's meanness is for you also to be mean. Mean, mean is consequently a stable Nash equilibrium.

If you find yourself in a game like Figure 31 where everyone plays mean, the best way to extricate yourself is to convince your opponent that you should both simultaneously start being nice. Keep in mind, however, that if you can't convince your opponent to change his strategy, you shouldn't change yours.

If we slightly alter the payoffs in Figure 31, it becomes impossible to achieve the nice, nice outcome. Consider Figure 32. The only difference between this and the previous game is the enhanced benefit of repaying kindness with cruelty. This change, however, results in nice, nice no longer being a Nash equilibrium. If one player is nice, the other is actually better off being mean, so nice, nice is no longer stable.

Consider a less abstract situation where you and a coworker are both being mean and undercutting each other to your boss. The key

Player 2

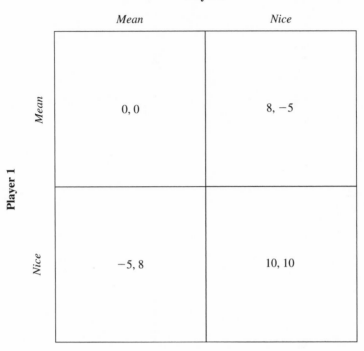

Figure 31

question for determining whether your game is like Figure 31 or 32 is this: If one of you is nice, should the other be mean or nice in return? It's possible that if one person were nice, your boss would disapprove if the other was not civil. Repaying kindness with cruelty, however, might be the ideal way of getting ahead in your firm. If both players benefit by being cruel to those who are kind, then you are stuck in a Nash equilibrium where you should be mean. The type of game where everyone is mean is called a prisoners' dilemma and is the subject of the next chapter.

NASH EQUILIBRIUM PRICING GAMES

The concept of a Nash equilibrium can also be applied to simultaneous games where players have many choices. Consider a game of price competition where two firms sell widgets.

The parameters for such a game are these:

Player 2

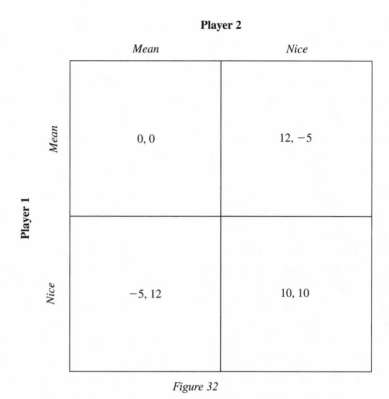

Figure 32

- Two firms can produce widgets of identical quality for $1 each.
- Both firms choose what price to sell their widget for.
- The customers will buy widgets from whomever charges less.

If the firms charge the same price, one-half of the customers will go to each firm.

If Firm One charges $100, and Firm Two charges $200, then all the customers would go to Firm One. Consequently, it's not a Nash equilibrium for one firm to charge more than its rival does. The firm charging the higher amount would get no customers and so wouldn't be happy with its strategy. If Firm One charges $100, what is Firm Two's optimal response?

- If Firm Two charges more than $100, it gets zero customers.
- If Firm Two charges exactly $100, it splits the customers with Firm One.
- If Firm Two charges less than $100, it gets all the customers.

Obviously, if Firm One sets a price of $100, Firm Two should charge $99.99. By undercutting its rival, Firm Two gets all the customers for itself. To have a Nash equilibrium, however, both players have to be happy with their choice given their opponent's strategy. If Firm One charges $100, and Firm Two, $99.99, then Firm One won't be happy, so we still don't have a Nash equilibrium. Once Firm Two undercuts Firm One, Firm One would then want to undercut Firm Two. This process will continue until both firms charge $1 a widget and make zero profit.

If Firm One charges $1, then Firm Two can't possibly do better than charge $1 itself. If it charges more than $1, then it will get no customers. If it charges less than $1, it will lose money on every sale. Given that Firm Two sets a price of $1, Firm One is destined always to make zero profit and will be as happy as it can be charging $1. Similarly, if Firm Two charges $1, Firm One can't do any better than charge $1 itself. Thus, both firms setting their price equal to their cost is the only Nash equilibrium.

The consumers were willing to pay any amount, yet the two producers still sold their product at cost. If both firms charged $1,000, then the consumers in this example would pay it, and the firms would make a large profit. The logic of Nash equilibrium, however, dooms both of these firms to make zero profit.

In our pricing game both firms greatly benefit from undercutting each other. If I sell my product for a penny less than you do, then I get all the customers. Because the benefit to undercutting an opponent is so large, both firms continue to do it until they are each selling the good at cost. This game provides another example of the damage that price competition can do to firms; damage that's magnified when the firms have high sunk costs.

Let's add to our example by assuming that to start making widgets a firm needs to spend $50,000 to build a factory. After building the factory, it will still cost $1 extra to manufacture each widget. What price will the firms charge? If both firms still end up charging $1, they will each lose $50,000. At a price of $1 the firms would break even on every widget sold, but would still have to pay the cost of the factory. Each firm charging only $1, however, is still the only Nash equilibrium. To see this, consider, is each firm charging $2 a Nash equilibrium? If they both charge the same amount, they must split the customers. Thus, if each firm is charging $2, one firm could acquire all of the customers by cutting its price to $1.99. Would a firm want all the customers if it could get only $1.99 per widget? Yes. Every additional customer you serve costs you $1. If you can sell a widget for $1.99 to a new customer you are better off by $.99. What about the $50,000 you spent building the factory? This is a strategically irrelevant sunk cost. Once you have built the factory you can't get back the $50,000 regardless of what you do. You should ignore this sunk investment and instead worry about your future gains and losses. Hence, if the other firm charges $2.00, you would want to charge $1.99 because this way you could acquire all the customers. Because of the $50,000 spent building the factory you may lose money if you charge only $1.99. You would lose less money, however, getting all the customers and charging $1.99 than you would by charging $2 and serving only one-half of the customers.

Industries with high sunk costs are extremely vulnerable to price competition because it is rational for companies to ignore their sunk costs when setting prices. As in the previous example, competition in the presence of high sunk costs can easily drive prices to a point where everyone loses money.

The airline industry suffers from high sunk costs because of the high cost of planes. Once you have an airplane and have decided to fly, it costs relatively little to add extra passengers.

Imagine that your airline always has one flight daily from New York to Paris. Assume that if this plane were always full, you would need to charge $400 a passenger to break even. What if, however, your flights were only one-half full, but you could sell additional seats for $300 each? Should you fill the extra spaces? Yes. Since you are already going to have the flight, you're better off getting $300 for a seat than leaving it empty. Of course, since everyone in the industry will feel this same way, the market price could easily be driven below $400. Nothing in game theory, however, guarantees that firms will make a profit or even survive.

The airline companies might go beyond the logic of Nash equilibrium, for in a Nash equilibrium the players never *cooperate*. The airlines might grasp how destructive competition could be. Should these companies formally agree to restrict competition, then they would be in violation of antitrust laws. Each firm, however, could decide not to reduce its price in hopes that other firms will follow course. The next chapter extensively considers the stability of firms' charging high prices.

SPAM, SPAM, SPAM, SPAM

I can't imagine that anyone still reads email spam, so why do we still get so much of it? Imagine that it costs a penny to send one million spams. What is the Nash equilibrium of the spam game?

We can't have spam equilibrium if some player regrets not sending spam. If the cost of sending one million spams were one penny, then a rational player would regret not spamming if it would earn her more than a penny. Consequently, game theory dictates that almost everyone must ignore inbox spam. If even 1 percent of the population regularly read their spam, then it would clearly be worthwhile for some retailer to spend a penny to reach 1 percent of a million users. Therefore if 1 percent of us read spam, more people will get spammed, which would reduce the number of spam readers. This process must continue until almost nobody reads the stuff.

How can we solve our spam dilemma? The best approach would be some technical fix that effectively separates out wanted email from spam. Email providers, however, obviously haven't mastered this trick. It would be impossible to get all spammers to agree to reduce their output, for even if some did, it would increase the benefits of others to spam. Spamming would decrease if the cost to spammers could be raised, but increasing the cost is challenging. If we impose legal penalties on spammers, then we will attract overseas spammers beyond the reach of American law. We have currently reached spam equilibrium, so if Americans spam less, some Americas would get less sick of spam and read more of it, thus increasing the benefit of foreigners to spamming us. Absent some anti-spam war (spammers, the next Axis of Evil?), we are unlikely to get other countries to prioritize stopping international spamming.

COMPETING ON THE LINE[3]

Like spam, political competition can be analyzed using the Nash equilibrium concept. Assume that two politicians compete for votes, and ideologically, the voters are equally distributed across a line from 0 to 100. Voters at 0 are far left, those at 50 are moderate, and those at 100 are far right. Assume that two politicians, labeled George and Al, stake out positions somewhere alone this line. Further assume that each voter will vote for the candidate who is ideologically closest to him. What is the Nash equilibrium?

Could Al = 0 and George = 50 be Nash? No. In this case Al would regret his choice since George would win by getting all the voters from 45 to 100. George would also regret his choice in this game because if Al = 40, George should pick 41 to maximize the number of votes he gets. Indeed, unless the candidates take near identical positions we don't have a Nash equilibrium. If Al takes X, George would always want to be right next to him at either X+1 or X-1 to get as many voters as possible.

The only Nash equilibrium occurs where both candidates take positions almost at 50. If one candidate wants to be at 52, the other could win by choosing 51. Competing on the line forces both candidates to the extreme center.

The logic of the line is applicable to business. Imagine that there is a town that consists entirely of one long road. Two gas stations must choose where to locate. Assume that customers will always go to the closest station. The gas stations will both locate at the population center of town next to each other for this is the only Nash equilibrium. If one gas station were a little off center, its competitor would be able to take more than half of the customers by locating right next to it on the center side.

SHOE STORES

Shoe stores and large-footed female customers play a coordination game that can be studied using the Nash equilibrium.[4] Shoe stores want to keep their inventories down so they stock only shoe sizes which customers request.[5] Women with large feet apparently get embarrassed when told that a store doesn't have anything in their size, so they avoid stores that don't stock large shoes.[6]

The coordination game played between the shoe customer and the store is shown in Figure 33 and it has two Nash equilibria. In the first, stores stock large sizes and women with big feet get their shoes from normal retail stores.

Player 2

	Go to retailers	*Not go to retailers*
Stock large sizes	Profits, Happy	Inventory costs, 0
Don't stock large sizes	0, Humiliation	0, 0

Figure 33

In the second equilibrium, the retailer doesn't stock large sizes, and the women don't shop at retail shoe stores. According to an article in Slate.com, this petite equilibrium currently predominates.[7] The no-large-shoe equilibrium is Nash because no one player can do better by deviating. If the store started to stock large sizes, it would just build up an inventory because the big-footed women wouldn't think to ask for them. If the women started asking for the large sizes, they would feel humiliated because the store wouldn't have their size in stock.

The shoe stores could break out of the bad equilibrium by advertising. In a Nash equilibrium you assume that your opponent's strategy is fixed and unalterable. This, of course, isn't always true. If it's possible for you to both change your own strategy and alter your opponent's move, then you could go to a better equilibrium.

In Figure 33 the shoe store and customer can end up in either a good or bad Nash equilibrium. The next chapter considers a class of games where there is only one type of Nash equilibrium, and it's a nasty one since it results in both players spending life in prison.

NASH EQUILIBRIUM

Look for the stable selfish outcomes, for they provide the Nash equilibria. The Nash equilibrium concept can help businesspeople because you can use it to make predictions. To predict with Nash, first determine all the players' possible strategies. Then, look for outcomes where everyone would be happy with their strategy given the outcome. Remember that multiple Nash equilibria can exist.

PRISONERS' DILEMMA

The next chapter explores a category of Nash equilibria: the *prisoners' dilemma*. In the prisoners' dilemma all players ruthlessly ride their own self-interest to collective ruin.

LESSONS LEARNED:

- A Nash equilibrium is an outcome where no player regrets his move given his opponent's strategy.
- A Nash equilibrium is a powerful game theory tool because it shows when an outcome is stable; it shows outcomes where no player wants to change his strategy.
- When trying to move to a new equilibrium, you should consider if the new outcome would be a Nash equilibrium. If it's not, then your new outcome is unstable and might be difficult to achieve.
- Seeing the movie *A Beautiful Mind* will not increase your knowledge of game theory.

7

PRISONERS' DILEMMA

Claw me, and I'll claw thee.

16th century proverb[1]

T HE MOST FAMOUS PARADIGM IN game theory is the prisoners' dilemma. Here's how it goes: The police arrest two criminals guilty of both murder and illegal weapons' possession. The police can easily prove that both men violated weapons' laws and could consequently imprison each criminal for one year. If the police could also establish that the criminals committed murder, however, they could send the men to fry in the electric chair. Unfortunately, the police can't establish that either criminal committed murder unless at least one of them confesses.

- If both criminals keep quiet, the worst punishment they could get is one year in jail.
- If either criminal confesses, both men could be sentenced to death.

The captured criminals realize the game they're in, so you might think that neither would ever confess. In the prisoners' dilemma story, however, the police use game theory to induce the men to turn on each other.

The police put the criminals, whom I will name Adam and Ben, in separate rooms. They tell Adam the following:

If Ben confesses, then:

- Adam gets the death penalty if he doesn't confess.
- Adam gets life in prison if he does confess.

The police need only one player to confess to convict either criminal of murder. Their threat to execute Adam if he does not confess and Ben does is credible. If Adam believes that Ben would confess, then Adam would himself benefit from confessing.[2] If Ben confesses, then by confessing himself, Adam gets life in prison rather than the electric chair. In their efforts to induce a confession the police have now made some progress. If Adam believes that Ben will confess, then it will be in Adam's self-interest also to confess.

The police then remind Adam that they already have enough evidence to convict him on weapons charges even if neither confesses. The police tell Adam that:

If Ben does not confess, then:

- Adam gets 1 year in prison if he doesn't confess.
- Adam goes free if he does confess.

If Ben does not cooperate, Adam still benefits from confessing. Adam, therefore, should always confess, since regardless of what Ben does, Adam benefits from confessing. Indeed, confessing is a dominant strategy for Adam. Recall that a dominant strategy is one you should play no matter what you think that other players might do.

Having been so successful with Adam, the police use the same strategy on Ben. Ben consequently finds confessing to be a dominant strategy. As a result of their clever implementation of game theory, the police induce both men to confess and put them in jail for life.

Figure 34 illustrates this prisoners' dilemma game. The result seems very counterintuitive. If both men had kept quiet, they would have gotten only one year in jail. By talking, both criminals get life. Shouldn't the men understand the game they are in and adopt different strategies? No! If Adam thinks that Ben is not going to confess, Adam is still better off talking. Even if Adam could somehow convince Ben to stay silent, Adam would still want to confess. Of course, when

Player 2

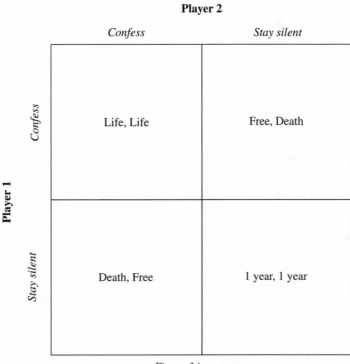

Figure 34

Adam does confess, he increases the punishment that Ben receives. Remember, however, in game theory land people care only about themselves. In the context of a prisoners' dilemma this assumption seems particularly realistic as someone who has just committed murder is probably not too interested in self-sacrifice.

Wouldn't Adam fear that his confessing would cause Ben to confess? No! The police separate the criminals. When Ben decides whether to cooperate, he has no way of knowing if Adam confessed. The police are certainly not going to tell Ben that he should not confess because his brave partner stayed silent. Whether Ben confesses will have nothing to do with whether Adam talks. Consequently, each player profits from cooperating with the police, even though this causes them to both receive life sentences. The key result in prisoners' dilemma is that even though all the players realize that the outcome is going to be bad, they still adopt strategies guaranteeing the bad outcome is achieved. Of course, the police are pleased with the results of the prisoners' dilemma.

What if the two criminals made an agreement never to confess if caught by the police? If you're about to commit a murder, you should always make such an agreement. This agreement, of course, shouldn't prevent you from cooperating if caught. Rather, you should make the agreement to keep your naive co-criminal quiet and then confess to escape punishment. True, this will mean that your partner in crime dies. But so what? He is, after all, a murderer.

If the police interviewed both men in the same room, then the logic behind prisoners' dilemma would collapse. Each man would suspect that if he confessed then his friend would too. If the men were interviewed together, then whether one player confessed would influence the probability of the other man confessing. This is why on television shows, at least, the police always separate suspected criminals when interviewing them.

Two rational criminals playing prisoners' dilemma would always confess. Two irrational criminals might both not talk and get a far lower prison term. Does this mean that rational people do worse in prisoner's dilemma games? No. You are always better off being rational. You are hurt, however, when your opponent is rational. While it's true that if both of you are rational, you might be worse off than if both of you were irrational. The best outcome would be if you were rational, and your opponent was not.

Joining the Mafia would allow the prisoners to overcome their dilemma. The depiction of the Mafia in movies suggests that they harshly punish those who cooperate with the police. This added punishment changes the prisoners' game by altering the payoffs. Figure 35 illustrates this Mafia modification of the prisoners' dilemma. In an effort to avoid the Mafia death penalty, both criminals should now not cooperate and will get only one year in jail. Interestingly, belonging to an organization that threatens to kill you if you break the rules can increase your payoff, so Mafia membership clearly has its privileges. Since Mafia membership will effectively lower your prison term if caught, we would expect members of the Mafia to commit more murders. The Mafia thus has a competitive advantage in the market for crime.

PRICING DILEMMAS

The prisoners' dilemma has numerous applications to business, and not just white-collar crime. Price competition often pushes firms into

Player 2

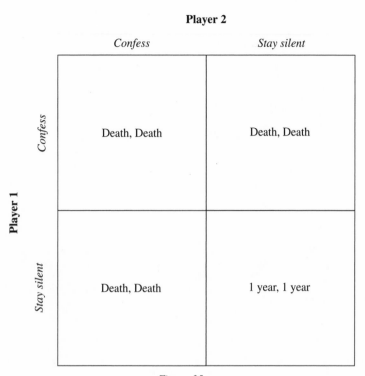

Figure 35

a prisoners' dilemma. A business can frequently increase its profits by lowering prices because reducing prices attracts new customers. Many of the new customers will be stolen from the business's rivals, however. Of course, when all businesses lower prices to steal customers from each other, they all suffer.

Figure 36 illustrates a prisoners' dilemma game with two firms that can each charge either a high or low price. In this game, regardless of what the other firm does, both firms are better off charging a low rather than a high price. If your rival is charging a low price, then he will get all the customers unless you too have a low price. If your rival charges a high price, you are better off charging a low price to get all of the customers. For both companies, charging a low price is a dominant strategy, so the likely outcome for this game is for both firms to charge low prices.

In the game in Figure 36, the two firms would be better off if they could make a binding agreement to maintain high prices. As with the cops and murderers version of prisoners' dilemma, however, such an agreement would be difficult to sustain. Each firm would like to pre-

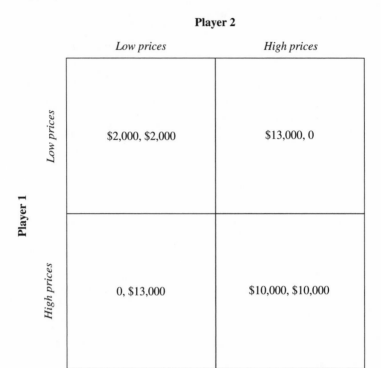

Figure 36

tend to go along with the agreement and then capture all the market by charging a low price while its rival charges a high price.

Another problem with making agreements in this prisoners' dilemma pricing game is that any agreement would be a violation of antitrust laws and punishable by prison. Antitrust laws were explicitly designed to make it illegal for firms to agree to keep prices high. Consequently, if you make an agreement with your business rival for you both to charge high prices, you might find yourself in a different kind of prisoners' dilemma. Also, because agreements to charge high prices are illegal, if you made such an agreement and it was violated, you couldn't sue for damages.

EVALUATING DILEMMAS

I recently read a large number of letters of reference for candidates applying for the position of Assistant Professor of Economics at Smith College. Most of the reference letters were very good. Indeed, they seemed, on average, a little too good. A significant number of reference writers said that the job candidate was one of the best he had ever worked with. I suspect that reference writers exaggerate the quality of the person about whom they are writing. Actually, I have written many letters of recommendation for students, and I know that I exaggerate their good qualities. Letters of reference play an important part in our economy by helping employers match positions with people, so great harm is caused when reference writers are not completely candid. I don't feel bad, however, about writing letters that are a little more glowing than they should be, because prisoners' dilemma makes me do it.

When you are writing a letter of recommendation you probably have two goals: You want to give an honest evaluation of the candidate to a potential employer, and you desire to help the candidate. Since one of these goals is best filled by being truthful and the other by exaggeration, on average, recommendation writers should embellish their recommendations at least a little. Of course, a problem arises when everyone plays this game. If everybody exaggerates, then when a reference writer indicates that his candidate is average, it will be taken to mean that the candidate is below average.

Now imagine that you have an average candidate, and you want to write her a letter that causes employers to think a little bit more highly of her than they should. Because everyone exaggerates, it's now not enough to say she is above average; you might have to label her as, say, extremely good. Alas, if all reference writers follow this trend, then even saying someone is extremely good does not signal quality. To help a candidate who truly is above average a reference writer is almost forced to say he is one of the best ever. Of course, all of this exaggeration causes recommendations to be taken less seriously. This is where the prisoners' dilemma manifests since all reference writers are worse off because they all exaggerate, even though it is in each reference writer's self-interest to exaggerate. Since we all exaggerate, the effects of exaggeration cancel out. Unfortunately, this still reduces the value of recommendations, so all reference writers would benefit from some binding agreement forbidding any embellishment. If, however, everyone else stopped exaggerating, then I could greatly benefit by being the only one to deceive, since such deception would then not be suspected.

This evaluating dilemma increases the importance of networking and personal connections. A letter of recommendation I write to a friend should be given more weight than one I sent to a stranger—not, obviously, because my friends know me to be particularly truthful, but rather because I have a greater incentive to be honest with my friends. I will probably never need anything from the strangers who see my recommendations, so I most likely wouldn't be hurt if they find out I had deceived them. A friend would probably be annoyed with me if I recommended a student whose performance was below what I promised. Since I don't want my friends to dislike me, I tend not to lie to them when I know that such lies will be detected.

When companies require internal reviews of employees by supervisors, they can also face evaluating dilemmas. The supervisors will want to be perceived as honest and effective evaluators. They will also, however, probably want to be considered nice people to work for. Thus, supervisors have some motivation to be honest and some incentives to exaggerate, causing them on average to be a little too kind when evaluating. To stop this evaluating dilemma, companies often require supervisors to rank employees. By mandating ranking, companies prevent evaluators from labeling everyone as above average.

THE EVALUATED ONES' DILEMMA

Companies often grade workers on a curve. Pretend that you develop a new product and hire 20 salespeople to push it. How do you determine each salesperson's quota? Since the product has never been sold before, you can't really know how much a competent, hard-working salesperson should sell each month.

The solution: evaluate each salesperson on a relative standard—compare him to his peers.[3] Relative performance standards create a prisoners' dilemma for employees. Consider the game between two employees where each can work either 40 or 60 hours a week. Assume that your company can't judge how much each employee works, but does observe how much they sell, with employees working 60 hours a week selling more than ones who put in only 40 hours a week.

If both employees work the same hours, then each will get an average evaluation. Obviously, to get the same evaluation, the employees would vastly rather put in 40 than 60 hours each week. Prisoners' dilemma, however, compels them to work more. If the other person works 40 hours, and you put in 60, you will get an excellent evaluation. Alas, if he works 60 hours a week, and you work only 40, then your continued employment will be at peril. Consequently, working 60 hours is a dominant strategy for both employees.

When judged by relative standards, your workers would all like to go for the easy life and underperform. Sadly, prisoners' dilemma makes it challenging for workers to credibly commit to collective laziness.

Workers judged by relative standards are like athletes considering taking steroids. Steroids increase athletic ability. Unfortunately, such drugs have harmful medical side effects. For a top athlete, however, it might well be rational to take performance-enhancing drugs. It could be worth suffering the side effects of steroids to win an Olympic medal or to get a multimillion-dollar professional football contract.[4] Alas, when all athletes use steroids, then none receives a competitive advantage. Figure 37 shows a prisoners' dilemma game where there are two equally matched runners competing for some prize. They each have the ability to take steroids, which would make them faster but would also give them health problems. If the athletes have equal ability, and only one runner takes steroids, then he will win. If it were worth enduring the health problems to win, then either athlete would be willing to take steroids if the other doesn't. Furthermore, if the other athletes take them, and you don't, then you would have little chance at victory. Therefore, it might well be in your interest to take steroids if your opponents also take them. Of course, if both athletes take steroids, then neither is helped in their competition, but both still suffer the drugs' negative side effects.

While most workers wouldn't enhance their career by ingesting health-imperiling steroids, they do benefit by putting in family-destroying hours. You can sometimes employ prisoners' dilemmas, however, to get your workers to put your needs ahead of their family responsibilities.

PROFESSIONAL SPORTS' DILEMMA

Why do some sports leagues pay their athletes so much? Leagues like the NFL and NBA need top talent to draw viewers. So you might think that it's essential for leagues to offer high wages to attract the best

Player 2

	Use steroids	*Don't use steroids*
Use steroids	50% chance win and health problems, 50% chance win and health problems	Win and health problems, lose
Don't use steroids	Lose, win and health problems	50% chance win, 50% chance win

Figure 37

players. The problem with this argument is that while it might justify paying an athlete $100,000 per year, it doesn't justify giving him a multimillion-dollar contract. A professional basketball player, for example, has very specialized talent. His skill in basketball can't transfer to other sports or professions. As a result, a professional basketball player probably won't make anywhere near his basketball salary in another job.[5] Though a high salary may be needed to attract a player to a particular team, a much lower salary, however, would be needed to ensure that this same person becomes a professional basketball player.

If all basketball teams offered much lower salaries, they would still attract the top talent since this talent would have no other place to go. Indeed, giving athletes multimillion-dollar salaries might even shorten their careers because such large salaries make it easy for players to retire early.[6]

Individual teams face a prisoners' dilemma with respect to their players' salaries. If all other teams offered very low salaries, your team could greatly benefit by paying high wages. Then you would get the best players, win all the championships, and always have sellout crowds. If all the other teams offered high salaries, you would have to also, because if you didn't, your team would have the worst players, and you would consequently sell few tickets. Thus, offering a high salary is a dominant strategy for each team. Unfortunately for the teams, they are all worse off if they all offer high salaries than if they were all to pay low wages.

Professional sports leagues realize the game they're in and try to limit athletes' salaries. The teams attempt to enforce salary caps that limit the total amount a team can spend on wages. Players, of course, benefit from their teams' prisoners' dilemma and so players' unions fight against salary caps.

Colleges have succeeded at eliminating the prisoners' dilemma that causes professional athletes' salaries to be so high. College athletes can get free room, board, and tuition, but not cash. Most college athletes don't deserve to be paid as they bring their school little extra revenue. A college with a nationally ranked team in a popular sport, however, can make a lot of money from ticket sales, merchandising rights, and increased alumni contributions. Top college athletes are very valuable assets to their schools. Nevertheless, colleges manage to avoid giving their best players cash payments. Prisoners' dilemma would normally compel colleges to pay these players because schools that did pay would have an enormous advantage over those that didn't. College sports leagues overcome their prisoners' dilemma by forbidding teams in the league to pay their athletes. If any college started paying its players, then it would presumably be kicked out of its league. No one school could benefit by paying its athletes, because it wouldn't be able to play against any other team. Even with an official ban on salaries, however, prisoners' dilemma manifests itself by creating incentives for colleges to cheat and secretly pay athletes or give athletes benefits that are as good as cash. These incentives to cheat cause periodic scandals involving colleges using improper recruiting tactics to acquire the best athletes. Overall, though, colleges seem to do an excellent job at overcoming their prisoners' dilemma and getting the services of their top athletes almost for free.

I have a suggestion for how colleges with mediocre teams could benefit from prisoners' dilemma. If around ten of these colleges started paying athletes, they could attract the best players. These schools would be kicked out of the traditional leagues, but then they could play against each other. Since these schools would attract the top players they would have the most interesting games so their sports revenues would significantly increase. Prisoners' dilemma would then force other colleges to pay their athletes. These first schools, however, would probably have a few glory years where only they would get the best amateur athletes money could buy.

Reputation is the most important recruiting tool colleges have. The top athletes want to go to schools with the best programs. Normally, it's nearly impossible for schools with mediocre teams to recruit the best players because these players eventually want to play professionally, so they want to get practice playing on teams which also have excellent athletes. If a few schools started paying students, they could attract a large number of top players, and so they could overcome the barriers to recruiting that their mediocre reputations create. Once other schools start paying, however, these schools would still benefit from having a good reputation and so they might be able to continue recruiting top talent. Of course, the colleges that currently have the best players would be devastated if the schools with mediocre teams started paying players.

CEO RECRUITMENT

The only salaried employees paid more than professional athletes are CEOs. In the age of Enron, Global Crossing, and WorldCom, we shouldn't necessarily assume that CEOs deserve their salaries. Perhaps CEOs get their millions through manipulation and control of the compensation process. Prisoners' dilemma, however, provides a more benign explanation of why rational companies need to pay astronomical sums to attract the best bosses.

A CEO candidate slightly better than the rest is worth a lot to your company. If the top candidate would increase the equity value of your $10 billion company by only 1 percent, then he's worth $100 million to you. Still, he would probably be willing to run a company for only $10 million, so why do you need to give him the extra $90 million he's worth?

As with the professional sports' dilemma, competition forces organizations to pay CEOs near what they bring to the firm. If all large companies agreed to limit salaries to, say, $10 million a year, then they would all probably still attract top talent. When companies compete, however, every firm finds it a dominant strategy to pay high salaries. If only your firm does, you get the best. If everyone but you does then, well, I bet Ken Lay is willing to work cheap.

CONTRACT LAW'S SOLUTION TO PRISONERS' DILEMMA

Imagine you want to buy a house and need a mortgage. You are obviously better off if you can convince a bank to lend you money. Of course, you would be even better off if you could get the loan, and then not have to pay it back. Absent binding contracts, a bank probably wouldn't lend you money because you would have an incentive to betray them and not repay. Similarly, you wouldn't borrow from a bank that could foreclose on your house even if you made all the payments. Consequently, even though your taking out a loan could make both you and the bank better off, the loan would not be made unless contract law forced both of you to behave properly toward each other.

Parties often use legally binding contracts to overcome prisoners' dilemmas. In many business situations you must trust someone with money or goods. Without contracts, the person you must trust would often be better off keeping your stuff. Contract law allows us to trust other people because if we are betrayed, we can sue and reclaim what was lost (minus attorney's fees).

Prisoners' dilemma limits investments in countries where many are exempt from the rule of law. Imagine that you are a mayor of a small town in a poor country. To increase your town's prosperity you try to attract foreign investment by begging a colossal multinational firm to build a factory in your town. Your plan works and they construct a $10 million factory. Before the factory was built, you were dependent upon the mighty multinational. After the factory is completed, however, they are dependent upon you. The vulnerable multinational's $10 million investment will be worthless if, say, they are denied the right to use water or electricity. Why shouldn't this greedy multinational be forced to invest another $3 million in your town as the price for getting access to local roads? There are three outcomes to the game between you and the multinational:

1. No factory is built.
2. A factory is built and the multinational is treated fairly.
3. A factory is built and the multinational is exploited.

Outcome 3 is obviously the best for you and your town. Of course, the multinational won't build the factory if they suspect that outcome 3 will manifest. To induce them to build, therefore, you promise never to exploit them. After they have built the factory, however, why not exploit them anyway? Shouldn't the welfare of your town take precedence over a promise made to a foreign multinational?

Of course, the multinational should understand the game and not build the factory unless they know you couldn't exploit them. Consequently, the multinational should invest only if the rule of law in your country prevents you from moving from outcome 2 to 3.

DO THE RICH ALWAYS WANT TO WIN LEGAL CASES?

Some leftist legal scholars argue that the U.S. legal system is biased because "the rich guys always win."[7] Let's pretend that the wealthy are in complete control of the U.S. courts and could ensure victory in every case. Would the rich always want to win? If the rich always won, no one would ever trust them because they could renege on any deal. Because fairly administered contract law allows parties to avoid prisoners' dilemma, the rich would actually be worse off if others thought that wealth would always prevail.

ACCOUNTANTS' HONESTY

Accountants, like the ones who used to work for Arthur Andersen, are supposed to act as referees between companies and their shareholders. These accountants theoretically ensure that companies honestly report their business activities so shareholders can make informed investment decisions. Accountants, however, are hired by only one team, the companies. Consequently, accountants always face a conflict between their ethical obligations to ensure fair reporting and their desire to win favor by assisting the firms they audit.

Once a few accountants become dishonest, prisoners' dilemma may ensure that honest bookkeepers are driven from their profession. Imagine a world where all accountants are completely honest. You live in this world and are competing for some auditing business. Would it be so bad if you promised to be a little helpful to some prospective client? After all, accounting rules are ambiguous. Why not promise that if hired, you will shade this ambiguity toward your clients' interests?

Of course, once a few accountants start being overly helpful, others will have to either alter their ethics or perish. Now, to get a competitive edge you might have to go beyond shading ambiguity. Don't worry, though: As long as the stock market continues to increase no one is likely to uncover your imaginative bookkeeping.

Dishonest bookkeeping can actually be a dominant strategy for accountants. If everyone else does it, and you don't, then you will get little business, while if only you do it, then riches await. Of course, if everyone is dishonest, then no one gains a competitive edge, but prisoners' dilemma could still force all accountants to adopt dishonest practices.

The collapse of Arthur Andersen will do much to solve this accountants' dilemma. In essence, the SEC and plaintiff lawyers are going to impose the Mafia's solution to the prisoners' dilemma whereby the misbehaving player is terminated.

OILMEN'S DILEMMA[8]

Oil doesn't respect property rights. Often a pool of oil will lie below the land of several drillers. Oil extraction can never remove all the oil from an underground pool. When one company owns the land above an oil pool, it carefully extracts as much oil as possible. When multiple players own this land, however, they all have an incentive to extract oil as quickly as possible. If you take the cautious approach while I go for speed, I'll get much more oil than you. Much of a shared oil pool becomes permanently lost to extraction when parties attempt to remove the oil too quickly.[9] The landowners consequently find themselves in a prisoners' dilemma. Regardless of what the other landowner does, you are always better off with rapid extraction. All landowners, however, would be better off if they all proceeded more cautiously.

WHY DO WE GET IN TAXICABS?

Oddly, prisoners' dilemma should manifest whenever you get in a cab. After having taken a cab ride why should you pay? "Because it's the right thing to do" is not a legitimate answer in game theory land. You should pay only if it's in your self-interest to pay. There is only a self-interested reason to pay: if you didn't pay, the driver might get upset and cause you trouble. Perhaps he would hit you or call the police and charge you with theft of services. Now imagine, however, that you have paid; why doesn't the driver pretend that you didn't and ask for payment again? If the reason you initially paid was to prevent the driver from getting upset, then you should be willing to pay again to avoid the same problem. Even if you pay once, you probably wouldn't be able to prove that you paid, so the driver could still charge you with theft of services. Of course, people ride in cabs all the time and there is rarely a problem with nonpayments or double payment demands. I'm not really sure why the prisoners' dilemma doesn't afflict cab rides. If it ever does become a problem, then everyone would start paying for cabs with credit cards so whether someone paid becomes provable.

RUN AWAY, RUN AWAY

Running away is often the best way of avoiding death in combat. If everyone on your side runs away, then you will probably all get killed. And thus is a cowards' dilemma born. Imagine that you and many others have been drafted. You are now in combat facing enemy troops. Let's assume that none of you are very patriotic, and your paramount objective is personal survival. The best way to avoid danger would be if you ran away, but all your fellow soldiers stayed and fought. Of course, if everyone else on your side ran away, then it would be even a better idea for you to abandon your combat position, for you certainly don't want to be the only one facing the enemy when they cross your lines. Running away is therefore the safest strategy you could follow regardless of what your fellow soldiers do.

A prisoners' dilemma arises because if everyone on your side runs away, it will be easy for the enemy to hunt you all down and kill you. Thus, you all might be better off if everyone stayed than if everyone ran away. Individually you are all better off being cowards. Collectively you're all better off being brave. Armies solve this cowards' dilemma much as the Mafia solves the classic prisoners' dilemma. In most armies if a soldier runs away while in combat, the soldier can be court-marshaled and executed. The potential for being killed for cowardice thus actually helps solders as it saves them from a prisoners' dilemma.

NUCLEAR DILEMMA

As Figure 38 shows, prisoners' dilemma might someday cause a nuclear holocaust. In this game there are two adversaries armed with nuclear missiles. The situation is volatile because each side has only a few missiles. If one side launches a surprise attack, it will be possible for this attacker to eliminate all of its enemy's missiles. Therefore, the side that attacks first achieves victory, while its opponent suffers defeat. Imagine that a crisis arises between these two nations. The generals on both sides realize that the country to strike first wins. Each country would have a strong incentive to launch.

In the Cold War between the United States and the Soviet Empire, much thought was given to avoiding this nuclear dilemma. The United

Player 2

	Launch	*Not launch*
Launch	War, War	Victory, Defeat
Not launch	Defeat, Victory	Peace, Peace

(Player 1 labels the rows)

Figure 38

States spent massive sums of money developing a survivable deterrent by having a large number of missiles, many of which were in submarines hidden deep in the oceans, safe from Soviet attack. The United States always wanted the Soviets to believe that they could never win a nuclear war merely by striking first.

Currently, India and Pakistan are adversaries who both have nuclear missiles. Neither country appears to have a survivable deterrent. Consequently, generals in both nations might think that a surprise atomic attack could lead to victory. An atomic war between these two countries could kill far more than died in the Holocaust. What is truly terrifying about the prospects for such a war is that a general might order an attack not because he is evil and wants to kill his enemy; rather, he might launch his weapons because he fears his enemy will do the same. If both sides fear that their enemy might launch a surprise attack, then the fears of both sides become justified. Tragically, a rational response to the fear of being hit with a surprise attack is to attack your enemy first.

TRAGEDY OF THE COMMONS

When a resource is commonly owned, it will be overused. Consider a fish-filled lake that everyone has the right to use. If overfished, the lake will die. Unfortunately for the fish and fishermen, however, overfishing is probably a dominant strategy. Imagine you are one of 1,000 fishermen, and each of you can fish at a low or high level. If most people fish at a high level, the lake will become depleted of fish. If just you choose the low level, however, it really won't make any difference. Consequently, you will always catch more fish, in both the long and short run, by extensive fishing. Since everyone will overuse this lake, it will be depleted, so the fishermen would be better off if they all fished at a low rather than high level. As with other prisoners' dilemmas, however, game theory dooms the fisherman to take selfish actions that collectively make everyone worse off.

The tragedy of the commons manifests when no one has the right to exclude. If you owned the lake, it would be in your self-interest to ensure that enough fish survived to breed and replenish the stock.

The tragedy of the commons could also strike a commonly used secretary. Imagine one secretary has been assigned to five firm attorneys. Each attorney has high- and low-priority work to give the secretary. If nearly everyone gives the secretary all possible work, the secretary will become overburdened and unproductive. Consequently, the attorneys would collectively be better off if they all give their secretary just high priority work rather than giving both high and low priority work. Each attorney, individually, however, might always be better off giving the secretary all his work. Consequently prisoners' dilemma and the tragedy of the commons doom the secretary to low productivity due to overwork. The solution to this secretarial dilemma is the same as to all tragedy of the commons: limit use. Someone needs to have the power to limit the secretary's workload.

Internet Pricing

The tragedy of the commons afflicts fixed-fee Internet pricing plans. Many Internet users share a common network, so the more users on a network, the slower the network becomes. Consequently, one surfer's viewing of graphic-rich pornography increases the time it takes another user to download pirated music.

When a user pays a fixed fee, the extra cost of spending another hour on-line is zero. Consequently, all users will download low priority materials, clogging up the Internet. All users on a common network might be better off if everyone limited their on-line time. Individually, however, users are better off spending as much time as they like on the net. When users pay per minute, however, this tragedy of the commons ends, for surfers now have an economic incentive to restrict their usage to high priority browsing.

REPEATED PRISONERS' DILEMMA WITH A LAST PERIOD

What would happen if you played the prisoners' dilemma game in Figure 39 100 times with the same opponent? If you played the game only once, you should always be mean. If your opponent plays mean, you score 1 if you're mean and 0 if you're nice. If your opponent is nice, you score 3 if you are mean and 2 if you are nice. Thus, regardless of what your opponent does, you are always better off being mean if the game is played just once. What if you are going to play it 100 times? Would it be reasonable for you to use the following logic?

Player 2

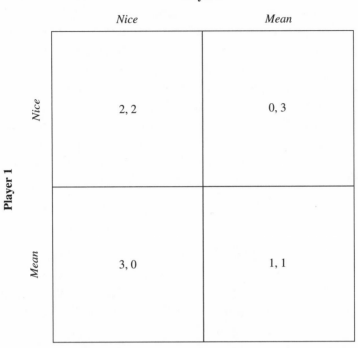

Figure 39

If we are both mean throughout the entire game, we will both get a payoff of only 1 each period. If, however, we are both nice all the time, our payoff per round will be 2. If I start out playing mean, my opponent will be mean to me, and we will be stuck getting a payoff of only 1. I would rather start being nice and hope that he too is nice. It's true that if he is nice, I could take advantage of him and be mean for one round. After this one round he would not keep being nice, however, and then I would be stuck with getting only 1 each period because he would probably always be mean after that. As a result I should play nice at least until he is mean to me.

Unfortunately, last-period problems would prevent parties known to be rational from being nice to each other even in round one. Consider what strategy you should employ in period 100, the last period. Playing mean always gives you a higher payoff in the round you played it than being nice would. The only possible reason you might play nice in a given round is so your opponent will play nice in the next round. (Recall that in simultaneous move games such as this, your opponent can't see how you're going to move when you move; thus, your choice in any given round can't influence your opponent's move in that same round.) In the last period, however, there are obviously no other rounds to care about. Thus, you should always play mean in round 100 and so should your opponent. Knowing this, what should you do in round 99? Playing mean will always give you a higher payoff in period 99. The only reason you might not want to be mean in round 99 is so that your opponent will be nice to you in round 100. We have already concluded, however, that your opponent should be mean to you in round 100 no matter what. Thus, everyone should be mean in round 99. Of course, this means that in round 98 both of you should also be mean because both players will always be mean in rounds 99 and 100. You can continue to apply this logic backward to establish that you should be mean in round 1! Consequently, even if this prisoners' dilemma game is played 100, 1,000, or a billion times, rational players should be mean in every round.

Irrationality and the Prisoners' Dilemma

Game theory teaches that when two people play a finitely repeated prisoners' dilemma game, they should always be mean. Economics, however, is supposed to be a science, and in science you test your theories. Unfortunately for game theory, when real people play a finitely repeated prisoners' dilemma game they often are nice to each other, especially in the early rounds.[10] Why the divergence between theory and reality?

Obviously, reality is wrong and should adjust itself to theory. Of course, it's also possible that game theorists are in error in assuming that people are always rational.

Imagine that you are playing a repeated prisoners' dilemma game 100 times with someone you know is not entirely rational. Many people, outside of game theory land, are nicer than they should be, but don't like to be taken advantage of. Let's say that you think your opponent will start out playing nice. You suspect that if you start being mean to him, however, he will be mean to you. How should you now play? You should probably play nice until the last period. In the last period, of course, you should always betray your fellow player.

This betrayal in the final round is why two parties who are known to be rational could never be nice to each other in a finitely repeated prisoners' dilemma game. Since a rational opponent would always betray you in round 100, you should betray him in round 99. Similarly, since you will betray him in round 99, he should be mean to you in round 98, which, of course, means that . . . . If some doubt exists as to your opponent's rationality, however, you might want to play nice in round one. This doesn't mean that your opponent would benefit from being irrational, but rather that he would benefit from being *seen* as irrational.

Interestingly, even if you both are rational, it's possible to get the nice, nice outcome until the last rounds. If both players are rational but neither is 100 percent sure that the other is rational, then both players might, rationally, play nice until the last few rounds.

Repeated Prisoners' Dilemma with No Last Period

If a prisoners' dilemma game has no last period, then the nice, nice outcome is achievable. Since the final period always brings betrayal, a final period makes it impossible for players ever to be nice. Many games in real life, however, have no final period. If you play a prisoners' dilemma game forever, you might reasonably adopt a strategy of always being nice unless your opponent is mean to you. If both players adopt this strategy, they will achieve a good outcome every round. The nice, nice outcome is reachable even if the prisoners' dilemma game doesn't go on forever. All that's needed is no definite ending date. For example, imagine two people playing a prisoners' dilemma game and then flipping a coin to determine if they should play again. If they don't stop playing until their coin comes up heads, then the game has no known last period where betrayal must manifest.

In a repeated prisoners' dilemma game with no last period, your ideal outcome would be for you always to be mean and your opponent always to be nice. This outcome is almost certainly not achievable, however. What might be obtainable is for both players always to be nice. Remember that the only reason any rational person should ever be nice in prisoners' dilemma is to induce his fellow opponent to be nice in the next round. Consequently, to induce your opponent to play nice, he must think that you will be mean if he turns mean. In game theory land people will be nice only if it's in their interest to be nice. Unfortunately, just because a repeated prisoners' dilemma game goes on forever doesn't mean that the players will always be nice to each other.

It's easiest to betray those who trust you, though once you have betrayed someone they are unlikely ever to trust you again. Treachery is justified, however, if it brings you a large enough one-time benefit. Let's compare the games in Figures 40 and 41. Both are prisoners' dilemma games. In these two games the players get 5 each if they are both mean and 10 each if they are both nice. Obviously, the players would rather be in a situation where they are always nice to each other than always mean. The difference between the games manifests if one player betrays the other. If you are mean, and he is nice, you do far better in the game in Figure 41 than in the one in Figure 40. Thus, there is a much greater incentive to betray your opponent in the game in Figure 41.

Smoking gives pleasure today and causes health problems in the future. Smoking can be a rational decision for someone who places far

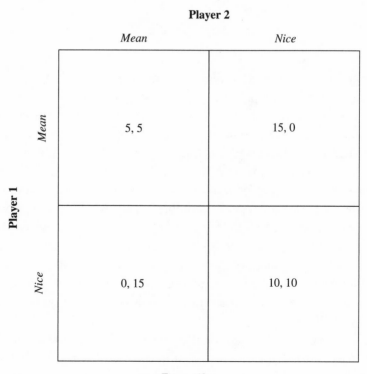

Figure 40

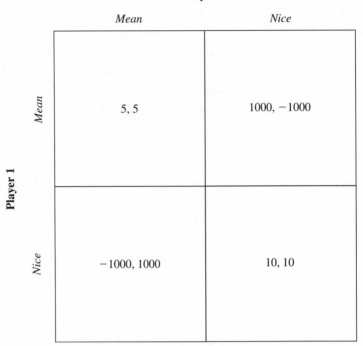

Figure 41

greater value on the present than the future. Like smoking, betraying someone in a repeated prisoners' dilemma game helps you today but harms you in future periods. Thus, the less someone cares about the future the more likely he is to betray you in a repeated prisoners' dilemma game. For example, a supplier who might go bankrupt or a lawyer considering retirement would value the present more than the future because he won't be playing in future periods. You should consequently place greater trust in someone who has a long time horizon.

People's actions often betray how much they care about the future relative to today. For example, you should have limited trust in smokers because they obviously care far more about the present than the future. Conversely, someone who exercises is willing to make sacrifices today for future benefits and thus is less likely to betray you for a short-term gain.

If you are convinced that another player will soon cheat you, don't necessarily try to change his mind. It might well be in his self-interest to be mean to you. If you suspect that your fellow player is someday going to betray you, your optimal response is probably to betray him first.

ENVY, THE DEADLIEST OF SINS[11]

The goal of business is profit maximization, not making more money than your competitor. To maximize your profit in a repeated prisoners' dilemma, you must cooperate with your competitor. If both players' objective is a higher payoff, however, then cooperation is unachievable since then only one can win.

Anything that helps your opponent in chess hurts you because chess is a fixed-sum game. Games like chess, football, and poker are called fixed-sum because whenever one person wins, another necessarily loses. Consequently, you should never bother cooperating with your opponent in a fixed-sum game because your interests are diametrically opposed. While business games usually aren't fixed-sum, they can be transformed into fixed-sum games by envy. If both players perceive that their opponent's gain is their loss, then their game will always be fixed-sum. Since in a fixed-sum game there is no benefit to cooperating, envious players in a repeated prisoners' dilemma game will always be trapped in the mean, mean outcome.

Just as you should be less trusting of smokers, you should also be wary of envious players. Consider how envy affects the cost/benefit calculation of optimal betrayal. The benefit of betrayal is a higher payoff this period while the cost is a lower payoff in future periods. For envious players, however, a further benefit of betrayal is that your opponent gets a lower payoff. Since envious players get a higher benefit from betrayal, they are more likely to engage in it. Therefore, you should be less trusting of envious people and others should have less trust in you if they perceive you as envious.

IMPLICIT AGREEMENTS

How do you achieve a good outcome in a repeated prisoners' dilemma game which has no last period? If possible, you should talk to your fellow player and convince him that both of you should play nice. Unfortunately, for two firms in a pricing dilemma it would be a violation of antitrust laws for them to explicitly agree to maintain high prices. Fear not, however, for in game theory land actions dominate words.

Imagine that you're repeatedly playing the game in Figure 42 with another firm. Currently, both firms charge low prices. Figure 42 is a prisoners' dilemma game in which individually you are both better off charging low prices, but collectively you would both benefit by jointly charging high prices. If you explicitly proposed to your competitor that both firms raise prices, you could go to jail. You should instead send a legal signal to your competitor, such as unilaterally raising prices this period.

For the game in Figure 42, charging high prices always makes you worse off this period. Thus, if your rival has always charged low prices, what possible motive could he assign to your setting high prices? He should interpret your price increase as an invitation for both of you to permanently raise prices. Of course, your rival might choose to tem-

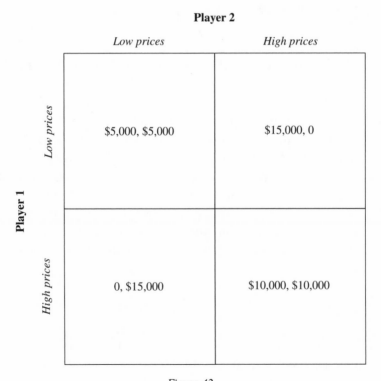

Figure 42

porarily take advantage of your high prices to make a high profit for himself. Your competitor might, however, accept your implicit invitation to move to a better outcome.

Let's imagine that your rival joins you and increases his prices, too. Several periods go by while you both earn higher profits by jointly charging high prices. Why is your rival continuing to charge high prices? Is it because since you were nice to him he feels obligated to be nice to you? The only reason your rival would charge high prices in this game is because he fears that if he lowers his prices, you will too. Fear of retaliation, not obligation or kindness, keeps your rival in line.

Having a reputation for swift retaliation is vital to being able to sustain a good outcome in repeated prisoners' dilemma games. Wimps can never achieve the "nice, nice" outcome, for their rivals will always exploit them. If others fear your wrath, however, the nice, nice outcome becomes obtainable since fellow players will grasp the consequences of betraying you.

COOPERATION IN THE TRENCHES

You're in a six-foot trench in sight of the enemy. Poison gas, bullets, shrapnel, and artillery shells put your life in constant danger. Sure, you're patriotic and hope for victory, but what you really crave is survival. You have been told that your enemies are inhuman, baby-killing scum; however, you suspect that they are just as scared as you are. The high commands on both sides are going for victory, not peace, but perhaps there is a way to give peace a chance in your little corner of the war.

Your battalion has faced the same enemy troops for quite some time.[12] Up until now, both sides have tried to inflict maximum damage on their foes. What would happen, however, if you stopped trying to kill? What if your snipers stopped trying to hit enemy soldiers, and then instead aimed at rocks? What if your artillery fired at the exact same spot each time so that the enemy could easily avoid getting killed?[13]

If you stop trying to hurt the enemy, they will obviously be thrilled. They might at first ascribe your actions to treason or stupidity. If they believe that you are rational, however, they will realize that the only reason you are being nice is to get reciprocity. Once they understand your motives, your enemy will have a choice: either accept your implicit deal and stop trying to kill you, or reject the bargain and put their own lives back in extreme peril.[14]

In *The Evolution of Cooperation,* Robert Axelrod writes about how troops in World War I found themselves in a repeated prisoners' dilemma game and often responded by not trying to kill the enemy.[15] The military leaders on all sides opposed and attempted to suppress these informal truces. The soldiers received such massive benefits from escaping their prisoners' dilemma, however, that they formed a separate, if temporary, peace.

As we have previously discussed, companies sometimes try to create a prisoners' dilemma situation among their employees. Axelrod's accounts of World War I show the perils of this tactic in repeated play. In a one-shot prisoners' dilemma game, the workers will always lose, but if the game is played repeatedly they have a chance.

Imagine, as discussed previously, a boss who tries to motivate his workers by setting them up in competition among each other. The boss could create a prisoners' dilemma game by announcing that employees who get the best results will be rewarded, while those who do below-average work will be terminated. If the employees go along with the game, their lives will likely be dominated by hard work and stress. What if they all played lazy, however? If the boss judges individual performance by relative standards, then if everyone plays lazy, everyone is considered average. Sure, all employees will lose out on the chance to be the star, but perhaps it's worth losing this opportunity in return for having a comfortable working environment. Furthermore, if some employee does try to defect by putting in long hours, the other employees could punish this nonlaggard defector by ostracizing him. Consequently, by working together, our employees could escape their trenches if they play their game repeatedly.

If the employees adopt collective laziness, how could our boss now motivate these employees? He would have to impose an objective standard on performance and be willing to fire everyone if everyone underperforms. In repeated games, employees can always overcome the prisoners' dilemma inherent in relative standards if they cooperate and effectively identify and punish defectors.

Recognizing that employees might embark upon deliberate collective laziness increases the difficulty of creating employee incentive systems. If there is no chance of collusion, a boss need only ask if he has created incentives for individuals to put in their best efforts. If you allow for collusion, however, you must ask whether all employees would be better off if they all were lazy compared to if they all worked hard. If you base your incentive scheme upon relative performance within a small group the answer might be that collective laziness is your employees' smartest strategy.

HIDDEN ACTIONS

Cheaters flourish in shadows. Hidden actions in a repeated prisoners' dilemma game increase the chances of betrayal. In all simultaneous move games you make your move before you know what strategy your opponent will employ this round. In studying repeated prisoners' dilemma games, however, we have previously assumed that the other player can see your move after you make it. This means, for example, that if you cheat in round five, your opponent will realize you betrayed him before he makes his move in round six. Sometimes, however, a player does not notice an opponent's move until long after it has been played.

What if it would take your opponent 10 rounds to figure out you had betrayed him? You would have a massively increased incentive to cheat, for now you could exploit him for 10 rounds before he would have a chance to retaliate.

OPEC's Hidden Action Problem

Hidden actions drain the strength of OPEC, a cartel of the world's major oil-producing countries. Countries in OPEC agree to limit their production of oil to increase their total oil-exporting profits.

Should an OPEC member like Kuwait restrict its oil production? Obviously, by reducing production Kuwait would sell fewer barrels of oil. Supply and demand governs the world price of oil: the lower the supply of oil, the higher the price. If Kuwait reduces its production of oil, the world supply of oil would shrink, causing the price of oil to increase. The price will decrease, however, regardless of whether Kuwait or Saudi Arabia reduces its production. Kuwait, therefore, would ideally like to sell large quantities of oil while all the other OPEC members cut production. Of course, all OPEC members would like other OPEC countries to be the ones that reduce their oil output.

Recognizing their dilemma, OPEC countries jointly agree that they should all reduce oil production. Each OPEC member, however, has an incentive to cheat. If all the other countries constrain their oil output, then the cheating country could produce a lot of oil while still enjoying the benefits of high world oil prices. Of course, if every country cheats, then the price of oil will plummet. OPEC members are consequently in a repeated prisoners' dilemma game with no clear last period. For any given period it's in each individual country's self-interest to cheat. The reason that a country might not cheat in this period, however, is because if it gets caught, other countries are more likely to cheat in the future. The harder it is to get caught, the more attractive cheating becomes. Because OPEC countries can't perfectly monitor each other's output, they frequently cheat by producing more than they agreed to. One of the justifications that Iraq gave for invading Kuwait in the Gulf War was that Kuwait was cheating on its OPEC oil production quota. Oil-importing countries like the United States, of course, benefit when OPEC members cheat.

BENEFITING FROM PRISONERS' DILEMMA

If you're being charged too much, you should consider exploiting prisoners' dilemma. Prisoners' dilemma creates varying degrees of pressure for firms to betray each other and lower prices. Imagine that two firms supply your company with widgets and the following facts hold:

- You buy 1,000 widgets a week from each of two suppliers.
- Both suppliers sell widgets for $10 each.
- Both suppliers can make widgets for free.
- Your firm is a major purchaser of widgets.

The widget companies are making significant profits from you, since it costs them nothing to make each widget. I imagine that you would first try to negotiate a discount with each supplier. The suppliers, however, prefer charging high prices and should lower their prices only if you can make it in their interests to do so by, say, plunging them into a prisoners' dilemma. A prisoners' dilemma must involve both a reward and a punishment. To create a prisoners' dilemma for the widget firms, you should reward a firm if it is the only company to lower prices, and punish a firm only if it does not offer a discount.

Currently, both firms sell you 1,000 widgets a week for $10 each, making a profit of $10,000 a week. To create a prisoners' dilemma you need to offer a firm a profit of more than $10,000 a week if only it lowers prices. If only one firm cuts prices, you should (a) buy all your widgets from this firm and (b) offer this firm a price so that it will make more than $10,000 a week in profits.

Let's say you give this firm a profit of $6 a widget. So you tell both firms that if only one of them lowers its price to $6, you will buy all 2,000 widgets from that firm, giving it a profit of $12,000 a week. Clearly, since it costs nothing to produce this good, both firms would prefer to sell 2,000 widgets at $6 each than 1,000 widgets at $10 apiece. If one firm lowers its price and the other does not, the firm that doesn't cut prices will get zero profit. If both firms lower their price to $6 each, assume that you will still buy 1,000 widgets from each firm. Figure 43 shows the new prisoners' dilemma game you have created in which both players have a dominant strategy to charge $6 per widget.

Unfortunately, your task may not be finished, for you have just created a repeated prisoners' dilemma game. If a repeated prisoners' dilemma game has no definite ending date, then it's still possible that the two firms will continue to charge $10 a widget. Each firm may reason that yes, it could make more this week by charging $6 a widget, but it's better off in the long run if both firms keep charging $10 a widget and split the market. If the game had a definite ending date, then the logic of prisoners' dilemma would compel the firms to immediately lower their price to $6.

Even if it would be a lie, you might want to tell both suppliers that after a certain date you would no longer want any widgets. A last period would make it much more difficult for the firms to maintain high prices. Remember, in the last period in a prisoners' dilemma game rational players will always betray each other and knowledge of this future betrayal will cause the players to betray each other in every previous period. Unfortunately, if these two suppliers also sell widgets to other companies, then the game won't end when you leave the market. The fewer widgets the firms expect to sell in the future, however, the greater incentive each firm has to betray its competitor today.

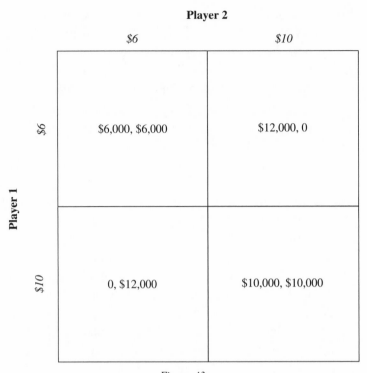

Figure 43

Thus, your falsely announcing that you will soon leave the market will increase the incentives for both firms to cheat by lowering prices. You could also induce the firms to cheat by exploiting hidden action problems.

Imagine that in this example both firms refused to lower their price to $6. What would happen if you started buying all your widgets from just firm one? You would still have to pay this firm $10/widget, but what would the other firm think? Firm two might suspect its luckier rival was really giving you a discount. Even if firm one promised its rival that it wasn't cutting prices, the rival might still suspect treachery. After all, if firm one really were charging you $6 a widget, it would obviously have an incentive to lie about it to firm two. To add to the mistrust you might even want to lie to firm two by asking it to match firm one's price of $6. If firm two thought that it was being taken advantage of, it would almost certainly lower its price. Of course, even if firm two did not believe that firm one had lowered its price, firm two would still be upset if you gave firm one all of your business and might lower its price anyway.

Chaos is your friend when seeking lower prices. If you are an important customer to your suppliers, then they strongly benefit from charging you high prices. Whenever suppliers are charging you high prices they are in a repeated prisoners' dilemma game. All suppliers know that they could significantly increase their sales to you by lowering their prices a bit. Fear of retaliation may prevent a supplier from cutting its price. Each supplier, however, also knows that if it could secretly charge you a lower price, then perhaps it could increase its sales without having other firms lower their prices too. Since all suppliers realize the game they're in, they should never fully trust each other. Random fluctuations in prices could cause a supplier to believe it is being betrayed. If market prices just happen to fall, a supplier might suspect its rival is giving secret discounts and respond by lowering its price. To multiply suppliers' mistrust you should do something strange like giving all your business to just one supplier so the other suppliers might suspect treachery. Perhaps you should even give all of your business to the supplier who appears to be charging the most. The other suppliers might then become convinced that they are being taken advantage of; otherwise why would the high-price supplier be getting all of your business? By creating chaos you can multiply the mistrust the suppliers have toward each other and perhaps cause them to betray their competitors by decreasing prices.

MOST-FAVORED-CUSTOMER AGREEMENTS[16]

Your supplier could get smart and protect itself from chaos by adopting most-favored-customer agreements. Under these agreements you promise a customer that you will never sell to him for a price more than what you sell to any other customer for.

If a supplier gave all of his customers most-favored-customer status, it would be much harder for him to secretly lower his prices, because he would have to lower prices for all customers if he did so for just a few. He wouldn't be able to offer lower prices to just those customers he was trying to steal from his rival. Furthermore, it's much easier to determine if a firm is giving discounts to all its customers rather than if it is just cutting prices for some. When one supplier issues most-favored-customer agreements, therefore, its rival can have much more confidence that it is not being betrayed. So, even though most-favored-customer agreements sound like they favor customers, they can really help producers by reducing price competition.

EVOLUTION AND PRISONERS' DILEMMA

The power of the prisoners' dilemma paradigm extends even to evolutionary biology. When humans play games, we usually assume that we rationally choose whatever strategy maximizes our payoff. Biologists sometimes apply game theory to animals and assume that the animals' genes dictate how they play their games.[17] Imagine that some creatures are repeatedly playing the prisoners' dilemma game in Figure 44. A creature's genes will tell it to play either nice or mean. The creatures receive food as their payoff. The more food a creature has, the more offspring it produces, and the more its genes will spread. The genes that are best for playing the game will survive while those that receive consistently poor scores will become extinct.

Imagine that there are two colonies of creatures separated by some considerable distance. In one colony all the creatures have genes telling them to play nice, while in the other, the genes dictate that the creatures be mean. The offspring in both of these colonies would always have the same genes as their parents. The creatures in both colonies repeatedly play the prisoners' dilemma game in Figure 44. The nice colony would appear to have an advantage. Because everyone in this colony is always nice to each other, everyone gets a payoff of 5 foods each round. In the mean colony everyone always gets a payoff of only one food. The nice colony should expand relative to the mean colony.

The colony of the creatures with mean genes, however, has one critical advantage over their nicer rivals. Consider what happens when the nice colony expands to the edge of the means and competes directly against them. The mean creatures will do very well in this game, and the nice creatures will die. When the nice colony creatures play only against each other, they beat the mean colony. When they play against the mean creatures, however, the mean creatures domi-

Player 2

	Nice	Mean
Nice	5 foods, 5 foods	0 food, 7 foods
Mean	7 foods, 0 food	1 food, 1 food

Figure 44

nate. This contest between nice and mean shows that nice guys finish first only when they don't have to compete against mean people.

Let's apply our evolutionary game to business cultures. Imagine that two divisions in a company have radically different cultures. In one culture, everyone is nice to each other, and in the other, everyone is always mean. These cultures are not the results of rational choice, rather they simply persist. When someone is hired in the nice culture, their surroundings automatically make them nice, and similarly anyone recruited into the mean culture becomes mean. The employees in the nice division will do better since they all cooperate with each other, while employees in the mean division always undercut each other to get ahead.

The theory of prisoners' dilemma, however, shows that the nice culture is extremely unstable. If just a few mean people start playing in the nice division and aren't converted, then the nice employees will starve. A cluster of nice employees will make higher short-term profits for your company, but their culture is unsound, for even a few meanies can destroy it.

WHAT TO DO WHEN TRAPPED IN A PRISONERS' DILEMMA?

A prisoners' dilemma game manifests whenever everyone individually would be better off being selfish, but collectively all would benefit from being nice. In a one-period prisoners' dilemma, you should always be mean to your rival, for meanness maximizes your score. Indeed, businesses must recognize when they are in such a game so they don't waste time trying to find a "win, win" outcome, for none exist in one-shot prisoners' dilemma games. In repeated games with no last period, however, you should strive to cooperate to achieve a better outcome. To obtain this outcome you most need your rival to believe in your capacity to detect and punish cheating.

SELF-INTEREST LEADS TO BAD OUTCOMES

Economics used to be called the "dismal science" because of the pessimistic predictions of some 19th-century economists concerning the inevitability of mass starvation. Economists' present day use of prisoners' dilemma to model different real-life situations perhaps shows that economists are still obsessed with predicting doom. The topic of the next chapter, adverse selection, provides yet more evidence of economists' tendency to focus on the dark side of capitalism.

LESSONS LEARNED

- In a prisoners' dilemma game, competition will harm both players. The players would be better off if they worked together, but if the game is played only one time, then self-interest will always force them into ruinous competition.
- In a repeated prisoners' dilemma game, the players might be able to work together to achieve a good outcome. Hidden actions, short time horizons, and last period problems might still make cooperation impossible, however.
- If your suppliers are charging you high prices, you could benefit from creating a prisoners' dilemma.

ADVERSE SELECTION

I refuse to join any club that would have me for a member.

Groucho Marx

L ET'S SAY THAT AFTER READING this book you feel compelled to learn more about business, and so you apply to 10 MBA programs. You get into nine but are rejected by one. Tragically, you most wanted to attend the school that rejected you. Bad karma? No, adverse selection. Adverse selection manifests when you attract those with whom you least wish to interact.

You probably want to attend the most exclusive MBA program that will have you. An exclusive school, by definition, is difficult to get into. Therefore, the lower a school's admissions standards, the less you should want to attend.

What would it signal if an MBA program really wanted you? It might show that the school believed you were a good match for its program. More likely, however, the school believed that admitting you would significantly increase the quality of its student body. Of course, if you were far better than the program's average students, you should probably look elsewhere. This means that if you were a bad enough student, you would not want to attend any school that would admit you, for by admitting you, the school signals its exceptionally low quality.

I attended a law school that admitted me from its waitlist long after it had made most of its admission decisions. Of all the schools that accepted me, it considered me the least worthy. This law school therefore was obviously the best that I could get into, and naturally the one that I decided to attend. When adverse selection applies, you should want most those who least want you.

From the viewpoint of a college, the students most likely to accept an offer of admittance are the ones the school probably least wants. Imagine that a college randomly chooses 100 high school seniors and guarantees them admittance. Which students would be most likely to accept the offer? The ones with really high SAT scores? Unfortunately, no; they would be the students who wanted to attend college but couldn't get into any other college. They would be the students whom the college probably least desired.

Employers also need to worry about adverse selection. Imagine that your company advertises to hire a computer programmer for $80,000 a year. Twenty people apply for the position. Which of these twenty would most want the job? The answer is, obviously someone whose talent would ordinarily bar him from making anywhere near $80,000. Adverse selection would manifest because the least qualified person would have the greatest desire to get hired. The person you would most want to hire would probably not even bother applying because she would be such a talented programmer that she could easily make more that $80,000.

To combat the appearance of adverse selection, a job candidate should avoid appearing overeager. Rather, a candidate should consider playing hard to get and let his prospective employer believe that he has many attractive offers. If a job candidate really is hard to get, then he is not desperate, and an employer doesn't have to worry about adverse selection.

Hidden information causes adverse selection. Because of hidden information, players often need to rely on signals. To see the value of signals, consider the following silly example: Your boss wants to reward you and punish either Rachel or Fred. He says you can have all the money in either Rachel or Fred's wallet. Your boss won't completely reveal the contents of each person's wallet, but he does say that Rachel's wallet contains 14 bills while Fred's contains only 9. Assuming you know nothing else about Rachel and Fred's wallet, which do you choose? I imagine you would pick Rachel's because it has more bills. Of course, you care about the total dollar value of the bills, not the total number of bills. While you can't directly observe what you care about, the number of bills in each wallet does provide you with some information about the total value of the bills. Thus, although this information is, by itself, irrelevant to you, it would still help you make your decision because on average, the more bills a person carries the more money he has. Consequently, the total number of bills provides a signal as to the value of each wallet. This signal might be faulty because Fred's wallet could easily contain more money than Rachel's does. For a signal to be useful, however, it need only be right on average.

When you consider hiring someone, you don't have complete information about his qualities, so you must guess based upon signals. A candidate's desire to work for you provides a useful signal about her quality. On average, job candidates who would be the happiest with your salary would be the candidates who are of the lowest quality since the marketplace values them the least.

Adverse selection is a powerful force in the universe that illuminates many strategies such as avoiding telemarketers offering investment advice.

TELEMARKETING INVESTMENT ADVICE

I hope you're already smart enough not to take investment advice from a stranger who cold-calls you. In case you're tempted, however, consider how adverse selection affects the type of person likely to offer unsolicited investment advice over the telephone.

Imagine a highly successful investor who has had a string of great ideas that have earned her lucky clients millions. Everyone on Wall Street desperately wants to lunch with her. Now, is this woman likely to cold-call you to let you in on her latest deal?

The type of person most likely to make random calls to strangers probably lacks the knowledge to give you intelligent investment advice. If your cold caller makes a low salary, then he obviously doesn't have a lot of marketable skills. Even if your cold caller prospers at his job, you still shouldn't trust him.

I suspect that a sophisticated understanding of finance does not help someone become a successful telemarketer. Rather, being a good telemarketer probably requires great salesmanship skills: the ability to sell things to people that they really don't need. Telemarketing companies probably attract either people who have very little ability to make money outside of telemarketing, or people skilled at selling unneeded products. Either way, the people most likely to cold-call you are the people you should least trust for financial advice.

USED CARS[1]

Adverse selection should make you wary of used-car sellers as well as telemarketers. When buying a used car you should most want to attract sellers of very high quality automobiles. Alas, sellers would most want to part with pre-owned vehicles of low quality. Used-car buyers need to take adverse selection into account and question the motives of used car sellers.

To simplify matters, assume that you are considering buying a 1996 Honda Civic that will necessarily be of either excellent or low quality. The car's quality determines its value to you.

Table 2

Car's Quality	Car's Value to You
Excellent	$10,000
Poor	$3,000

A mechanic who can determine the value of the car need not worry about adverse selection because he won't care why the car is being sold. Hidden information about the car's quality causes adverse selection. If you're not a mechanic, then you should worry that the seller most wants to sell his car when its quality is poor. Consequently, you should be reluctant to pay more than $3,000 for it.

Iteration magnifies the power of adverse selection. Assume that 90 percent of all 1996 Honda Civics are of excellent quality. Further assume that current owners know their car's quality, but prospective buyers don't. You would err in thinking that if you bought a used 1996 Honda Civic, there would be a 90 percent chance of getting one in excellent condition, since owners of poor quality cars will most desire to sell you their automobile. If all buyers are aware of adverse selection, then the price of used cars will be far from $10,000. Of course, this low price for used cars will mean that owners of excellent cars will be even less willing to sell them. Adverse selection thus creates a vicious circle.

> As adverse selection lowers the price of used cars, fewer used cars of excellent quality are sold, which by definition increases the strength of adverse selection, which further lowers the price of used cars, which causes even fewer used cars of excellent quality to be sold, which . . .

As a result, even though 90 percent of 1996 Honda Civics are of excellent quality, almost all of the used cars on the market will be of poor quality.

What if an owner of an excellent quality used car wants to sell his vehicle? An owner unwilling to accept a low payment needs to convince the buyer of the car's high quality. The buyer or seller could pay for an independent mechanic to inspect the vehicle. An inspection removes the hidden information that causes adverse selection. The owner could also perhaps explain his reason for selling the car. For example, if the seller could prove that he had to sell the car because he was moving to a different continent, then the buyer might believe that adverse selection isn't the reason the owner put his car on the market. The seller could also offer a warranty that covered some repair costs. The warranty would reduce the harm of hidden information because if the car was not of excellent quality and consequently broke down, the buyer would receive some compensation.

OLD COINS SOLD ON EBAY

People frequently sell bags of old coins dating back to the Roman Empire on eBay. Many of the sellers dug up the coins themselves. The eBay description will often state that the coins have not been examined and are still dirty. Sellers don't normally highlight the dirt on their wares. Adverse selection, however, could rationally cause you to place a higher value on dirty, unexamined coins.

Coins from the Roman Empire have vastly different values depending upon many factors, including whether they are composed of bronze or gold. If the seller had carefully examined the coins, he would have removed any gold ones before the auction. If the seller has information about the different coins' values, adverse selection would cause him to sell only the coins that he values the least. When the coins are unexamined, however, the seller has no more information about them than the buyer does, and consequently adverse selection doesn't come into play, and the buyer has a chance at getting gold.

FIRE SOME RATHER THAN CUT WAGES FOR ALL[2]

Imagine that your firm faces a budget shortfall and absent salary reductions you soon won't have the funds to meet your payroll obligations. You have two choices: Give everyone a 10 percent wage cut or fire 10 percent of your workers. Adverse selection shows why you should prefer the firing option.

If you give everyone a 10 percent wage cut, some of your workers will probably leave for better-paying jobs. Unfortunately, your most productive workers will probably have the best job opportunities and will consequently be the most likely to quit. Cutting everyone's wages by 10 percent will cause adverse selection to come into play, since those whom you would most want to stay will be the ones most likely to leave. In contrast, if you fire 10 percent of your employees, you could obviously eliminate your least-productive workers.

SECURITY DEPOSITS AND SELECTION FOR DEADBEATS

Most landlords require their tenants to provide security deposits. What if you own an apartment building and consider no longer requiring a deposit since you have never before had a problem with tenants? Every other landlord in your area requires security deposits, so up to now you have too. Over 95 percent of the prospective tenants in your area are honest and responsible, however, so you figure there is no need to inconvenience tenants with security deposits. Unfortunately, if you become the only landlord to not require security deposits, then adverse selection will cause you to get all of the deadbeats.

Irresponsible, destructive deadbeats would most like to rent an apartment for which they don't have to provide a security deposit. If, alone among all the landlords, only you don't require one, then adverse selection will manifest since you will attract most of the deadbeat renters.

MILDLY CARELESS BANKS

Banks run credit checks on loan applicants. What if your bank had a reputation for being slightly less thorough than other area banks? Applicants who had the most to hide would be the most attracted to your bank. You would thus attract the customers you least wanted to lend to. Most banks strive to overcome adverse selection by gathering information about loan applicants. If your bank did not diligently seek out this information, adverse selection would increase your default rates.

FAILURE TO SETTLE LAWSUITS

Adverse selection causes court battles. It should initially seem strange that all lawsuits don't settle out of court. Since lawyers are very expensive, it might seem litigants could always do better if they settled their case rather than pay their attorneys to take them to trial.

Assume that you're suing me. You have strong witnesses and a great case. If you go to trial you will probably win a million dollars. Even if you win, however, you will have to pay your lawyer $100,000, so you want to settle before trial to avoid attorney's fees. You suggest to me that we should settle the case for a million dollars. If I knew everything that you knew, I should accept your offer. After all, I would have to pay you one million dollars at trial, so settling for a million would save me from attorney's fees too.

Unfortunately, I would be unwilling to settle if I suspected that your case wasn't that strong. Adverse selection should cause me to ask why you wanted to settle. You would most want to settle when your case was weak. Of course, it's when your case is poor that I would most want to go to trial. Consequently, your willingness to settle is a signal to me that I shouldn't settle. If I become informed about the case and realize you really would win one million dollars at trial, then I would be amenable to your offer. If I never learn about the strength of your case, however, I would always suspect that you wanted to settle because you were afraid to fight me in court.

"AT A GREAT BARGAIN, PAUSE."[3]

If a litigant offers to settle a case on overly favorable terms, you should question his kindness. Similarly, you should be wary of accepting any business offers that seem too generous. Imagine that an acquaintance starts a new business. You have studied the venture and estimate that it should be worth $10 million. Your acquaintance offers you 10 percent of the business for only $500,000. You had previously thought that 10 percent of the business was worth one million dollars, so should you accept? When you were offered 10 percent of the business for $500,000, you gained a valuable piece of information. A person who knows more about the business than you would be willing to trade 10 percent of it for $500,000. Perhaps this is because she needs the money, but it's also possible that your acquaintance knows that 10 percent of the business is not worth what you had thought, so you should study the business further before investing in it.

Adverse selection comes into play when the seller knows more about the good than the buyer. The seller is always going to be more willing to sell an item the lower its quality. If the seller knows more about the quality of the good than you, you should assume that the seller's willingness to part with the item signals that he might think the item is of poor quality. This doesn't mean that you should never accept any offer. There are many instances where it's possible for you to benefit from a deal that also would benefit your potential partner. It could be that your potential partner needs your financing or expertise so she is really willing to make an offer that would make you better off. When a prospective partner knows more about a deal then you do, however, you should always examine her incentives for interacting with you.

ADVERSE SELECTION, CHILD PREDATORS, DICTATORS, AND PRESIDENTS

Organizations that work with children need to be especially concerned about adverse selection. Only a very small percentage of the population sexually abuses children. Unfortunately, these abusers are attracted to jobs that allow them to interact with children. Consequently, organizations such as day care centers and elementary schools need to vigilantly screen out undesirables.

Undesirables are likely attracted to dictatorships as well as daycare centers. Those who most lust for power are often the ones who should be least trusted with it. Joseph Stalin became leader of the Soviet Empire only after crushing his enemies. Given that thugs ruled the new Soviet Empire, brutality was the only means by which anyone could have risen to the top. This meant, however, that the supreme leader of the early Soviet Empire would necessarily be a man comfortable killing for personal gain.

To gain power in a dictatorship, one must be willing to kill. It's not surprising, therefore, that almost all dictators have been evil scum, for most dictators would never have risen to power if they had been nice. Adverse selection affects dictatorships because those who are the worst for the people are often those best able to take power.

Adverse selection also explains why most revolutions go bad. The Russian, Chinese, and French revolutions all produced narcissistic, brutal governments. This should not be surprising, as all the revolutions started in blood. The only types of people capable of acquiring power in these revolutionary environments were people skilled at murder and betrayal.

Monarchies are usually superior to dictatorships because of adverse selection. A man born to be king is, on average, likely to be average, while adverse selection results in dictators usually being men of exceptionally low morality.

Americans consider George Washington to have been not just one of their best presidents, but also one of the greatest leaders the world has ever known, and adverse selection justifies this assessment. President Washington was a skilled general who used force of arms to expel the British. He had the strength and ruthlessness necessary to lead a colonial insurrection against what was then the world's greatest power. George Washington, however, did not lust for power himself. Yes, he became President, but he respected the limitations on presidential power inscribed in the U.S. Constitution. Furthermore, he voluntarily chose not to seek a third term as president, even though he would almost certainly have won reelection. President Washington, therefore, had the personality that allowed him to both take and abdicate power. This combination has seldom been seen in world history. Usually the only men strong enough to take power through blood are men like Lenin, Mao, and Napoleon: men who do not give up spilling blood once they seize control. The unique success of the American Revolution is due to its escaping adverse selection.

Adverse selection is the reason that men seeking power often deny their desires. Bill Clinton had clearly wanted to be President his entire life. Yet when campaigning he often said he didn't really want to be President and would have been happy staying in Arkansas. He claimed to be running only because the country needed him. Clinton recognized that the American people did not trust someone who lusted for power. Thus, he at least attempted to hide his ambition when he sought the presidency.

SELECTION FOR STOCK ANALYSTS

Most dictators are scum, because scum has a comparative advantage in the competition for dictatorships. Which types of individuals are most likely to be successful stock analysts? It depends on how analysts are judged.

Analysts are supposed to study stocks to advise which should be bought, sold, and held. Analysts almost always issue positive recommendations for stocks, however, so we should be somewhat suspect of their motives.

Although the SEC has cut back on this practice, analysts often get inside information from companies. Naturally, companies most like analysts who say nice things about them. Analysts work for investment banks, and investment banks constantly woo companies for new business. As a result, investment banks are most likely to promote analysts who please companies. Consequently, if an analyst is successful, it probably means he toddies to big public companies.

RATIONAL PESSIMISM

Adverse selection means that what you don't know is probably worse than you thought. Businesspersons must often make decisions about people when they don't have full information. When faced with uncertainty, however, the rational businessperson makes intelligent guesses. This chapter showed that the reason someone wants to interact with you should educate your estimate of their value. When considering forming a new commercial relationship, ask why your potential partner wants to interact with you and what this motivation signals.

MORE TALES OF HIDDEN INFORMATION

Adverse selection comes about when a party does not know everything about those with whom he might deal. As the next chapter explains, limited information has far more consequences for game players than just causing adverse selection.

LESSONS LEARNED

- Adverse selection occurs when you attract those with whom you least want to interact.
- When you make offers to job applicants or customers, you should consider the type of person most likely to accept your offer. Will they be more likely than average to have undesirable traits?
- People desperate to interact with you are often the ones with whom you should least want to deal.
- Playing hard to get can overcome adverse selection by convincing others that you are not desperate and thus not undesirable.
- Adverse selection is caused by hidden information and so can be remedied by information acquisition.

Surviving with
Limited Information

A man surprised is half beaten.

Proverb[1]

AMES OF LIMITED INFORMATION are both varied and interesting. Because there are so many different types of games involving incomplete information, this chapter will explore several unrelated topics. I assume that my readers mostly want to learn about business, but will excuse digressions if they are entertaining. Consequently, I trust that you will forgive my ramblings on the relationship between game theory and dating. Before we get to dating theory, however, we must first further study signaling.

BRING ME A SHRUBBERY!

When Singapore was still desperately poor, its prime minister used neatly trimmed shrubbery to attract foreign investment.[2] The prime minister ensured that the roads from the airport to the hotels were well kept and nicely groomed. He did this so foreign businesspeople would think that Singaporeans were "competent, disciplined, and reliable."[3]

The existence of sharply pruned shrubbery in a host country doesn't usually enhance a multinational's foreign investments. The shrubbery from the airport to the hotels was highly visible to potential investors, however, and was far easier to judge than, say, Singapore's level of corruption. What makes things interesting is that the foreign businesspeople knew that Singapore knew that they would observe the quality of the road between the airport and hotels. Consequently, if Singapore couldn't even go to the trouble of keeping up this road, it would signal that it wouldn't make future accommodations to foreign capital.

These shrubberies were Singapore's easily viewed cover, and as we all know, it's pretty easy to judge a book by its cover. While evaluating a book's contents takes some time, the message of the cover can be grasped in seconds. A book's cover provides a signal as to its contents.

BRAND NAMES

Brand names act as covers for your products and should provide helpful signals to customers. For example, when picking a movie, parents know that if they go with a Disney cartoon, their children will not be exposed to sex, but probably will see lots of violence like Bambi's mother being shot. Brand names help consumers because they are easy to understand. People, as well as products, can acquire brand names.

EDUCATION AND SIGNALING

College degrees can signal a job applicant's intelligence and, consequently, separate productive from unproductive workers. What's the purpose of a college education? College might expand your mind and make you more enlightened, but I suspect that most people attend college to increase their lifetime income. Why, however, does going to college increase one's earning capacity? The standard answer is that college teaches people useful things. A signaling theory about college, however, shows that college could increase a student's earning capacity, even if it taught him nothing of value.[4]

It's somewhat challenging to graduate from a decent college. To graduate, you must first be accepted by the school and complete all the required work. Graduating from college signals to a future employer that you have a decent level of intelligence, responsibility, and diligence. Imagine that you want to hire a high-quality employee. You believe that students don't really learn anything useful in college. You think that college students just memorize lots of stuff and write papers on theoretical issues of no importance. You do, however, believe that it's difficult to do all of this memorization and writing. Consequently, the fact that someone graduated from college signals to you that they have high intelligence even if you believe that college did not enhance this intelligence. Hopefully, students do learn a few useful things in college. The point of this paragraph, however, is to explain that even if college teaches you nothing of value, it would still be valuable to attend, for graduating from college would signal to some types of employers that you might be worth hiring.

SIGNALING AND RACISM

Racial stereotyping illuminates the dark side of signaling. People judge books by their covers because the covers are visible and easier to grasp than the book's contents. Similarly, individuals' physical characteristics are easier to evaluate than their personalities. Unfortunately, therefore, people sometimes make decisions based upon race when ignorant of a person's vastly more significant qualities.

Although perhaps not moral, using race as a signal can be rational. This rationality is not predicated upon genetic differences among the races. Using race as a signal is rational if race is merely correlated with less visible characteristics. For example, imagine that your company wants to hire a recent Malaysian college graduate. You want the smartest student you can find. Let's assume that Malaysian colleges discriminate against ethnic Chinese in admissions. Consequently, it is harder for an ethnic Chinese than an ethnic Malay to be admitted to a Malaysian college. Given this discrimination, you would expect in Malaysia that, *on average*, Chinese college students are more capable than Malaysian college students. If the colleges discriminate against a group, then the school must have higher standards for that group,

implying that students from this group will be *on average* better than
the rest of the college's student population.

So, you want to hire a Malaysian college graduate, and you believe
that on average, Chinese graduates are more capable than the
Malaysian graduates. How important is this racial difference? It's of
absolutely no importance if you can determine each job candidate's
quality. You care about competence, not race. If you can determine a
candidate's competence, then race becomes irrelevant. If, however,
competence is difficult or even costly to evaluate, then it becomes
rational for you to use race as a factor when hiring, because race is correlated with competence. Even if a book's cover would have no effect
per se on how much pleasure you would derive from reading the book,
it's still rational to base your purchase decision on the cover if it tells
you something about the contents. Signaling theory shows that if colleges discriminate against some race, then employers might desire to
discriminate in favor of this race. Alas, the reverse also holds true.

Affirmative action can harm racial groups to the extent that a college is a signal of quality. Assume that high school students can be
academically scored from 0 to 100. Let's say that some highly selec-
tive college admits students from race X with a score over 90 and,
because of affirmative action admits students from race Y with a score
over 85. Imagine that the primary benefit of attending this college is
that it signals your high rank. Unfortunately, if this school's affirmative
action policies are known, the signaling benefit of attending this college will be lower for group Y than X. Tragically, even members of
group Y who have scores of 100 will be hurt by affirmative action,
because potential employers could more easily judge their race than
their intelligence or score.

SIGNALING FITNESS

Animals sometimes evolve traits that allow them to signal information. For example, when a gazelle sees a cheetah, it sometimes tries to
run away for fear of being eaten. Often, however, the gazelle will
instead jump 18 inches into the air when it notices a cheetah.[5] An
explanation for this behavior is that the gazelle is signaling to the cheetah that the gazelle could easily outrun the cheetah. Because the
gazelle's jump separates it from unhealthy animals, the cheetah should

not waste its energies trying to kill the gazelle. A cheetah can't directly observe its potential prey's fitness, but it can observe its acrobatics. Assuming that the cheetah would have little chance of catching a gazelle that could perform such an acrobatic feat, the cheetah would be "rational" to not chase a jumping gazelle. If the gazelle consumes less energy jumping than running away, then jumping is an evolutionarily sound strategy.

You can use this jumping gazelle strategy to deter a potential business rival. Imagine that you are currently the only seller of snow tires in Buffalo, New York. Another firm starts trying to sell snow tires. You know that almost none of your customers would ever switch brands. You are certain that in the end, your rival would be unable to compete successfully. Unfortunately, you can't convince your rival of his doomed fate. Because competing against even a feeble rival is costly, you desire a strategy that quickly causes your competitor to exit your market.

Normally, when you face a new competitor, it's optimal to increase advertising to prevent any of your customers from abandoning you. What if, however, when this rival enters your market, you stop all advertising? If your rival has any chance at long-term survival, this "no advertisement" strategy would be disastrous. If, however, you are confident that no one would buy your rival's snow tires even if you stopped advertising, then you might indeed want to stop. Your rival will realize that if he can't beat you when you weren't even trying that hard, he has no hope of prevailing when you start advertising again. Succeeding even without advertising is the equivalent of a gazelle's jumping 18 inches in the air. It's an impressive feat that should deter would-be predators.

WARRANTIES

Warranties and money-back guarantees act as powerful signals about your product's quality. Imagine that there are two types of cars a buyer could purchase from a used car dealer: lemons and high-quality vehicles. A lemon would require a lot of future repair work while a high-quality car would require little or none. Assume that the dealer, but not the buyer, knows the car's quality. If the seller knows that his car is of high quality, he should offer a free warranty, promising to pay all repair costs. The seller of a lemon would be reluctant to offer a warranty that would impose expensive obligations upon him. The buyer should thus believe that a free warranty offer signals that the car is no lemon. Note that if the car is of high quality, the warranty will cost the seller nothing and provide no benefit to the buyer once the car is purchased. The warranty would still, however, serve an important function. It would signal the car's quality.

SIGNAL JAMMING[6]

Sometimes you want to prevent your competitor from acquiring useful information. Imagine that a potential business rival test-markets his product in a few stores in your area. The results of these tests will provide your rival with a signal as to whether he should enter your market. When should you interfere with these tests? If you could secretly interfere, then you could always forestall competition by surreptitiously causing your rival's test marketing to fail. But what if you couldn't interfere without your rival finding out?

Say the only way that you could mess with his test marketing would be to drastically alter your prices in the stores in which he was selling his products. By randomly varying your prices, you prevent your rival from getting any useful information from his test marketing. Before engaging in visible signal jamming, however, you need to determine what your rival will do in the absence of any new information. Perhaps he is 90 percent sure he should enter. He is just test marketing to guarantee that he is not making a mistake. In this case, visible signal jamming would just ensure that he would enter. What if your rival is almost certain that he should not enter, but is test marketing to see if you are weaker than he previously thought? If he was almost certain that he shouldn't compete, and you prevent him from acquiring any new information, will he now stay out of your market? Unfortunately, if you visibly interfere with his test marketing, your rival would necessarily gain valuable information. He would learn that you are scared enough of him to go to the trouble to mess with his signal. Your rival might interpret your signal jamming as a sign that you are weak, and he should enter.

Signal jamming is most effective when your rival hopes to receive a multidimensional signal. Let's assume that there are many different types of products your rival could sell, but he's not sure which to offer in your market. At a significant expense, he manufactures multiple prototypes and sells each type in a separate store. If you now were to signal-jam by, say, radically lowering prices in some stores and raising them in others, you would make it very difficult for your rival to formulate an entrance strategy. He wouldn't know which prototype would sell best in your area. When your rival's decision is binary, enter or not, it's difficult to visibly signal-jam, for such jamming tells him that he should enter. If your rival's decision is multifaceted, then signal jamming can be very effective because while it does show your fear, it also prevents your rival from determining how to best compete against you.

VALENTINE'S DAY

Why do men give flowers to their girlfriend(s) on Valentine's Day, and why do women who don't receive flowers on Valentine's Day get depressed? Flowers on Valentine's Day signal love, and many of us are worse off for it.

Women are often uncertain if any of the men in their lives are romantically interested in them. Since it's customary for men to give women whom they desire flowers on Valentine's Day, women who don't receive flowers learn something. They learn that it is not likely that any of their male acquaintances are romantically pursuing them. Valentine's Day is a day of judgment for many women, and so those who don't receive flowers sometimes feel damned.

Game theory almost forces a man to give flowers to his girlfriend on Valentine's Day. Flowers, particularly roses, are expensive (especially on Valentine's Day). Men who don't really care about their girlfriends consequently won't spend the money to get them flowers. Could a man who did care about his girlfriend convince her that he didn't need to buy her Valentine's Day flowers? Yes, but this would be like a smart person convincing his employer that he is intelligent even if he didn't graduate from college. Recall that graduating from college separates a smart from an unintelligent person, because only the smart person can go to college. Thus, if almost every smart person goes to college, it would be extremely unlikely that someone who didn't graduate is still intelligent.

Similarly, if almost all men buy flowers for their girlfriends whom they still care about, then most women will believe that not getting flowers signals their boyfriend's disinterest. Men are thus in a trap, for we are actually made worse off by not giving flowers. Men who (a) don't care about their girlfriends and (b) don't buy their girlfriends flowers have an incentive to lie and pretend that they still do care about their girlfriends. Consequently, it's difficult for men who care but don't buy flowers to convince their girlfriends of their devotion Furthermore, if a woman knows that her boyfriend knows that she would be upset if she didn't get flowers, then the woman is automatically justified in getting upset if she doesn't get them, for now her boyfriend has knowingly hurt her. We are all in a horrible Valentine's Day game theory trap with no solution but for all of us men to waste large sums of money on expensive, soon-to-wither, thorn-studded vegetation.

CELEBRITY ENDORSEMENTS

Why do some companies pay celebrities piles of money for product endorsements when the celebrities usually aren't qualified to evaluate the products? Celebrity endorsements resemble flowers on Valentine's Day: a costly method of signaling. Celebrities are expensive to rent. A company would be willing to spend lots of money only on a product it was devoted to. Consequently, a celebrity endorsement signals commitment.

SEXUAL INFORMATION STRATEGIES

Success in the dating market comes not from mastering fashion or foreplay, but from managing *information*. Attracting a mate is like selling a used car: In both cases you want to play hard to get. Buying a used car is somewhat of a mystery. You can't be completely sure of the car's quality when you purchase it. The buyer has a lot more information about what's under the hood than you do. Since in some situations it's highly inappropriate to check under the hood before taking a drive, buyers must often rely upon signals to assess the car's quality.

If a buyer was extremely eager to sell you his car, you should wonder why. The worse the car's quality, the greater the buyer's desire to sell it. If I offer to sell you my 1994 Honda Civic for $500, you won't think I am offering you a great bargain. You'll question what information I have about the car's condition that causes me to be so desperate to part with it. What mechanical dysfunction am I hiding?

People should play hard to get in the dating market to avoid transmitting negative information. If you express an extreme desire to date someone, she may question why you can't do better than her. If Debbie is an 8, and the best that I can do if she rejects me is to date a 4, then I would obviously be very eager to date her. The marginal value added I would receive from interacting with her would be high. But if Debbie ever finds this out, she would realize how much better she could do than to date me. The strategy I should adopt is to convince Debbie that while I normally date 9s, I would be willing to make an exception with her. Ideally, I want Debbie to think that I would barely consider dating her.

Of course, if Debbie is a 10, then none of this applies. Anyone would be eager to date a 10. Expressing intense interest in dating someone who could be on *Baywatch* signals that you're normal, not desperate. Therefore, when going after supermodel types, feel free to honestly express your desires, but be coy when pursuing ordinary mortals.

Unfortunately, if you have a justifiably low opinion about yourself, the economics of dating might dictate that you not date anyone who is interested in you. If you don't have any traits that a reasonably decent person would admire, you might want to avoid people who would consider becoming romantically involved with you. Yes, I realize this means a life of lonely desperation.

I have been told that single women sometimes pretend not to recognize available men whom they have previously met. This is a brilliant strategy, for it signals that they have so many options that they need not keep track of them all. Their feigned ignorance will impress not only the men they pretend not to know, but also people who find out about their deed. Obviously, the better-looking the men they pretend not to know, the higher opinion people will have of them.

Many people pursue someone, only to lose interest after the "capture." This is often thought to be the result of some deep psychological flaw. We want something just because we can't have it. Or worse, we don't really want sex or romance, so we run away when these things become obtainable. However, it's entirely rational to lose interest in someone who responds favorably to your advances. Your estimate of a potential mate should go down after you find out they like you. After all, this means they can't do better than you. If they're too eager to accept, then perhaps you should look elsewhere.

For some people (mostly women) romantic success is achieved more by dating someone who has a great personality than who is gorgeous. Let's say you want to attract a person who does care more about personality than appearance. What would be better to do: take bodybuilding classes or go to therapy to work on your personality?

Is it more important for restaurants to have clean kitchens or clean bathrooms? Obviously, since the patrons see only the bathrooms, it is far more important that they be kept clean. Even if most of a restaurant's customers would rather dine in a place with a clean kitchen than a clean bathroom, restaurant owners should still pay more attention to the cleanliness of their bathrooms because this is what is observable. Similarly, it is easier for others to judge our looks than personality. Beauty may be skin deep, but it transmits information far more quickly than personality does.

We are judged not just by our appearance, but also by the company we keep. Looks take milliseconds to evaluate. But how can you convince someone that you are a deep, caring, sensitive soul? The best way is to be completely superficial in your choice of mates. What would you think if you saw a strikingly beautiful woman dating a below-average-looking man? You would think that he must have some desirable hidden traits. Perhaps he is smart, sensitive, or even rich. Seeing him with a beautiful woman would increase your opinion of his deep unobservable characteristics. Now, what would you think if instead you saw this same man dating an average-looking woman with a terrific personality? Probably nothing, because you wouldn't know she had a great personality. To convince others that you have a nice personality, you need to pick dates who have great observable traits. So if you want to trade up in the dating market, be superficial.

THE SOUND OF SILENCE

Silence can be a powerful signal. For example, imagine that you have a friend who is a female college student. You see your friend kiss a boy who looks like he is in high school. You estimate he is 13, 14, 15, or

16. It would be very embarrassing for a college girl to be caught kissing a boy that young.[7] Assume that your friend's honesty would prevent her from ever lying to you. If she told you the boy was 16, you would believe her. While she won't lie, she would be willing to tell you to "mind your own business." When you ask your friend how old the boy is, what should she say?

Obviously, the older he is, the less embarrassed she will be. She knows that there is no way you would ever think he is over 16. Thus, if he is 16, she will tell you. If he is 16, she wouldn't, by assumption, lie. If she says, "Mind your own business," you might think he is 16, but you also might think that he is younger. Consequently, if he is 16, she will always make herself look better by revealing it.

Now let's assume that the boy is only 15. What should she do? Her choice is either to say 15 or to tell you to "mind your own business." If she says, "Mind your own business," however, you will know the boy could not possibly be 16 because, recall, if he is 16, she would reveal it. Thus, if she employs her "none of your business" strategy, you will believe that the boy is 15, 14, or 13. Since she would rather you think him 15 than 13 or 14, she will reveal his age if he is indeed 15.

Now pretend that the boy is really 14. If she says, "Mind your own business," you will assume he can't be 15 or 16 and thus must be either 13 or 14. Since it will be better if he was 14 than 13, she should reveal his age if he is indeed 14.

We have established that your friend will tell you the boy's age whenever he is 14, 15, and 16. Consequently, if she says, "None of your business," you know the boy is 13. This is a stable outcome, for if you assume that "none of your business" means 13, it will be in your friend's interest to tell you his age, unless he is indeed 13. Since your friend can't lie, she must reveal the truth. Game theory thus establishes that she can't really stay silent, since silence tells you the boy is only 13.

The key result from this game is that when a player can't lie, she also can't stay silent, for silence communicates information. Silence signals that the situation is very bad because if it wasn't, you would have an incentive to say something. This result has strong applications to consumer product markets.

Imagine that widgets are a tasty food that comes in two varieties: (1) safe widgets, which cause no ill health effects, and (2) unsanitary widgets, which induce vomiting. You're in the grocery store and see some widgets labeled as safe and some with no label. Assume that consumer fraud laws prevent makers of unsanitary widgets from labeling them as safe. What should you assume about the unlabeled widgets? Obviously, if they were safe, their producer would benefit from labeling them as such. Thus, the lack of a label signals that the widgets are unsanitary. In a deep sense, therefore, all the widgets are labeled.

Now imagine that instead of being safe or unsanitary, widgets are either high or low in fat. Since most consumers prefer low-fat foods, manufacturers of low-fat foods will label their products as such. Thus, no label means high in fat.

When a product is not labeled for some characteristic, you should assume that either most people don't care about the trait, or that the product's trait is bad. Even if the trait were average, it would be labeled. Since good traits are always labeled, if a product is not labeled, customers will assume that its quality is well below average. Consequently, firms will find it in their self-interest to label products of merely average quality.

In U.S. criminal trials, defendants are not required to testify. A rational jury should conclude that if the defendant doesn't testify, he must realize that testifying would hurt him. Thus, a rational juror would learn a lot from a defendant's refusal to testify. In U.S. courts, however, juries are prohibited from drawing any inference from a criminal defendant's refusal to testify. Juries are thus supposed to be irrational and forget what a defendant's non-testifying signals.[8] (If you want to get out of jury duty, then when asked if you could fairly judge the defendant, you should warn the court that if the defendant doesn't testify, you will assume that he has something to hide.)

While juries are sometimes supposed to be irrational, business-people should always listen to the sound of silence. If information is not disclosed, you should often assume the worst. For example, if a job candidate has several holes in his résumé, you should assume that he was afraid to fill in the gaps.

PUTTING PEOPLE UNDER PRESSURE

Occasionally, people will reveal the truth accidentally when they are placed under pressure. As the story of Achilles' recruitment shows, this can sometimes be a useful tactic to employ.

The Greeks wanted Achilles, the greatest mortal warrior, to fight in the Trojan War. Achilles' mother, however, didn't want her son to fight, for if he fought he was destined to die. Consequently, when the Greeks came to recruit Achilles, his mother disguised him as a girl and hid him among the king's daughters. The Greeks were unable to determine who Achilles was, and they were unwilling to perform the necessary physical examinations to determine which "female" was hiding her sex. Odysseus, however, was able to trick Achilles into revealing his manhood.

> Odysseus placed in the courtyard of the palace women's goods, among which he put a shield and spear, and he gave the order for the trumpet suddenly to sound the call to arms. Achilles, believing the enemy was at hand, divested himself of his woman's clothing and seized the shield and spear. From this action he was recognized.[9]

Achilles momentarily forgot where he was and considered himself at battle. Odysseus fooled Achilles and got him to reveal more than he intended to. Odysseus recognized that when Achilles was put under pressure, he would crack and revert to form.

Practical applications of this trick include when an interviewer asks very hostile questions to a job candidate to see if he can handle the stress, or when a manager asks her employees which of them has a lot of free time to work on a new project. An unthinking employee eager to please his boss might volunteer to work on the project, not realizing what he has just signaled. The key in these examples is that when people have to act quickly, they might reveal more about themselves than they should.

You could apply this surprise principle to a supplier who has been providing you with low-quality goods and claiming that he couldn't possibly do better. Perhaps, in a meeting, you could tell the supplier that for just the next batch it's really important that there are zero defects, and you will pay him double if he manages it. If the supplier is not too sharp, he might comply, and then you will have proof of his true capacities.

LINES

You can learn a lot from the length of a line. In spring of 2002, my game theory class started at 2:40 P.M. Once, when I arrived exactly at

2:40, I noticed that many students were standing outside of the classroom. I assumed that the previous class had not yet left. After waiting for about three minutes, I looked inside the classroom and saw only my own game theory students. The previous class had left long ago. A student told me that she was talking outside of the classroom with a friend, and other people just assumed that the classroom was still occupied and waited outside.

Even though most everyone who waited outside the class was wrong, we all acted rationally. When we came to the room and saw people waiting, we gained information. It was reasonable to assume that they were waiting for a reason, the most likely reason being that the classroom was still occupied.

Lines can also provide you with useful information about restaurants. If you are new to a city, you might want to go only to restaurants with long waiting lists. Waiting lists signal that other people find the restaurant desirable. If you tend to like restaurants that other people like, then you might want to eat only at a restaurant that would take a while to seat you. Of course, an unpopular restaurant might manipulate this situation and deliberately close off much of their space to artificially set demand above supply.

Why is it so difficult to get tickets to popular Broadway shows like *The Producers*?[10] Normally, businesses increase prices when demand exceeds supply. Generally, the only cost of raising prices is that it results in fewer customers buying your product. If your product would sell out even if you set a higher price, however, there would seem to be no disadvantage to increasing prices. What if ticket fans use lines to judge a show's quality? Perhaps by having sellout crowds today, *The Producers* generates good press, ensuring it will have patrons far into the future.

Consequently, there is a shortage of tickets for popular Broadway plays, because patrons don't trust theater critics. If we could rely on critics to identify quality plays, we wouldn't need to rely on the information we gain from lines.

Lines can cause bank panics. Currently, most bank deposits in the United States are insured by the federal government, so even if your bank runs out of money, depositors can still get their funds back. Before the Great Depression, however, there was no deposit insurance. If your bank went under, your savings were lost.

Imagine that your bank has the funds to pay off only 80 percent of its depositors. If everyone finds out about this bank's insolvency, everyone will try to get their funds before the bank goes bust. Of course, if everyone attempts to get their money back, 20 percent of the depositors will be disappointed. Consequently, all the depositors will hurry to the bank to avoid being one of the left-behind 20 percent.

Let's say that you believe that your bank is doing well, but you see a very large line in front of the bank. What should you think? The long line might indicate that the bank is in peril, and thus you should join the line before the bank runs out of funds. Of course, once you get in line, the line's length grows and further demonstrates to other depositors that they should join the line.

Let's complicate this story and assume that the bank is fine as long as everyone doesn't immediately demand their money back. Assume that the bank has cash on hand only to cover 20 percent of deposits. The rest of its funds (like in the movie *It's a Wonderful Life*) are tied up in home mortgages. If the depositors are all patient, the bank will be able to cover all deposits. If, however, depositors all want the funds immediately, the bank will have to call in their loans at a loss and consequently won't be able to repay all depositors. If a large line starts to form, you should get worried and join the line. You are joining the line, because you know if many other people want to withdraw their funds, then so should you. If there were no line, you would be happy keeping your funds in the bank. It's only when many other people want to withdraw funds that you do too. Interestingly, if a line formed, and someone asked you why you were withdrawing your funds, the reason would be because many others were doing the same. The line therefore exists because the line exists: It's self-justifying.

Similar stampede effects can cause foreign currency crises. Imagine that there was a financially healthy third-world country that had attracted a lot of foreign capital. For whatever reason, however, many foreign investors decided to withdraw their capital. If most foreign investors took back their funds, the capital flight would devastate the economy and lower the value of the foreign investments. Consequently, if you suspected that other investors would withdraw their funds, you would want to get your money back as soon as possible. This healthy economy could thus be devastated merely by a belief that foreigners wanted to withdraw their funds because this belief would be self-justifying. If everyone believes it, everyone will want to get their money quickly, so the belief becomes valid.

VALUING OPTIONS

You're considering buying a business in one month. You estimate that the business is worth around $110,000. Which of these two options should you prefer?

(a.) Six months from now you must pay $100,000 for the business.
(b.) Six months from now you have the option of paying $100,000 for the business.

An option gives you the right but not the obligation to do something. Options are valuable because you can choose not to exercise them if conditions become unfavorable. In the previous example, arrangement (b) is far preferable to (a) because in six months if the business is worth less than $100,000, then under (a) you must still buy the business while under (b) you can forgo the transaction. If you are forced to buy the business in six months, you must purchase it whether the business is doing well or poorly. If you have an option to buy, you need only acquire the business when it is doing well.

Options mitigate the danger of uncertainty. With an option you are not locked into a transaction, so if circumstances move against you, you can withdraw. Options are valuable because they eliminate downside risk while allowing you to capture the upside benefit.

Options are more valuable the greater the underlying level of uncertainty. If, in the previous example, you know that the business will be worth $110,000 in six months, then arrangements (a) and (b) are identical, because you will always exercise the option in (b). If, however, there is some chance that in six months the business will be worth, say, $50,000, then you should much prefer having the option to having the obligation to buy.

Options are also more valuable the farther into the future they run. Uncertainty increases with time. The greater the amount of time that will elapse before your deal must be consummated, the higher the chance of something going wrong.

Options should cause you to take risks. Imagine that you are considering launching a very risky product. The product will either do well or poorly. If it does poorly, it will cost you $20 million each year it is being marketed. If it does well, it will provide you with $20 million a year in profits.

Table 3

Value If Product Does Poorly	Value If Product Does Well
–$20 million	$20 million

At the end of the year you will know how the product did and will have an option to keep the product in the market for future years. Assume that there is a 70 percent chance that the product will do poorly. Should you launch the product?

If you introduce the item, you will probably lose money. Any losses will be limited to one year. If the product does well, you can earn $20 million a year forever. Consequently, you probably should release the product.

Many business ventures have inherent option value because they can often be canceled if things go poorly and continued if they go well. You should be willing to try new ventures that have option value even if you believe they will probably fail.

Because of option value you should be more adventurous in trying new restaurants when at home than when abroad. It's rational to try a local restaurant that you will almost certainly hate. If you do dislike the restaurant you need never eat there again. If the local restaurant is surprisingly good, however, you can go back many times. You don't get option value from visiting a restaurant far from home, because even if you like it you may never go back.

Employees give firms varying degrees of option value. When you hire someone, you have some control over how long he will work for you. You should be more willing to take a chance on a new employee the greater their option value. Legally, it can be difficult to fire employees. If you can't fire an employee, you don't have an option on him. Regardless of whether you like or hate a difficult-to-fire employee, you may be stuck with him. This means that, paradoxically, antidiscrimination laws can hurt minorities.

Imagine there are two potential employees, one white and the other a protected minority. Both have exactly the same qualifications. Both employees are risky hires, and there exists a good chance that neither would work out. You know it would be much harder to fire the minority employee because of antidiscrimination laws. It might be rational (although not ethical) for you to hire the white employee because he can be more easily fired. It would be worth taking a chance on the white employee whom you could easily fire, because if he doesn't work out, you're not stuck with him. In contrast, if your legal department won't let you fire minorities, the profit-maximizing move might be to hire only a minority candidate if you are almost certain that he would be a productive employee.

It's much harder to fire workers in Western Europe than in the United States. Therefore, American workers have greater option value than their European counterparts do. Consequently, unemployment rates in the United States are lower because American businesses have a greater willingness to hire new employees.

WHICH CAME FIRST?

You can use options to solve chicken and egg problems. Imagine you want to make a movie staring Arnold Schwarzenegger. He will agree to star in your movie if you can get the $100 million needed for financing. Assume that you could get the $100 million, but only if Arnold commits to be your star. You need Arnold to get the money, and you need the money to get Arnold, so what should you do? You could convince Arnold to give you an option on his time. He could promise to star in the movie if you pay him a certain amount. Since you would not have to pay him until you exercised the option, it would be possible to get the option before acquiring the financing. With the option in hand, you could convince the money people to trust you with the $100 million.

You can also use options to solve more complicated coordination problems. Imagine that you want to build a shopping mall. Unfortunately, five people currently own property where you want the mall to be located. You want to build the mall only if all five people agree to sell. You don't want to start buying the land sequentially, because it would be a waste of money to get a few parcels of land if you couldn't get them all. One solution would be to negotiate with all five owners simultaneously. This might, however, be difficult to coordinate. Another solution would be to use options. You ask each of the five owners to give you an option on their land. You might have to pay only a small amount to each landholder. If you can't get options from everybody, you don't exercise any of the options. This way you don't have to buy any of the land unless you have the right to buy all of it.

Another advantage of using options is that you can back out of the deal if the mall becomes less profitable. Even if all five people agree to sell, you can choose not to exercise the option if real estate prices fall. Of course, the people giving you the options should take this into account.

For example, imagine that you own land worth $50,000. It's worth $50,000 because next year there is a 50 percent chance that land prices will rise to $60,000 and a 50 percent chance that they will fall to $40,000. On average, the land next year will be worth $50,000. What if you give someone an option to buy your land next year for $50,000? If land prices increase, the option will probably be exercised, and you will get $50,000 for land that is worth $60,000. If land prices fall, the option will not be exercised, and you will keep the land that is worth only $40,000. Thus, if you give someone an option on your land for $50,000, then half of the time you would get $50,000, and half of the time you would keep land worth $40,000. Hence, on average, you would get only $45,000 when before you signed the option, you had land worth $50,000.

PRICE DISCRIMINATION

Limited information often hinders firms' pricing abilities. To maximize profits, firms often need to set higher prices for customers willing to pay the most. What customers, however, will give you the most for your product?

LESSONS LEARNED

- Book covers, college degrees, and brand names can be quick ways of signaling quality.
- When a player can't lie, he also can't stay silent, for the sound of silence can be deafening.

- Placing people under pressure might cause them to be too honest for their own good.
- Lines can provide useful information about others' beliefs and intentions.
- Options can help solve "chicken and egg"–like coordination problems.
- You should take more risks if you have an implicit option.

10

PRICE DISCRIMINATION AND OTHER PRICING STRATEGIES

From each according to his ability . . .

Karl Marx

SINCE CUSTOMERS WILL PAY different amounts for the same product, you sacrifice profit when you set the same price for everyone. Price discrimination, which entails charging separate prices for different customers, can augment your profits.

Imagine that Tom is willing to pay $20 for your product, whereas Jane will pay at most $15. If you don't price discriminate, then you obtain the maximum revenue by charging both people $15. By price discriminating you can make an extra $5 by selling your product to Tom for $20 while still getting $15 from Jane.

Price discrimination is easy: Just ask each customer, "What is the most you would pay for my product?" You then charge each customer his answered amount. In reality, however, it is likely true that asking customers how much they value your product and charging them this amount is probably not a long-term winning strategy. Price discrimination creates a game between you and your customers in which they all try to get your lowest price.

MOVIE PRICES

To price discriminate, you need a means of forcing some customers to pay more than others. Movie theaters often give discounts to students. They usually can exclude nonstudents from these discounts by requiring students to show school IDs. From personal experience I know that this doesn't always work, however, for I have frequently been able to get a student discount by showing my faculty ID (from a women's college!).

Why would a theater ever want to charge students lower prices? Consider: When would it be profitable to cut the price of a movie ticket by, say, $1? Obviously, reducing the ticket price by $1 would reduce your profit per ticket by $1. Cutting your price, however, would increase the total number of tickets sold. You can't know exactly how many extra tickets you would sell if you reduced your prices, for this would depend on how *price sensitive* your customers are. Some customers might attend the same number of movies regardless of the ticket price. These customers exhibit very little price sensitivity. You want to charge price-insensitive customers high prices, since these high prices will not drive them away. In contrast, price-sensitive customers are greatly influenced by your prices and would be much more willing to attend your theater if you slightly lowered them. Movie theaters would like to charge price-sensitive customers less than price-insensitive customers. Alas, few customers have tattoos attesting to their price sensitivity.

Students, however, have less income on average than other movie patrons, so high movie prices are more likely to deter them from going to the theater. Although undergraduates inevitably think that they are extremely busy, they usually have more free time than most working adults do. Therefore, students are relatively more willing to travel a large distance to attend a cheaper showing of a given movie. This willingness to travel makes students particularly price sensitive and consequently worthy of receiving discounts from profit-maximizing theater owners.

FINANCIAL AID

Colleges often price discriminate with tuition. At many expensive colleges only about one-half of the students pay the full cost of tuition; the rest get some financial aid.

Many colleges use financial aid packages to attract favored students. Since colleges have limited financial aid budgets, they should maximize the recruiting benefit per dollar of financial aid.

Poor students care more about college prices than rich students, and so poor students are consequently more price sensitive than their more affluent classmates. Imagine that Smith College is trying to attract two students of equal talent. If Smith can give only one student a $10,000 tuition grant, then Smith should give it to the poorer student, since the grant is more likely to induce her to attend Smith.

Colleges can price discriminate far more easily than businesses. If a bookstore tried setting higher prices for lawyers than, say, economists, the economists would simply buy the books for the lawyers. When a college offers one student a substantial amount of financial aid, however, the student can't give her aid package to someone else. Furthermore, colleges require students to submit financial information such as their parents' tax returns, allowing the schools to figure out whom they can charge the most. Since businesses rarely have access to their customers' tax forms, firms must devise alternate means of determining which customers are worthy to receive discounts.

A HINT TO COLLEGE STUDENTS AND THEIR PARENTS

Sometimes you can negotiate with colleges for better financial aid packages. You can often use a financial aid offer from one school to get a better package from another. Make the college believe that your choice of colleges will depend upon financial aid; have the college believe that you are price sensitive.

SELF-SELECTION, PRICE DISCRIMINATION, AND GREEK MYTHOLOGY

Many businesses price discriminate through customer self-selection. Before we analyze this, let's consider a story from Greek mythology that uses self-selection as a truth-telling device.[1] Odysseus was one of many suitors for the hand of Helen, the most beautiful mortal woman in creation. To avoid conflict, the suitors of Helen agreed that she would pick her husband, and they would all support her choice and protect the rights of the man she choose. Helen did not choose Odysseus, but Odysseus had still sworn an oath to protect her.

After she got married, the Trojans kidnapped Helen from Greece. Helen's husband demanded that the men who had sworn an oath to protect his rights join him in a war against Troy. Odysseus did not want to keep his oath, however, for he was happily married, had an infant son, and had been told by an oracle that if he fought, he would not return home for 20 years.

When the Greeks came for him, Odysseus tried to dodge the draft by acting insane: He plowed his fields randomly. Since an insane Odysseus would be useless to their cause, almost all of the Greeks were ready to abandon Odysseus to his strange farming practices. One Greek, Palamedes, suspected that Odysseus was faking. Palamedes, however, still needed to prove that Odysseus was sane, so he took Odysseus' infant son and put him in front of the plow. Had Odysseus continued to plow, he would have killed his son. If Odysseus really had been insane, he would not have noticed or cared about his son's position and would therefore have killed him. Since Odysseus was rational, however, he stopped plowing and thus revealed his sanity.

Palamedes had made it very costly for Odysseus to continue to act insane. By increasing the cost to Odysseus of lying, Palamedes was able to change Odysseus' behavior, forcing him to reveal his previous dishonesty and join the Greek military expedition to Troy. Although the Greeks did conquer the Trojans, unfortunately the oracle was right and Odysseus needed 20 years to return to his wife and son.

To summarize the game-theoretic bits of this myth: there were two types of Odysseus, sane and crazy. By placing the baby in front of the plow, Palamedes ensured that a sane Odysseus and a crazy Odysseus would take different visible actions. Palamedes used a self-selection mechanism to get Odysseus to voluntarily reveal his type.

SELF-SELECTION OF CUSTOMERS

Businesses often use self-selection to induce different groups of customers to take different visible actions. By getting customers to voluntarily self-select into separate groups, businesses can enhance their profits through price discrimination.

Coupons

Coupons are a brilliant means of getting customers to self-select into two groups: (1) price-sensitive customers and (2) price-insensitive customers. Superficially, coupons seem silly. In return for slowing up the checkout line and turning in some socially worthless pieces of paper you get a discount. Coupons, however, effectively separate customers and give discounts to the price sensitive.

Coupons allow customers to trade time for money. To use a coupon you must usually go to the effort of finding, clipping, and holding a small piece of paper. Coupons therefore appeal most to those who place a low value on their time relative to their income. Coupon users are therefore the customers most likely to shop around to find the best price and consequently are exactly the type of people companies most like to give discounts to. In contrast, shoppers who don't use coupons are probably not that price conscious, and companies can safely charge these people more, confident that their high prices won't cost them too much in sales.

Movie theaters require students to supply identification so that theaters can determine which group a consumer belongs in. Colleges place financial aid applicants in different categories based upon submitted financial data. Coupons, in contrast, rely upon customers to sort themselves. Coupons sort customers based upon self-selection. The fundamental essence of coupons requires that those who use them are almost automatically the people who are the most price-sensitive.

Airlines

Airlines too rely upon self-selection to price discriminate. It's usually much cheaper to fly if you stay over a weekend. Business travelers generally don't want to spend weekends away from home, and thus by giving discounts to those who do stay over a weekend, airlines effectively charge business customers more than other travelers. Business travelers usually have more fixed schedules than other airline customers; consequently they are, on average, less price sensitive. Airlines, therefore, increase their profits by charging business travelers more than other flyers.

Ideally, the airlines would like to verify independently whether a passenger is flying for business or pleasure and charge the ones traveling for business more, but, of course, in such a game business travelers would hide their true purpose. The airlines therefore have to rely upon self-selection and assume that most travelers staying over a weekend are not flying for business.

Airline price discrimination shows that when firms in the same industry price discriminate, then they must, at least implicitly, coordinate their efforts. If two airlines had flights to the same city, but only one price discriminated, then consumers would always go to the lowest-priced airline, and any efforts at price discrimination would fail. Individual airlines can price discriminate only because nearly everyone in the industry does so.

Airline check-in counters usually have separate lines for first class and cattle. The lines the first-class customers wait in are invariably much shorter than those that coach passengers must endure. This seems reasonable, because first-class customers pay more. The greater the benefits to first-class customers, the higher the premium over regular tickets that they are willing to pay. Thus, airlines benefit by reducing the length of first-class ticket lines. Airlines could also profit, however, by *increasing* the wait for nonpreferred customers. First-class customers are concerned about the difference in waiting times, not just the speed of the first-class check-in line in. Hence, airlines can increase the demand for first-class tickets by either improving service for first-class customers (by increasing the number of first-class ticket agents per passenger) or through increasing the annoyance of those traveling by other means.

Further Examples of Price Discrimination Through Impatience

Book publishers get buyers to self-select based upon impatience. Books frequently come out in paperback about one year after they are first published in hardcover. Paperback books are significantly cheaper than hardcovers. Only a tiny bit of the difference comes from the extra cost of producing hardcovers. Publishers assume that customers who are most eager to buy a book are the ones willing to pay the most. Publishers make impatient customers, who are less price sensitive, buy expensive hardcover books and allow patient readers to acquire relatively inexpensive paperback copies.

The Universal Theme Park also price discriminates through impatience. Long lines are the bane of child-toting amusement park visitors. For an extra $130, though, Universal allows patrons to move immediately to the front of their lines.[2]

Supermarkets could benefit from Universal's price discrimination methods by offering speedy checkouts to those willing to pay more. All they would have to do is have one checkout line where prices were, say, 10 percent higher. A customer would go in this line only if he was price insensitive and willing to pay for faster service. The expensive line would be like a reverse coupon: customers could trade money for time.

Supermarkets could also charge different prices at separate times of the day. If a supermarket estimated that business people were most likely to buy at certain times (say between 5:30–8:00 PM), they could charge the highest prices at these times. By making prices time dependent, supermarkets would get customers to self-select based on when they shop. Clothing and department stores that offer sales only during working hours use this tactic.

Hollywood also uses impatience to price discriminate through self-selection. Movies first come out in theaters, then become available for rental and pay-per-view-TV, next are shown on premium cable channels, and finally are broadcast on free network TV. Customers who most want to see a movie, and are presumably willing to pay the most, see the film when it first comes out in the theater. More patient and thus more price-sensitive customers wait longer and pay less.

Gadget manufacturers also use impatience to price discriminate. Some consumers desperately desire the latest gadgets. How can a producer get top dollar from early adopters and yet still set a reasonable price for the masses who buy for more utilitarian reasons? The obvious solution: Set a high initial price, which will fall after six months or so.[3] The cost of such a pricing scheme, however, is that most consumers know not to buy recently released high-tech toys.

Upgrades

Software companies price discriminate when they charge different prices for product upgrades than for a full version of the new software. When Microsoft released Word 2002, it charged much less for an upgraded CD than for the full version of Word 2002. Obviously, it doesn't cost Microsoft anything extra to sell you a full rather than an upgraded version. Microsoft probably figures, however, that customers who already have a previous version of Word are willing to pay less than new customers.

The Future of Price Discrimination

While Big Brother probably isn't watching you, a massive number of corporations are. The supermarket cards that get you those discounts also allow stores to track your every purchase. When you venture onto many web sites, cookies are placed on your computer that keep track of where you have been. Every credit card payment you have made or missed has been recorded somewhere. Soon your cell phone will have a GPS chip that could allow others to keep track of your every move. This book even contains hidden cameras and transmitters that monitor and report on your breakfast cereal consumption. All of these data would be very useful to a company that price discriminates. In the near future, firms might put everything that they know about you into a computer program that scientifically gives you a custom-made price.

ALL-YOU-CAN-EAT PRICING

Most firms sell their goods individually. Some businesses, however, offer all-you-can-eat specials, where for a fixed fee you can have as much of their product as you want. Which pricing strategy is more profitable?

Imagine that you run an Internet company that sells news articles. You currently charge customers 10 cents a story. Say that one customer, John, buys 1,000 articles a year from you at a total cost of $100. How much would John pay for the right to read an unlimited number of your articles per year? He would definitely be willing to pay more than $100. We know that John is willing to pay $100 for 1,000 articles. Consequently, he must be willing to pay more than $100 for the right to read an unlimited number of articles. It's almost inconceivable that if John had already read 999 articles, he would pay 10 cents to read one more article but wouldn't pay more than 10 cents for the right to read, say, 1,000 more articles. Since it presumably costs you nothing to let John read as much as he wants, you would seem always to be better off selling John an all-you-can-read special.

If you didn't know how much John valued your product, however, you might be better off charging him per article. When you charge John per article, he will automatically pay more the more he values your product. Thus, you can be completely ignorant of how much John likes your goods and still set a good price when you charge per article. Setting one fee for unlimited access is riskier. If the fee is too high, John won't use your service. If it's too low, you will miss out on some profit. Consequently, the greater your ignorance about John, the greater the benefit of charging per article. Of course, since John will value your services more if he has unlimited access, charging per article reduces the value of your product to him and reduces the maximum amount of money you could get from John.

All-you-can-eat pricing plans naturally cause your customers to consume more of your product. Consequently, the main danger of all-you-can-eat plans for most goods is that they will cost you too much to supply the items. These plans are therefore best suited for products that are cheap to replicate. Therefore, as information goods become more important to our economy, I predict that these types of plans will proliferate.

BUNDLING[4]

Can a firm use bundling to increase profits? *Bundling* means selling many products in one package. Bundling can't be used to get a single customer to pay more. If different customers place separate values on your products, however, bundling might enable you to increase profits.

Extending Monopolies Through Bundling (Slightly Technical)

Microsoft has a near monopoly on operating systems for PCs and bundles lots of software into its operating system. Microsoft doesn't have a monopoly on all of this other software, because much of it has close alternatives produced by other companies. Does bundling permit Microsoft to extend its monopoly?

Consider the issue abstractly. Imagine that a firm has a monopoly on good M. This monopoly allows it to charge extremely high prices for M. The firm does not have a monopoly on good X. Could the firm enhance its monopoly profits by forcing consumers to buy X whenever they purchase M?

No, bundling cannot help a firm extend its monopoly. To understand this, assume that good M is worth $100 to you and good X is worth $20 to you.

Table 4   Value of Goods to One Customer

Product	Value To You
M	$100
X	$20

Sold separately, the most you would ever pay for M would be $100. Just because a firm has a monopoly doesn't mean that it can charge whatever price it wants. (If a monopoly could sell M at any price it would set the price of M at infinity!) Obviously, the most you would pay for X is $20. Consequently, if the firm sells the goods separately the most it will ever be able to get from you is $120. If the firm bundles the two products, it doesn't increase their value to you. Therefore, if the firm bundles, the most they could ever get you to pay would be $120. Hence, if you would have bought both goods anyway, bundling wouldn't help the firm increase its profits.

Assume now, however, that you would only have bought M but not X if the two goods were sold separately. Can the monopolist now use bundling to increase its profits? No! The only way the monopolist could ever get you to buy the bundle is if the bundle's price is $120 or less. By selling the goods separately at $100 for M and $20 for X, however, the monopolist could also have gotten you to buy both products. Thus, bundling doesn't allow the monopolist to do anything it couldn't do by selling the products separately.

While bundling can't get a single customer to pay more, it can be used to get more money from a group of customers who place different valuations on your products.

When Bundling Can Be Profitable

Imagine that two customers place different values on products X and Y.

Table 5   Value of Goods to Two Customers

Product	Value to Abe	Value To Bill
X	$100	$40
Y	$40	$100

Assume that the firm can't price discriminate. If the firm sold only product X, it could sell either to just Abe for $100 or to both Abe and Bill for $40 each.

Consequently, by selling both products separately the most revenue the firm could get would be $200, which would be achieved by selling both goods for $100 to one customer each. Now imagine that the seller bundles the two products and charges $140 each. Both consumers would be willing to pay $140 for this package, so bundling could gross this firm $280.

If some customers greatly value X and others place a high value on Y, then bundling can help a firm extract more total profits from its customers. The bundling doesn't increase the value of the product to one particular customer but rather evens out how much customers are willing to pay.

This type of bundling is most profitable when a company sells an easy-to-replicate good. Imagine that a company sells many different types of software packages. Each package has a small value to many and a large value to a few. Without bundling, this company faces a difficult choice. It can either set a high price and attract a few customers or a low price and attract many. Its best option would be to bundle all the software into a single package. True, many customers would get software they don't place a high value on, but since it's so cheap to give customers copies of software, software bundling doesn't significantly increase a company's cost.

Microsoft's bundling of so much software into its operating system can be explained not as an attempt to expand a monopoly, but rather as an attempt to put in something everybody likes.

PRICING GAMES

To extract the maximum rents from your customers, you need to charge different customers separate prices. Beware, however, because each customer will always resist paying more than another.

HOLDUPS

A clever pricing strategy will help increase your profits. Chapter 11 demonstrates, however, that to extract the maximum possible profits from your customers, you need to go beyond pricing strategies and make customers dependent upon you by holding them up. Holdups create an artificial monopoly that allows you to earn excessive profits.

LESSONS LEARNED

- You should charge price-sensitive customers less than other buyers.
- To price discriminate, you need to find a mechanism to exclude some customers from discounts given to others.
- To price discriminate, you need to identify which customers are the most price sensitive or devise a mechanism by which price-sensitive customers self-select.
- You can't use bundling to extend a monopoly, but you can use it to increase your profits by evening out how much different customers value your products.

11

HOLDUPS

Trust none. For oaths are straws, men's faiths are wafer-cakes . . .

Shakespeare, Henry V[1]

OU'RE WAITING IN THE HOSPITAL while your husband undergoes open-heart surgery. The operation has been scheduled for about a month. A doctor leaves the operating room and approaches you. He says you must pay $500,000 to have the operation completed. If the hospital doesn't get the money, then the doctors will stop working, and your husband will die. You ask why they need the extra money, and the doctor responds that they don't really need the extra money so much as want it. The hospital found out that you were rich and figured that you would pay another $500,000 to keep your husband alive.

You just experienced the "holdup problem." By going to the hospital, you made yourself artificially vulnerable to its doctors. Because you had a month to schedule the operation, you could easily have found other doctors who would have charged you less. Once the operation started, however, you became dependent on the doctors you selected, and they acquired an artificial monopoly over you. The doctors exploited your dependence by demanding extra money.

Imagine, instead, that there is only one doctor in the world who can perform your husband's operation, and she charges $1 million. This doctor is not holding you up, because she has a real monopoly that you couldn't have scheduled around. She didn't trick you into dependence; rather, her unique skills make her your only salvation.

The famous legal case of *Alaska Packers' Assn. v. Domenico*[2] also illustrates the holdup problem. A boat owner hired fishermen to catch salmon in Alaska. The fishermen were hired in San Francisco and agreed to work for a specific wage. When the boat arrived in Alaskan waters, however, the fishermen announced they would not work unless they received a substantial wage increase. The boat owner was in a difficult situation because it would have been very challenging for him to get new fishermen on such short notice. The boat owner agreed to the wage increase, but when the boat returned to port, he refused to pay the extra money. The fishermen sued but lost. The court held that the fishermen improperly tried to take advantage of the boat owner's short-term dependence upon them.

Figure 45 illustrates a generalized holdup game. In this game Player One can hire one of three people to complete a task. Once someone has been hired, however, only he can finish the job. From the viewpoint at the beginning of the game, three people could finish. Once Player One picks someone, however, he becomes dependent upon his hire, for it is now too late to pick someone else. Figure 46 shows another game where you are dependent upon someone, but there is no holdup. In this game person A is always the only person who can complete the job. Thus, you do not become more dependent upon person A after hiring her. In Figure 45 the act of hiring person A gives her considerable power over you, while in Figure 46 person A always has this power.

You should minimize holdup problems by avoiding dependence on those who could exploit you. For example, imagine that you are considering building a factory to produce widgets. After building the factory you will still need sprockets to manufacture widgets, and only one company produces sprockets. After the factory's completion, therefore, you will be dependent upon this sole sprocket supplier, and it will be able to charge you extremely high prices. To avoid this potential holdup problem, before building the factory you should enter into a long-term contract with the sprocket provider to ensure that it never charges too much.

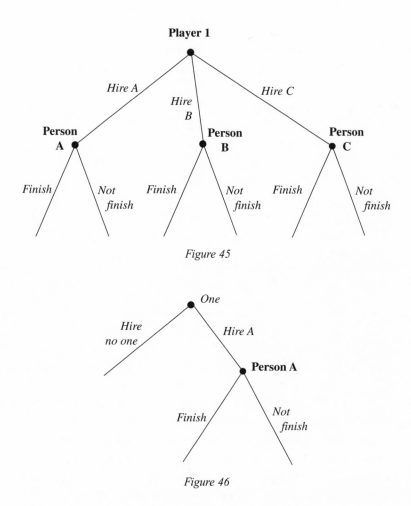

Figure 45

Figure 46

Second sourcing also mitigates holdup problems. If in the previous example you ensured that at least two firms could sell you sprockets, then neither would have a monopoly. Perhaps before you build the factory, you could convince another supplier to start making sprockets so that you would never be dependent upon just one firm.

SOFTWARE HOLDUPS

Holdup problems in software created the open-source movement. For a long time AT&T let people use its popular Unix software for free.[3] After AT&T was broken up by the antitrust police, it started charging for Unix. Unix programmers felt betrayed by AT&T's new pricing policy.[4] They had spend massive amounts of time mastering Unix when it was free, and now, after they were dependent upon programming in Unix, AT&T started charging for its use. Many of the programmers might not have spent the time needed to become proficient in Unix had they known that in the future it wouldn't be free.

To stop this holdup problem from occurring again, a programmer developed an alternative to Unix called GNU, "a recursive acronym meaning '*GNU*'s *N*ot *U*NIX.'"[5] GNU was designed to always be free, and thus programmers could use it without fear of someday being exploited. GNU is considered open-source software because its source code is available so that it can easily be modified by users.

AIRLINES[6]

Warren Buffett once said, "It would have been a blessing for shareholders if someone had thought to shoot down Orville Wright at Kitty Hawk."[7] Holdups, caused by strikes, make it difficult for airlines to sustain profitability. Airlines are especially vulnerable to holdups because of their high fixed costs and specialized workforce.[8]

Strikes are extremely costly to airline companies because strikes cause their expensive planes to sit idle. Furthermore, airlines have difficulty replacing striking workers because of their employees' specialized skills. Consequently, airline workers can do massive damage to their companies and can hold them up for high wages.

To understand the airlines' dilemma, consider the following highly simplified example. Assume that if there is no strike, your company expects to have:

1. $10 million in revenue
2. $9 million in costs

Absent a strike, you will make $1 million in profits. But what happens to profits if your employees strike? Ideally, you would replace your workforce and suffer no harm. If easy to replace, your employees could not hold you up since you wouldn't be dependent upon them. Now assume, however, that your workers have specialized skills, so if they go on strike, you must shut down and lose the $10 million in revenue. Your workers now can hold you up because they have an artificial monopoly over you. After being trained, your current workers are the only ones who can complete the needed tasks, so you are dependent upon them. But how much would a strike hurt you?

The strike would cost you the $10 million in revenue, but it would also save you some of the cost since you would no longer have to pay your workers. If your entire $9 million in costs were from salaries, then a strike would hurt you by only $1 million. What if, however, you normally paid only $2 million in salaries and the other $7 million in costs was attributable to equipment expenses? Now a strike would cost you the $10 million in revenue but save you only $2 million in costs. The lower the percentage of your costs represented by wages, the more costly a strike would be. When a few workers are needed to operate many expensive machines, and these workers can't be replaced, the workers have you in their power. This is the situation for airlines, because it takes specialized skills to operate and maintain their extremely expensive planes.

MANY ATTEMPTS, FEW SUCCESSES: HOLDUPS IN THE MUSIC INDUSTRY

After MCA records spent $2.2 million promoting a new recording artist, her album sold only 378 copies.[9] According to *The Wall Street Journal*, such failures are commonplace in the music industry. Record companies spend millions on new talent, knowing that most of their money will be wasted. These companies hope to make enough from their few successes to pay for their many failures. Relying on the successful few, however, makes record companies vulnerable to holdups from their profitable artists.

Imagine that you spent $1 million on each of 10 new artists. You know that nine of these artists will probably fail, but the 10th will bring you $11 million in revenue. Further assume that you don't know which of the 10 artists will be successful. What would happen if the one successful artist wanted to keep most of the $11 million in revenue she generated for herself? This artist might reason that since you spent only $1 million promoting her, it's unfair that you get $11 million in revenue from her work. If you couldn't "exploit" your own successful artists, however, you would suffer massive losses.

To avoid holdups, record companies force new artists to sign long-term contracts. These contracts ensure that the few marketable artists must stick with their record companies. Of course, from the artists' viewpoint, once they have been discovered and proven marketable, they would rather be free to keep all their profits and not have to compensate record companies for the companies' failed endeavors.

ARTIFICIAL ACTORS

Computer-generated actors might soon dominate the entertainment business because of holdup problems. Imagine that you want to hire an unknown actress for a new TV show that you will be producing. Thousands of qualified candidates apply. Most are so desperate to get acting work that they would actually pay for the privilege of starring on your show. If your show becomes a hit, however, you will be dependent upon the show's stars. This year any of a 1,000 pretty actresses would do. After Debbie has been starring in your show for a couple of years, however, you will be desperately dependent on her staying.

Long-term contracts somewhat mitigate this actress holdup problem. You sign up the unknown actress only if she agrees to work, say, for five years at some agreed-upon salary. Contracts can't provide a complete solution to actress holdup problems, however. First, a contract forcing someone to work for you for life at low wages probably wouldn't be enforceable because it would too closely resemble slavery. Second, even if the actress is under a legally binding contract, she can still hold you up by suggesting that she will get sick, gain weight, or lose her acting talent if you don't drastically increase her salary.

I suspect this actress holdup problem will someday be eliminated by computer-generated actors, because digital talent can be owned by the TV producers. Virtual slavery will thus protect producers from being held up by those annoying and greedy human beings.

WEAPONIZING PATENT LAW[10]

Patent law can be used to hold up inventors. Imagine that your company has decided to develop a new product called a gaunkulater. Once you have designed a gaunkulater, it will cost you a few hundred dollars to make each one. You will incur a substantial research and development cost, however, before you can produce even your first gaunkulater.

Your engineers have determined that there are three substantially different methods of researching and developing a gaunkulater: Path A, Path B, and Path C. You estimate the following:

Table 6   Research Paths

Path Followed	Research and Development Costs
A	$50 million
B	$52 million
C	$53 million

Since Path A is the cheapest, you provisionally decide to follow it. Your lawyers, however, warn you that following Path A would necessitate using a patent owned by Hogan Inc. Hogan Inc. doesn't have a patent on a gaunkulater; rather, one of the products it has a patent on would be a critical subcomponent of a gaunkulater if you use Path A. Consequently, without Hogan Inc.'s permission, you could not produce the gaunkulater if you used Path A.

Because of holdup problems, if you use Path A, it's vital that you get Hogan Inc.'s permission before you start to build the gaunkulater. It would cost you an extra $2 million to follow Path B rather than Path A. Consequently, *before you start researching the gaunkulater,* $2 million is the most that Hogan Inc. would assume you would pay for their patent rights. Imagine, however, that you stupidly spend $50 million for research and development on Path A before getting Hogan Inc.'s permission. Now, if it doesn't give you its patent rights, you will have to spend $52 million more to develop the gaunkulater using alternative means; $52 million is now the maximum amount that Hogan Inc. expects you would be willing to pay if you have already spent $50 million developing the gaunkulater using Path A.

Let's imagine that you tried to get Hogan Inc.'s permission before you started research and development, but it demanded $3 million for its patent rights. Consequently, you decided to abandon Path A and worked on Path B.

Unfortunately, just after you have spent $52 million on Path B, Hogan Inc. is granted a new patent. This patent is on a critical subcomponent of a gaunkulater that is built using Path B. Hogan Inc. had been working on this Path B component for some time. When you came to it asking about patent rights, it was within weeks of getting a patent on this subcomponent. The clever lawyers at Hogan Inc., however, decided to slow down their patent request. When your attorneys did a search to see if using Path B would violate any patent rights, they didn't find out about Hogan Inc.'s patent, since it had not yet been granted. Hogan Inc. decided to wait until just before you started selling your product to get its patent finalized. Now, without Hogan Inc.'s patent, it would cost you an additional $53 million to develop the gaunkulater using Path C. Consequently, it would be worth it for your company to pay Hogan Inc., say, $40 million for its patent rights, bringing your total cost of development to a total of $92 million ($40 million + $52 million). If you had known that Hogan Inc. could block the production of a gaunkulater by Paths A and B, you would have used Path C and paid only $53 million.

Companies developing patents often have incentives to keep their patent rights submerged by not getting the official patent until they have trapped some other inventors. Because of holdup problems, patent holders can get far more money for their patent rights if negotiations begin after the company that needs its patent has developed its product.

FIRM-SPECIFIC HUMAN CAPITAL

Firms can hold up their workers. Imagine that you are a highly productive employee because you have mastered a manufacturing process vital to your company. What if, however, no company but yours uses this manufacturing process? If your company fired you, your skills would not be transferable.

Experience is one of the rewards most employees get from working. Experience increases what economists call a person's "human capital," which measures a worker's worth. Usually, the greater your human capital, the higher your wage. If your human capital is company specific, however, then you might not get paid what you are worth.

For example, imagine that today you are worth about $50,000 a year to many companies in your field. You are considering working for Acme. Acme provides great training, and after three years you will be worth $100,000 a year to Acme and many other firms. This means that after three years, Acme will have to pay you at least $100,000, or else you will quit for a higher paying job.

Now imagine that Acme's training is job specific. After three years, you will still be worth $100,000 a year to Acme, but only $50,000 to other companies. Perhaps Acme will teach you how to run its unique computer system. If, after three years, Acme pays you only $52,000, then you will be unable to find another company that will pay you more. Employees should always be cautious of working for a business where the experience they gain would not be transferable to other companies.

Of course, there is an advantage to having firm-specific skills: You are harder to replace. If your skills aren't transferable to other companies, then your firm couldn't easily train someone from another company to do your job.

SPECIFIC VERSUS GENERAL INVESTMENTS[11]

Workers are more vulnerable to holdups when they have job-specific human capital. Similarly, capitalists can more easily be exploited when their investments have but one use. Imagine you agree to set up a manufacturing plant to make automobile parts for Hondas. Once you have built the plant, how much power does Honda have over you? If you could easily retool to make auto parts for, say, Ford, then you're not desperately dependent upon Honda. If, however, your investment is lost if Honda no longer wants your parts, then Honda can hold you up because you are dependent upon it. If your investment will have only one use, you need to guarantee, probably through long-term contracts, that you will always be able to sell your wares. If, however, your investment has many uses, then you can take a less cautious attitude since you're not artificially dependent upon your old partner.

FISHER BODY AND GENERAL MOTORS[12]

Around 1920 General Motors asked Fisher Body to manufacture closed metal automobile bodies for its cars. Fisher Body needed to make substantial firm-specific investments to comply with General Motors's request, so to protect itself from being held up, it required General Motors to sign a long-term contract under which General Motors would buy its closed metal automobile bodies only from Fisher Body. If Fisher Body had not entered into such an agreement, then after they made their firm-specific investment, General Motors could have exploited them, because Fisher Body's investment would have been nearly worthless if they couldn't sell auto parts to General Motors.

After this exclusive agreement was signed, consumer demand for automobiles with closed metal bodies substantially increased, putting Fisher Body in a very strong position. General Motors now needed far more of these bodies, and by contract it could get them only from Fisher Body. Fisher Body, therefore, had the potential to hold up General Motors.

After demand increased, General Motors made several requests of Fisher Body. They asked them to build a plant closer to General Motors's production facilities and to reduce their expensive labor costs. Fisher Body refused, however. Since General Motors was locked into Fisher Body, they couldn't retaliate against this refusal by getting another supplier. Fisher Body had intelligently used contracts to avoid the holdup problem, while General Motors had failed to grasp how its long-term contract would create an artificial monopoly for Fisher Body. General Motors eventually solved its holdup problem by buying Fisher Body.

OPTIMAL SIZE OF FIRMS

How big should firms get? Should companies like General Motors make all the parts for their cars, or should they purchase components from other manufactures? While most of the answers to this question are beyond the scope of *Game Theory at Work,* an understanding of holdups provides some help in determining the optimal size of a firm. This chapter has discussed what holdups are and how they can sometimes be stopped. Occasionally, however, dependencies are necessary, and potential holdups can't be avoided. In these special situations, your only solution might be to purchase the company that will have an artificial monopoly over you.

For example, imagine you are considering building a new product that will require a subcomponent made by Acme. No other firm but Acme can make this critical subcomponent. Obviously, building the factory without first coming to an agreement with Acme would make you extremely vulnerable. Unfortunately, if you can't be certain of what you will need from Acme, then even a long-term contract wouldn't eliminate this vulnerability.

Perhaps the exact nature of your needed subcomponent will change over time in ways that you can't predict. Even if Acme agrees contractually to supply you with a certain subcomponent, you will be vulnerable when your needs change. If you're not sure what you will need, you can't specify your needs in a contract.

Assume, for example, that today you buy the subcomponents for $12.95 each. If you will always need this exact same subcomponent for 15 years, you could get Acme to agree contractually to always supply you with this subcomponent for $12.95 plus inflation. What if, however, you will need a slightly different kind of component in five years, but you're not exactly sure what this component will look like? Obviously, Acme would never agree to give you anything you wanted at $12.95 each, because you would then demand platinum-plated, jewel-encrusted subcomponents. A contract forcing Acme to always charge you a reasonable price might not be enforceable because courts have difficulty with reasonableness. Even a contract mandating that Acme charge you its costs plus 10 percent would leave you vulnerable since Acme would have an incentive to inflate costs to maximize their 10 percent. Your only solution to this holdup dilemma might be to acquire Acme. But make sure you buy it before it gets an artificial monopoly over you.

FATE AND CHOICE

Fate often forces us into dependencies. Sometimes, however, we voluntarily follow a path that gives others artificial control over us. Whenever you are about to enter into a deal that would give someone great power over you, ask yourself what they might gain through your exploitation.

OTHER PEOPLE'S MONEY

A holdup creates an artificial monopoly that allows you to extract a massive sum of money from your victim. An even more effective way to get someone else's money, however, is simply to acquire the right to spend it. Chapter 12 will explore the implications of what happens when one person has the right to spend someone else's money.

LESSONS LEARNED

- Holdup problems manifest themselves when you become artificially dependent on one person or organization to perform a task.
- Holdup problems can be mitigated by long-term contracts or second sourcing.
- Employees should be wary of developing skills that are highly company specific.

12

SPENDING OTHER PEOPLE'S MONEY

It is rather a pleasant experience to be alone in a bank at night.

Willie Sutton, bank robber[1]

BUYING STUFF IS MORE FUN when it's done with other people's money. Most of us like nice things, but we don't like paying for them. Consequently, when we are spending other people's money, we often buy goods we wouldn't ordinarily purchase.

FREQUENT FLYER MILES

Frequent flyer miles exploit business travelers' willingness to spend other people's money. Airlines give their passengers frequent flyer miles, which they can exchange for free flights. Frequent flyer miles are a great deal for business travelers, because while the business pays for the ticket the traveler often can use the miles for personal travel.

Imagine that you have a choice between two flights. The first is cheaper, but the second gives you more frequent flyer miles. If you're paying, you would probably take the less expensive ticket. If, however, your company pays for the ticket, but you get to keep the frequent flyer miles, wouldn't it be tempting to pick the flight that gives you the most miles? After all, if you're spending other people's money, what do you care about the ticket price? Frequent flyer miles can be a bribe for employees to waste their company's money.

It's cost-effective to bribe those who spend other people's money. If I'm spending $1,000 of my own money, then to get me to spend it on your product, you would actually have to give me something worth at least $1,000. If I'm buying for my company, with my company's money, however, I should be willing to give you $1,000 in return for you giving *me* only, say, $100.

SPENDING STUDENTS' MONEY

The Wall Street Journal bribes college professors to get us to spend our students' money. The *Journal* gives college professors free subscriptions if the professors force their students to subscribe. In fairness, the *Journal* is often a useful classroom tool, and students buying it through their college classes get reduced rates. Still, by giving professors free subscriptions, the *Journal* creates incentives for professors to misappropriate their students' money.

Textbook-choosing time provides professors with their best opportunity to waste students' money. When professors buy books with their own money, they certainly take price into account. When we choose books for our students, however, it doesn't cost us anything extra if the books are expensive, especially since publishers always provide us with a free personal copy. Professors have no reason to worry about prices when deciding which textbook to use. Consequently, college textbooks are, page per page, several times more expensive than other hardcover books. The greatest potential for abuse manifests itself when professors assign their own books for class. In return for making my students pay $30 each for this book, I might get $1.20 in after-tax royalties. While I would of course be fired for forcing my students to directly give me $1.20, few would object if I required them to purchase *Game Theory at Work*. Indeed, students are often impressed when their professor wrote the textbook. Private liberal arts colleges like Smith don't charge that much in tuition, so it seems only fair that I be able to use my textbook-assigning power to extract a little more money from my students' parents.

To reduce the problems caused by professors' spending their students' money, colleges should give professors financial incentives to minimize the cost of the books we make our students buy. To amplify this problem, publishers should bribe professors to assign expensive textbooks. Perhaps McGraw-Hill could give professors five frequent flyer miles for every dollar our students spend on their textbooks.

BRIBING PILOTS

A few years ago *The Wall Street Journal* ran an interesting article on how airline refuelers bribe pilots of corporate jets.[2] Since corporate jets can be refueled at multiple airports along their routes, there is intense competition for their business. Normally, you might think that these refuelers would compete on price. These refuelers, however, realize that the pilots decide where to refuel, but the jets' owners pay for the gas. The refuelers take advantage of the pilots' sending other people's money by bribing the pilots. One company "hands out one 8-ounce steak for every 100 gallons of fuel purchased."[3] The steaks are given to the pilots by attractive, scantily clad women. The pilots are usually given their freebies only "if [they] forgo discounts on fuel."[4] The refuelers are careful to give the pilots their freebies secretly, thus proving that the pilots and refuelers fully understand the game being played.

Why don't the refuelers simply give direct cash bribes to pilots? These bribes would probably be illegal, so pilots, fearing criminal prosecution, would be reluctant to accept them. Bribing pilots with meat is more effective because it's legal.

CONFERENCES IN EXOTIC LOCATIONS

Many businesses forbid their employees to accept gifts from suppliers. Suppliers, of course, attempt to circumvent restrictions by making their gifts seem business related. For example, imagine that Maria negotiates with several suppliers to buy expensive equipment for her company. Maria's company would probably be smart enough to not let her accept free tickets to Hawaii from a supplier. What if, however, a supplier held a conference in Hawaii and offered to send Maria there for free?

Even if a supplier doesn't pay for the ticket, companies should still be suspicious of conferences in exotic locations. Firms often pay for travel to conferences. Conference organizers occasionally take advantage of this by holding their events in attractive vacation spots. An employee is far more likely to waste his company's money attending a conference in Hawaii than, say, Buffalo, N.Y. Consequently, the nicer the conference location, the more scrutiny a travel-funds request should be given.

SELFISH CHARITY

Many consider corporate charity a noble undertaking. When you consider who really pays for this charity, however, its morality becomes questionable. Charitable donors usually get both pleasure and pain. The pleasure results from knowing you have helped someone and from getting recognition for your good deeds. The pain comes from actually having to give away your own money. When you give away other people's money, however, it's all pleasure.

Stockholders own public companies. Consequently, when an executive donates some of her company's money to charity, she is really giving away her shareholders' money. Imagine if a college professor forced each of his students to donate $100 to some charity of the professor's choice. Few would praise the professor's generosity.

Knowing that it's easier to give away other people's money than one's own, charitable groups often look to corporations for money. Charities often reward those who contribute to them. When charities seek corporate money, however, they should focus more on rewarding the giver than the stockholders. After all, the person who controls the money is far more important than the person who merely owns it.

POLITICAL BRIBES

Politicians get to spend taxpayers' money. Imagine that the U.S. Congress is considering awarding your company a contract worth $10 million in profit. How much money would you be willing to pay to get this contract? Obviously, if you paid anything under $10 million, you would come out ahead. Such is the reason why corporations are so willing to donate money to politicians.

"Good governance" advocates are always trying to reduce the influence of campaign contributions. Reducing political contributions, however, is like stopping water from flowing downhill. When a politician gives away other people's money, the potential recipients become desperate to influence the politician. If a congressman's actions could increase your profits by $10 million, it would be stupid not to give him at least a few thousand dollars. Influential politicians therefore almost gravitationally attract campaign contributions.

SPLITTING BILLS

A group at a restaurant can either equally divide the bill or have everyone pay for the food he got. When the bill is divided equally, everyone is spending everyone else's money. If there are five people in your group who will equally split the check, then the cost to you of spending an extra $1 is but 20 cents. Thus, when considering whether you should get a pricey $10 appetizer, remember that the appetizer will only increase what you pay by $2. True, you will have to help pay for everyone else's appetizers. You will, however, have to do this regardless of whether you get an appetizer yourself.

Obviously, restaurants should encourage their patrons to split checks equally because this creates incentives for everyone to order more. Restaurant customers often have difficulty splitting the check so that everyone pays for what he ordered. Given the widespread use of computers, it would be easy for most restaurants to separately calculate the cost of each person's food. Since restaurants want customers to equally divide the bill, however, they have little incentive to provide these data.

When college roommates sharing a phone equally divide the bill, they are likely to make too many toll calls. If two roommates know that they will equally split the bill, then the cost to each of them of making an additional call is halved. This, of course, results in both roommates making far more calls than they would if they were each paying their own bill themselves. Consequently, to keep down telephone expenses roommates should agree to specifically calculate the cost of both people's calls.

INSURANCE

Insurance policies give you the right to spend the insurance company's money, and whenever someone else is paying you should buy the best.

Let's say that you typically buy $30 worth of drinks when you go to your neighborhood bar. One night the bar has a $30 all-you-can-drink special. Will this special cause you to consume more or less alcohol?

After you get the special, each drink is free. The $30 purchase price represents a sunk cost that you should ignore because you have to pay it regardless of whether you have that next drink. Consequently, the special should intensify your intoxication.

Health insurance resembles an all-you-can-consume medical care special. You pay a fixed amount for insurance, but then pay little for the medical services you subsequently use. The problem for health insurance companies is that their insurance causes customers to spend too much on health care.

After your car gets stolen, it's reasonably easy to calculate how much your insurance company should reimburse you for. What if, however, you buy health insurance and you get sick? How much of your health bills should the insurance company pay? If the insurance company agrees to pay for everything you could possibly call a medical expense, you will obviously have incentives to overspend. If the insurance company is paying, why not get that expensive massage chair to help your back or the ergonomic keyboard you need to alleviate carpal tunnel syndrome? When you have health insurance, you purchase medical care with other people's money. Consequently, health insurance companies need to constantly monitor their customers' medical expenditures.

The more price sensitive the demand for a service, the more health insurance companies need to monitor. A service is very price sensitive if a decrease in price causes consumers to buy much more of the service. Heart operations probably aren't that price sensitive since a reduction in the price of bypass surgery is unlikely to induce you to get another heart operation. Consequently, insurance providers don't have to worry that health insurance will cause customers to get unneeded bypass surgery. Of course, even if you must have a bypass operation, you don't necessarily need to have it performed by the world's top surgeon. If someone else is paying, however, why not get the best?

Consumers are in a strange game with insurance companies in which we want them to rigidly monitor everyone else's expenditures but our own. The better job insurance companies do at keeping down everyone else's costs, the less we have to pay. Of course, once we have paid our premium we want our insurance company to give us the best, and often most expensive, care.

Insurance companies are especially challenged at providing mental health coverage. There are, I imagine, objective ways to determine whether someone needs a heart bypass operation. It's much more difficult to figure out whether someone needs psychotherapy. Furthermore, while almost no one would get a bypass operation just for fun, a lot of mentally healthy people would enjoy spending a few hundred hours talking to a friendly psychotherapist. Since it's difficult for an insurance company to determine how much mental health care a customer needs, it's tough for them to control mental health care costs by stopping fraud and abuse.

CO-PAYMENTS

Insurance companies frequently require their customers to pay part of their medical bills. A customer might, for example, have to pay the first $20 of a bill or 10 percent of the total amount. Co-payments, however, can never cause the customer to be as financially responsible as if he were paying all the bills himself.

You are deciding whether to buy good X for $100. Obviously, you will buy the good if it is worth more than $100 to you. Now assume that if you get good X, the insurance company will pay part of the cost, so the cost to you of good X is now lower than $100. This must necessarily make you more willing to buy good X. If the insurance company pays for 10, 30, or 90 percent of the cost, you are still more likely to get X when insured. By definition, health insurance lowers the price of medical services to the sick. The greater the co-payment, the less likely the customer is to buy the service. As long as the co-payment isn't 100 percent, however, the individual's insured state makes him more likely to buy medical services.

Which type of co-payment causes consumers to buy fewer medical services: (1) a fixed co-payment or (2) a percentage co-payment? Once you have made the fixed payment, it becomes a sunk cost and should rationally be ignored and thus will have no effect on inhibiting wasteful spending. In contrast, if you have to pay 10 percent on all bills, you always have some incentives to reduce costs.

HMOs

Insurance companies use health maintenance organizations (HMOs) to control costs. Imagine that a doctor is about to prescribe some pills for an insured patient. There are two kinds of pills the doctor could prescribe. They're both approximately of the same quality, but one costs a lot more. If the patient is fully insured, he won't care about the pill's expense. If the doctor has no incentive to worry about the pill's cost either, she might prescribe the more expensive pill. The health insurance company probably wouldn't be able to tell for certain that the patient didn't need the expensive medication and consequently they might end up paying for the costly medicine.

Now imagine that this same doctor is part of an HMO. This HMO both provides care and insurance to its patients. The HMO will pay doctors more if the doctors keep expenses down. The doctor now has an incentive to reduce costs. What if the patient really needed the more expensive treatment? Well, the doctor would still have an incentive not to prescribe it, but at least the patient's health insurance costs would be lower.

INSURANCE AS GAMBLING

Are you willing to bet that your house will burn down? You are if you own fire insurance. Buying insurance constitutes gambling. When you purchase fire insurance, you are betting with the insurance company that your home will burn down. If it burns down, you win, and the insurance company pays off. If your house doesn't go ablaze, you lose your bet, and the insurance company keeps your premium payments and gives you nothing.

Although insurance is gambling, it's a form of gambling that actually reduces your risk. Imagine that for some strange reason you were forced to bet $50,000 that the Buffalo Bills will win their next football game. This bet is obviously very risky. If you can't cancel this bet, another way to reduce your risk would be to make another $50,000 bet that the Buffalo Bills will lose their next game. If you bet $50,000 that the Bills will both win and lose the game, then you are assured of breaking even. Your two bets cancel out and you have eliminated the risk from the first bet. When gambling, two bets are sometimes safer than one.

Owning a home automatically forces you to take a bet that your house will not burn down. If you own a home but don't have insurance, then you are far worse off if it burns. When you buy fire insurance, you are making an opposite bet that your home will burn down. These two bets mostly cancel each other out and reduce the risk in your life.

INFORMATION PROBLEMS

Imagine that you're a bookie who takes football bets. A player on the Buffalo Bills wants to (illegally) bet that the Bills will lose their next game. Should you take this bet? This player has inside information about the game. He also has some ability to influence the chance of their losing. You might refuse this bet because you suspect the player would make it only when he is certain of defeat. It's dangerous to bet with someone who knows more about the underlying event than you do.

Whenever insurance companies sell policies, they are issuing them to people who have superior information. When you buy life insurance, you are betting with your insurance company that you will die. You obviously have information about your health that the insurance company lacks. The insurance company should suspect that the reason you want to buy life insurance is because you know you are sick. Indeed, if you find out you are going to soon die, it would be a good strategy to buy lots of life insurance. The people who would most want insurance are inevitably those people whom the insurance company would least like to have as customers.

SEARCH AND RESCUE

You are considering scaling a dangerous mountain on which you could easily get injured and stuck. If you were trapped on the mountain for a few nights, you would die of exposure. You're not a particularly advanced mountain climber, nor are you suicidal. Should you attempt the climb? You should if you bring a cell phone and are confident that if you get trapped, a government search-and-rescue team will save you.

If this search-and-rescue team didn't exist, you probably wouldn't consider going up the mountain. Consequently, while the purpose of the team is to save climbers, it paradoxically might cause climbers to endanger themselves. The search-and-rescue operation is a type of insurance, and like all insurance it causes people to take on excessive risks.

TOO MANY RISKS

Do motorcycle helmet laws kill? A study found that between 1987 and 1999 states with helmet laws had more deaths per motorcycle accident than states that lacked such laws.[5] Helmets are designed to protect riders' skulls in the event of accidents, so how could laws mandating helmets increase the number of deaths per accident? The helmets undoubtedly provide some head protection, but they also change riders' behavior.[6] Knowing you have more protection should cause a rational driver to take more risks, and these risks increase the death rate. Helmets function as insurance against accidents because they reduce the harm of an accident. But, like all types of insurance, they enhance the insured's willingness to take risks.

Insurance companies also have to be wary of people taking additional risks because they have insurance. For example, having your car stolen is not so bad if you have auto theft insurance, so rational people insured against theft will take more chances with where they park their car. They won't deliberately cause their car to get stolen. But, like mountain climbers who count on the park rangers or like the motorcyclists who wear helmets, the existence of auto insurance will cause car owners to take additional risks.

Workers' compensation provides benefits to workers if they are injured on the job. Since this compensation reduces the financial harm of being injured, it decreases the incentive for workers to take care to avoid injuries and thus increases the number of injuries. I realize that this seems far-fetched, a theory thought up by an out-of-touch professor, but consider: Everyone takes risks all the time. When you go to the movie rather than staying at home, you are slightly increasing your risk of death through a car accident. When you eat high-fat foods, you increase the risk of suffering a heart attack. The number of risks we all take is determined by the chance of something bad happening and the harm that results from an accident. Since workers' compensation reduces the damage of an accident, it should cause us to take more risks.

DEPOSIT INSURANCE

The U.S. savings and loan crisis of the 1980s was caused by deposit insurance. Imagine that I was the type of person who liked to make very risky and sometimes silly investments. Would you be willing to lend me money? Now imagine that the government promised to repay your loan to me if I couldn't repay. This governmental guarantee would mean that you wouldn't have to worry about my solvency. With the guarantee, you could feel comfortable lending me money, even if you knew that I would squander it.

Savings accounts in U.S. banks are guaranteed by federal deposit insurance. When you put your money in a savings account, the bank uses it to finance investments. If these investments go bad, the bank might not have the funds to give you back your money. Because of deposit insurance, however, the government guarantees to pay depositors of insolvent banks. Consequently, deposit insurance allows banks to attract depositors even if the bank makes extremely risky investments.

Imagine you were about to go gambling and a rich friend promised to pay any of your losses. If you won $10,000, you could keep the money. If you lost $15,000, your friend would compensate you for your loss so you would break even. Your friend's guarantee would create incentive for you to take massive risks. You should bet everything you have because if you win, you win big, whereas if you lose, you always break even.

Deposit insurance causes banks to take risks because it guarantees that at worst depositors break even. Consequently, banks have incentives to take depositors' money and make huge gambles. If the investments pay off, everyone gets rich. If they fail, the taxpayers pay.

To combat the ills of deposit insurance, the federal government must constantly monitor banks to ensure that they don't make overly risky investments. Sometimes, however, federal oversight fails, as it did in the savings and loan crisis. In this crisis savings and loan institutions made risky real estate gambles and lost, costing U.S. taxpayers billions.

FLOOD INSURANCE

The U.S. federal government offers subsidized flood insurance to many homeowners. By subsidizing flood insurance, the government reduces the cost to homeowners of building in flood plains and consequently increases the total amount of flood damage in the United States.

LIFETIME EMPLOYMENT

Tenure is the ultimate insurance. College professors with tenure are guaranteed a job for life.[7] Tenure functions as insurance because if something bad happens to the professor's career (for example, he stops publishing and becomes a terrible teacher), he still gets to keep his job. Other types of employees, such as U.S. government workers, effectively have tenure as they are almost impossible to fire. Lifetime tenure creates two problems. First, it decreases the incentives of those with tenure to work hard. The second problem manifests from adverse selection. The type of person most attracted to a job with lifetime tenure would be someone who suspected that she would need protection from getting fired because her job performance might not always merit continued employment.

DISCRIMINATION

Insurance companies often discriminate on the basis of age, sex, health, and other observable characteristics. If insurance companies didn't discriminate, then most of their market would disappear. To see this, consider a very simple example of health insurance in which two people want to buy health insurance, a healthy person and a sick person.

Table 7   Insurance

Person's Health	Most Person Is Willing to Pay for Insurance	Cost of Insurance to Insurance Company
Healthy	$500	$400
Sick	$2,000	$1,900

This table shows how much it would cost to insure the people and what they would be willing to pay for insurance. First, notice that the insurance company should be able to make money from both customers, who are willing to pay $100 more than it would cost the insurance company to provide them with coverage. Consider what happens, however, if the insurance company can't discriminate. If it wanted to sell to both people, it would have to charge at most $500 because that is all a healthy person would be willing to pay. If, however, the insurance company charges $500 to both, it would obviously lose money since its expenses would be far greater than $500. Consequently, the insurance company can't profitably sell to both at the same price. If it sells at too low a price, it will lose money, and if it sells at too high a price, the healthy person won't buy any insurance. The only way in this example that the insurance company can sell to everyone is if it discriminates and charges the sick person more.

Governments don't like the sound of the word "discrimination," so they often place restrictions on insurance companies' ability to discriminate. To preserve their markets, however, insurance companies have strong incentives to get around antidiscrimination laws. Health insurance companies naturally attract the sickest people, whereas they want to sell to the healthiest. To repel sick people, insurance companies try to exclude those with preexisting conditions.

GENETIC TESTING AND THE DISMAL FUTURE OF THE HEALTH INSURANCE INDUSTRY[8]

Genetic testing might someday destroy the market for health insurance because testing holds the promise of determining which diseases people will get. The health insurance industry, however, depends upon blissful ignorance and might be decimated by genetic testing.

Imagine there was some magical test that could determine who would win the next Buffalo Bills football game. The mere existence of this test would probably prevent people from betting on the Bills. Everyone who didn't run this test would fear making a bet because they would suspect that the person on the other side of their bet did use the test.

People buy health insurance because they don't know whether they will get sick. For example, assume that 1 percent of 35-year-olds will incur significant health care expenses over the next year. It's worthwhile for almost every 35-year-old to get health insurance. Those who don't get sick will pay a little to the insurance company, which will give most of these funds to those who did need medical coverage. The insurance company effectively transfers money from those who turn out to be healthy to those who end up sick.

Now imagine that there was some genetic test that could determine whether you would get sick the next year. If you took this test, you would only buy insurance if the test indicated that you would get sick. Of course, if the only people who buy insurance were those who will get sick, then the insurance companies would go bankrupt.

If there were genetic tests that could determine when someone would get, say, cancer or heart disease, then the insurance companies would be reluctant to sell coverage to anyone they had not tested. These companies would fear that the people who wanted coverage had been tested themselves and knew they would get sick. The genetic tests would increase the adverse selection problems inherent in the insurance industry because the people buying insurance would have even more private information about themselves.

If the insurance companies tested applicants, it would still not solve this genetic problem. The insurance companies would be unwilling to sell insurance to someone whose genetic test reveals will get cancer next year unless this person pays the full cost of cancer treatment. This person would thus not buy insurance; he would be paying for cancer treatment.

True, with genetic testing one could still insure against accidents. Also, a genetic condition might mean one has, say, only a 50 percent chance of getting some disease. You could still insure against this 50 percent risk. To the extent that genetics determine your future health expense needs, however, genetic testing will destroy the health insurance industry.

THE POWER OF THE PURSE

Businesses often must give others the ability to spend their money. You can never completely eliminate people's desire to waste and misappropriate your funds, but you can mitigate the harm by instituting appropriate safeguards.

MANAGING EMPLOYEES

Stopping others from exploiting you is a fundamental problem of business. Much of this chapter considered why insurance companies need guard against being taking advantage of by their customers. Chapter 13 will explore how businesses can mitigate the harm of being exploited by their employees.

LESSONS LEARNED

- An employee spending her company's money has an incentive to spend the money in a way that benefits her, not her company.
- Bribing those who spend other people's money can be a cheap means to make sales.
- Companies need to employ appropriate safeguards to ensure that employees don't misallocate company funds. Many types of bribery are legal, so you can't rely upon fear of criminal prosecution to stop your employees from taking noncash bribes.
- Insurance creates incentives for people to take too many risks and spend too much money.
- To combat the negative incentive that insurance creates, insurance providers need to monitor, regulate, and carefully screen their customers.
- The people who most desire insurance are those to whom the insurance company would least like to sell.

C H A P T E R

MANAGING EMPLOYEES

The eye of the master will do more work than both his hands.

Proverb[1]

JUST BECAUSE YOU PAY AN EMPLOYEE it doesn't mean you have his loyalty. Rational employees will always put their own interests ahead of your firm's needs. Consequently, salaries should not be seen as a way of gaining a worker's allegiance; rather, they should be viewed as a mechanism to alter an employee's incentives to align his interests with yours.

The great economist Adam Smith described how an invisible hand causes selfish capitalists to act as if they were altruistic. A capitalist produces products not to satisfy your needs, but to make money for himself. Manufacturers can only prosper, however, by making products that consumers want. Consequently, the invisible hand of capitalism causes business owners to care about their customer's needs. The invisible hand of capitalism, however, does not automatically make your employees care about you. It's your job as an employer to create a visible salary structure that forces employees to adopt your concerns. No salary structure works perfectly, however.

ATTORNEY FEE STRUCTURES

Your company's lawyers, like all employees, will do their job based on how you pay them. Attorneys usually get paid by one of two methods:

- They are paid by the hour.
- They receive contingency fees, which are a percentage of any amount that you win at trial.

If attorneys are paid by the hour, then they have an incentive to work too much, because the more they work, the more you pay. When you pay by the hour, your attorneys have the incentive to spend time considering every single legal subissue. This means, however, that you should be most afraid of suing a company whose lawyers are paid by the hour.

Attorneys paid by contingency fees have an incentive to work too little. Success for a contingency fee lawyer comes from putting a small amount of time into many cases to get as many contingency fees as possible.

Neither paying attorneys by the hour nor paying with contingency fees provides for ideal incentives. When picking a fee structure, however, you must decide which would do you the least harm. Perhaps you want to win at all costs, so you would want to pay by the hour. Or, say, you fear attorneys padding their bill; then you should go with contingency fees.

DOCTORS AND HMOs

Like attorneys, doctors don't always have appropriate incentives to serve your interests. Imagine that you are considering undergoing an expensive operation. You're not certain if the operation will improve your health, so you consult your doctor for advice. First, assume that the doctor who would perform the operation is an independent service provider who gets paid based on how much he works. Getting the operation would increase your doctor's salary, and so he has an economic incentive to advise you to get the procedure.

Now, imagine that your doctor works for an HMO. You pay the HMO a flat fee, and the HMO takes care of all your medical needs at no additional cost. Obviously, the HMO would like to minimize these costs. Many HMOs, understandably, provide economic incentives for their member doctors to keep expenses down, so your HMO doctor would probably have some interest in recommending that you forgo the operation.

Independent doctors and HMOs also have different incentives with regard to preventive care. It's usually much cheaper to stop a medical problem from occurring than it is to fix a medical condition once it manifests itself. An HMO, therefore, has a massive incentive to encourage its patients to take preventive care. HMOs should also want their patients to live healthy lifestyles. Selfish, profit-hungry HMOs should desperately try to convince their patients to exercise, eat right, and not smoke, for the less medical care you need, the greater your HMO's profits.

Independent doctors, by contrast, are actually better off when their patients become sicker, so they have negative economic incentives to give their patients lifestyle advice.

TAXES AND INCENTIVES TO WORK

Combating worker laziness often provides the paramount challenge for employers. Economists have long understood that government taxes reduce individuals' incentives to work. Understanding how taxes affect effort will help you motivate employees.

Consider a game where you must decide how much to work. The more you work, the more money you get. Unfortunately, for every extra hour you work, you actually have to work one more hour. For mortal man, time is the most precious commodity. When we work, we trade time for money, and the more money we earn per hour, the more most of us are willing to work.

When the government taxes you, it reduces the benefit you get from working. If you must pay, for example, 40 percent of your earnings in taxes, then for every extra dollar you make, you really get to keep only 60 cents. This is one of the reasons why high taxes slow economic growth, because they reduce incentives to work.

For example, assume that a college professor has the opportunity to teach a summer class for $10,000. The professor would be willing to do it for only $8,000, but if he does teach the course, he will net only $6,000 after paying taxes. Consequently, the professor doesn't teach the course, choosing summer leisure over high-taxed employment.

TENANT FARMERS

Companies often tax their employees. For example, imagine that you rent land to a farmer. You are considering three ways of extracting money from your worker:

1. You pay the farmer a fixed amount to work for you, but you keep all of the crops he grows.
2. The farmer gives you a percentage of everything he grows.
3. The farmer pays you a fixed fee, but he keeps everything that he grows.

The farmer has the least incentive to work when paid a fixed fee. Under the first scheme, the farmer gets paid the same amount regardless of his effort, so it's in his self-interest to work as little as possible. Taking a percentage of what the farmer grows it the equivalent of taxing him. Under the second plan the farmer still has some incentive to work, but this incentive is greatly reduced by your implicit tax. The farmer has the greatest incentive to work if he must pay you a fixed fee. Under this scheme, if the farmer works a little harder, he captures all of the benefits of his efforts.

Imagine that the farmer could work an extra hour and produce $30 more in crops. Under plan (1) he would get none of this extra money, under plan (2) he would get some of it, while under plan (3) he would get the full $30.

It might therefore seem then that you should always use plan (3) and have the farmer pay you a flat fee. The problem with the third plan, however, is that it puts all the risk of crop failure on the farmer. If he has a bad year, the farmer absorbs all of the losses. Since most workers dislike risk, workers usually accept risk only if they are compensated for assuming it. The farmer will agree to the third plan, therefore, only if he gets a high average income. Under plan (3) the farmer must expect to make a lot of money in good years to be compensated for a low income in bad years.

This tradeoff between risk and work always exists for employers. To motivate employees to work, you usually need to make their salary dependent on how well they perform. Employees, though, usually dislike risk and prefer steady, consistent paychecks. Firms face a difficult choice. If a firm forces its workers to take on high risk, the workers will be motivated to work, but will dislike this risk. If the firm pays employees a constant amount, the workers will be happy with their safe jobs but may have little incentive to work hard. The following game illustrates this employers' dilemma.

Assume that a salesman can either (a) work hard or (b) slack. The employer can't observe the salesman's efforts. The salesman will either do well or poorly. If the salesman slacks off, he will always do poorly. If, however, the salesman works hard, he will do poorly half of the time and do well the other half.

Table 8

	Work Hard	Slack Off
Low Sales	50% of the time	100% of the time
High Sales	50% of the time	0% of the time

How should the firm pay the salesman? If it always pays the salesman the same amount, the salesman obviously has an incentive to slack off. If, however, the salesman's salary is based on his outcome, then he will be forced to take on a lot of risk, for even if he works hard, he still might have a bad year. If you make employees take on too much risk, they will demand greater salaries or will seek safer jobs.

The one way around the risk/motivating tradeoff is for employers to carefully monitor efforts, not outcomes. In the previous game, you could achieve an ideal result if you paid the salesman based on how hard he worked, not his total sales. An employee willing to work hard would then face no risk. Unfortunately, determining effort is always subjective and much more challenging than monitoring outcomes. There is consequently no always-right solution to the risk/motivation problem; rather, each company must accept that any pay structure will cause some inefficiency and seek to determine which inefficiencies cause the least harm.

The tradeoffs between risk and reward are also an important topic in finance; this book further explores them in Chapter 16, The Stock Market.

OUTSIDE CONTRACTS

We can apply our risk/reward structure to outside contracts. Imagine that your company hires another firm to construct a building. You can adopt one of three contracts, as noted below.[2]

1. You pay the builder a fixed amount.
2. You pay him a fixed amount plus a percentage of any cost overruns.
3. You pay the total cost of construction.

The contractor obviously has the greatest incentive to minimize cost in the first contract. The first contract, also, puts the most risk on the contractor, so he would probably demand the higher fee under this arrangement.

VENTURE CAPITALISTS[3]

Imagine that you're a venture capitalist considering lending me money to start an Internet company. My business plan entails enacting implementations that utilize the synergies of leveraged . . . and then going public. Obviously, you would love to fund me. Your main worry, however, is my reputation for laziness. Fortunately, I'm also known to be greedy, so you intend to structure a deal under which my greed will overcome my laziness, causing me to put in maximum effort.

You agree to put $10 million into the business, but only if I put in $70,000 myself. The $10,070,000 will go to setup costs, and I won't get any of it if my business fails. True, my $70,000 is trivial compared to what the business needs, but it represents a large sum to a college professor. You want failure to cause me a massive amount of pain so that I will be motivated to succeed. In return for the $10 million, you ask for 40 percent ownership of the company.

I suggest an alternate arrangement. You see, besides being lazy and greedy, I'm also fearful. I offer you 80 percent of the company in return for you giving my company $10 million and giving me $1 million. I want to guarantee myself a profit if the company fails, so I'm willing to trade 40 percent of this company for $1,070,000 . Should you go along? Under my arrangement, I own a smaller part of the company and do much better if the company fails. Consequently, I have a far lower incentive to work hard under my arrangement than yours. Under my proposal, however, you double your share of the company. Which proposal better serves your interests?

It depends on how lazy I am and how much my laziness could hurt the company. If my level of commitment will determine the success of the company, then your arrangement is preferable to mine. In contrast, if the company's prospects for profits are largely independent of my efforts, then you should accept my proposal. Note that it's not just the risk of the venture that's relevant to your decision but rather how my actions might affect this risk. If, say, the venture is extremely risky, but my efforts matter little to the company's success, then you should go with my fearful proposal.

FREE RIDER GAMES

Most people like material goods but prefer not to work for them. Many humans besides me are both lazy and greedy. This dangerous combination creates trouble when people work in teams. Everyone benefits when a team succeeds, but most everyone would prefer if the team succeeded based on the hard work of others. People living together often are supposed to work as a team.

No one likes cleaning bathrooms, but most people like their bathrooms to be clean. When several people share a bathroom, a free rider game is consequently created. As its name suggests, free rider games manifest themselves when someone attempts to free ride on another's efforts. There are three outcomes to the bathroom free rider game:

1. Everyone shares the work.
2. One person gives in and does all the cleaning.
3. The sanitary conditions in the bathroom steadily deteriorate.

As of this writing, my fiancée is concerned that when we get married and live together I will have the advantage in this game since I'm vastly more willing to tolerate outcome (3) than she is. Of course, dirty bathrooms are far from the worst consequences that arise from free rider games.

Imagine life on some perfectly egalitarian agricultural commune where all the food produced is equally divided up among members. Let's say there are 10,000 people, and each tills a small share of land. When the harvest comes, all the food is brought to the center of town and distributed evenly. How much should each farmer work? The more you work, the more food everyone has. If you grow, say 10,000 carrots, however, you get to keep only one of them. True, you will also get some carrots that other people grow. Under the rules of egalitarianism, though, you get the carrots other people grow regardless of whether you grow any yourself. If you live to serve the collective good, then you will produce as much as possible. Outside of a socialist fantasy-land, however, people care mostly about themselves and their families. The cost to you of growing 10,000 carrots will be the large amount of effort their production requires. The benefit *to you* is only one carrot. A self-interested person would probably not go to the effort of growing 10,000 carrots just to keep one.

I suspect some readers are thinking that this analysis can't be right because if everyone on the commune thought this way, no one would produce anything, resulting in mass starvation. Actually, when collective agriculture was tried in China under Mao and the Soviet Empire under Stalin, the result *was* mass starvation. Was this just because the farmers did not realize the game they were playing and thus didn't grow enough food? Actually, the economic system destined them to die.

Imagine you were one of these farmers and realized that if everyone were lazy, many (possibly even you) would perish. What could you do? The best option, actually, would be to emigrate to America, but let's stay within the context of this game. What if you decided to grow lots of carrots? Your efforts would increase your food allotment by only a trivial amount. It would also make you more tired, so you would probably now be among the first to die. Your best chance at survival would lie in working as little as possible while praying that you survive to play another game. Of course, since everyone will probably follow this strategy, little food will be produced. If only Mao and Stalin had understood game theory, millions of lives could have been saved!

Underlying the theory of communism is the assumption that people will work for the common good, not their self-interest. Communists like Mao and Stalin presumably believed that a worker would be at least as motivated to work for the common good as he would to work to fill his own stomach. Since most people primarily care about themselves and their families, however, communism failed.

If you're not sure whether you're self-interested, then take the following test, which is somewhat adapted from Adam Smith's *The Wealth of Nations*. Imagine that two bad things happen today: First, there is a devastating earthquake in a country you have previously never heard of. One hundred thousand people die. Second, while cooking, you cut off the tip of your pinky finger. A close friend calls you tonight and asks, "How has your day been?" You reply, "This day has been terrible, one of the worst in my life." You then proceed to explain to your friend why your day has been so bad. What are you most likely to mention to your friend, the earthquake or your finger? If you would be more likely to discuss your finger, then you care more about the tip of your pinky finger than you do about 100,000 fellow human beings. This doesn't make you a bad person, just one who is primarily focused on what is in your, and perhaps your family's, self-interest. As the comedian Mel Brooks once said, "Tragedy is [if] I cut my finger. Comedy is if you fall into an open manhole and die."[4]

Communism caused economic ruin because it failed to take into account that most people are self-interested. Companies too can err when they don't consider how self-interest motivates workers.

Firms often try to motivate workers by giving them stock in the company. The logic behind employee stock ownership programs is that if the employee owns a piece of the company, he will get more of the rewards of his labor. Game theory, however, would predict that, at least for large companies, employee stockholding would fail to motivate workers for the same reason that communist communes failed. In a large company each employee could get only a tiny part of the whole company. Consider a worker whose stockholdings give her $1/1,000,000$ of the company. If she improves profits by $1 million, she gets only a dollar of benefit. Since $1 is unlikely to motivate anyone, her stock ownership will not influence her behavior. It's true that owning stock will cause the employee to care more about the company's profits; it just won't cause her to take any additional actions to actually increase these profits.[5] Perhaps owning shares in their company gives workers some warm and fuzzy feeling that somehow transforms them into better employees. Warm and fuzzy feelings, however, are beyond the scope of game theory.

A far more effective way to motivate workers is to pay them based on their own performance. When your salary depends on the performance of the whole company, you have little incentive to work as long as what you do does not significantly affect company profits. In contrast, when you are paid based on your own contributions, you have a tremendous incentive to work hard.

While stock ownership is not an effective way to motivate most employees, it can motivate the chief executive officer. A company's CEO has a tremendous influence on his company's fortunes. Consequently, giving him a slice of the company (and thus a claim on the company's future profits) will cause him to care a lot about the fortunes of the company. For example, most businesspeople don't like to fire employees. If a CEO knows, however, that firing 10 percent of his workforce will increase the company's stock price, then owning a lot of that stock would make her more willing to order the terminations. In contrast, if the CEO doesn't have a large position in the company, it might not be in her self-interest to get rid of the people just to help some outside shareholders.

Free Rider Problems Between Companies

Different companies that try working together can face free rider problems. Imagine several companies have agreed to conduct joint research and development. They agree to fully share the patent rights to anything developed. Each company should try to get the others to do all of the work and pay all of the expenses. Of course, if all the companies understand game theory, then they might be able to figure out some way of overcoming the free rider problems. The companies could specify in advance what everyone will do and contractually agree to penalties if one company doesn't accomplish its share. This free rider problem might disappear if the companies expect to work on future projects together. Each company might avoid taking advantage of its collaborators on this project, so they might have the opportunity to work together on future ventures.

Free Rider Problems with Teams

Companies often can't avoid free rider problems among their employees because teams can accomplish many tasks better than individuals. Companies often assign a group of employees to work on a joint project. Whenever they do this, however, there is always the danger that some employees will free ride. The free rider problem doesn't mean that joint tasks shouldn't be given, only that managers should recognize that free rider problems will manifest when people work in teams. Whenever possible, managers should try to assess individual members of the team so that no one person can benefit from laziness.

In a free rider game the key to winning is to be as lazy as possible and hope other people will take up the slack. When creating working environments involving teamwork, the key to success is recognizing free rider problems and doing your best to minimize them by punishing laziness and rewarding hard work.

THE AGENCY PROBLEM, STOCK MARKET MANIPULATION, AND ENRON

Although CEOs are usually considered bosses, not employees, they are in fact employees of the stockholders. Like all employees, they have an incentive to put their interests above those of their employers. On her web site, www.JaneGalt.net, Megan McArdle provided a highly readable analysis of this issue.[6] Since she's letting me use her writings for free (I'm greedy), and even approximating her level of quality would require my putting in tremendous effort (I'm lazy), I quote her at length.

> The agency problem is the fancy economic term for what most of us already knew intuitively; what benefits the stockholders doesn't necessarily benefit management. For example, I can think of many executives I've worked with on "re-engineering" projects, who, if they wanted to be honest about what would make their department work better, would "re-engineer" themselves right out the door and let somebody competent take over. Somehow, however, it was always one of their minions, usually one they didn't like too well, who was found to be superfluous. There are all sorts of ways in which this agency problem affects managers' actions to the detriment of their shareholders, but one of the most widely known is in compensation.
>
> If you know anyone in corporate sales, you probably already know of the hilarious shenanigans in which the sales force engages in order to meet their quotas. The purchasing manager at my old job was good for 10K or so of thoroughly bogus orders at the end of the month or the quarter to help our sales reps meet their quotas; in return they gave us a little extra off our regular purchases. These orders were invariably cancelled, after a decent interval, due to the whims of our fictitious clients. None of this was good for the companies for whom these sales reps worked; it benefited only the sales force.
>
> But trying to prevent these gymnastics has proved futile. Change the quota from orders to sales and they'll ship the stuff out and have it

"returned," incurring shipping charges both ways; change sales to "final sales" and they'll leave, because no one's willing to have their income that dependent on the whims of people they don't know. This applies even more to executives, who have much more power to manipulate matters so that they keep their job.

Now, being say, the CFO, is inherently riskier than being a clerk in accounting. It may not seem like it, but really, at the lowest level of a corporation, all you have to do in many jobs is show up on time and breathe. Even the most incompetent CFO gets made responsible for a lot of stuff, some of it out of his control, and not all of which can be blamed on his subordinates. If enough things go wrong, he'll be fired. This is why most senior executives spend so little of their time doing anything that looks like work to the clerks in accounting, and so much of their time sucking up to the board.

So executives do anything in their power to minimize that risk. Often, this makes them unwilling to make risky but high-expected value choices, because a bad bet could cost them their jobs. At other times, such as when the company is on the rocks, it makes them prone to shoot the moon on highly speculative ventures because, what the hell, they're going to lose their job anyway, so why not plunge all the firm's assets into that deep-sea titanium mining venture and hope they strike it rich? Entire consultancies, like Stern Stewart, have evolved around various metrics for structuring compensation so that the managers either get rich with the shareholders, or go down with the ship.

One of the original ideas was the bonus, predicated on performance. Of course, you can't just say "performance"; you have to give a metric, or a combination of them, that dictates what performance is. And there's the rub. They tried all sorts of things. If revenue growth was used, you got revenue growth—but much of that revenue was unprofitable, as the executives slashed margins to move product. Tell them to cut costs, and they'd stop making stuff to sell. Tell them they had to improve net income, and games were played with the financial statements to maximize net income.

So what became popular? Stock price. Seemed perfect; put the bulk of an executive's compensation in company stock, and watch those incentives align!

Well, not quite.

First of all, notice that all those managers made out like bandits in the recent bull market, even though they probably contributed little to its root causes, such as good monetary policy and the conviction of the American public that they'd finally found a sure thing. (Although probably a lot of them helped found their company's 401K, so perhaps we should give them some of the credit.)

Second of all, stock prices are . . . ahem . . . not immune to manipulation. No! I hear your stricken cry, Tell me it isn't so, Jane! Say it ain't so! But I'm afraid I cannot, my little chickadees. Stock prices do not represent some platonic ideal of the actual, true, total current, and future value of the company; they represent the market's idea of that value, which is something very different. Thus, they can be manipulated.

If you've wondered why all the Enron executives seemed to have such outsized amounts of stock given in consideration for doing nothing but sitting in meetings all day talking about what a great company Enron was, this is why. And if you've wondered why they played all those games with the company's income, this is also why.

Share price is determined in large part by analysts. Analysts like certain things in certain types of companies. In Enron's case, they liked things like rapid growth, both in asset base and earnings. They liked them a lot. So much, in fact, that the executives knew that unless they continued to produce this growth, the next time the analysts went up on the mountain where God delivers the share prices to them on stone tablets, the burning bush would deliver a punishing verdict that would send Enron's stock price, and hence the executives' incomes, falling.

Now, the first time they fudged the numbers, it probably seemed innocuous; just smoothing out a little dip this quarter. The problem is, the more quarters the rising income went on, the more the analysts grew to expect it, and the worse the punishment if they failed to deliver. Thus the ever-expanding web of deception that has now ensnared us all in a gray future of mediocre returns and endless congressional hearings on exciting topics like foreign earnings deductions. But I digress.

We're now seeing more and more such items hit the headlines; Xerox is the latest perp, and the charges are a predictable mélange of little accounting fudges here and there which together conspired to wildly misrepresent the state of the company's earnings. Which brings up two interesting points.

The first is that economists and financial wizards got it wrong. The best minds of a generation convinced themselves, to some extent, that the law of unintended consequences would not apply to something as obvious as stock-based compensation. It's a healthy reminder that no matter how good an economic idea seems, we should always try to figure out how we'd manipulate the system, if it were us.

The second is that it's easy for us all to say that we wouldn't have done the same thing in the place of those Enron executives. And from the safety of my little closet on the Upper West Side that's an easy call; no one's yet offered me hundreds of millions worth of stock for ranting at you guys all week. But try to think of it another way: if you could have half your income taken away unless you delivered a growing number of whatever it is you make, be it computer programs or payroll reports, every single quarter, you'd be pretty desperate to make that number grow, wouldn't you? When you hit the natural limits of your ability to produce those programs or reports, and it was a choice between lying to the bean counters or telling your wife to cancel that vacation to the Bahamas and plan on spending the week re-painting the house, it might not be so hard to convince yourself that a little fudging, just this once, wouldn't hurt.

So it's back to the drawing board on executive compensation. Which is the beauty of capitalism, really. We got it wrong this time. It may take us a few more tries to get it right. But we don't expect to set up the perfect system once and for all; capitalism is just the system for finding the perfect system. So when something goes wrong, the almost-instant response is "we're working on it."

THE BENEFITS OF TRADE AND OPTIMAL ALLOCATION OF EMPLOYEES

After Adam Smith's paradigm of the invisible hand, the most influential concept ever developed by an economist was probably David Ricardo's theory of comparative advantage. Comparative advantage explains why countries always benefit from free trade. His theory, however, also has applications for how businesses should allocate their employees.

To understand comparative advantage, consider the following:

Table 9   Absolute Advantage

	Jane	Bill
Time it takes to cook	10 hours	5 hours
Time it takes to clean	5 hours	10 hours

In this example Jane and Bill live in adjoining apartments. It takes 15 hours for both people to do all their cooking and cleaning. Jane, however, is better at cleaning, and Bill is better at cooking. If the two work together, and have Jane do all the cleaning and Bill, all the cooking, then it will take each only 10 hours to do their work. This result may seem unimportant, but it's really magical!

Think: By trading their services, each person can save 5 hours. No one besides these two people need get involved, and obviously no one gets hurt. Just by trading, these two can be made better off. This result has widespread implications for companies and countries. When you have two people, each of whom is best at one particular task, there are considerable benefits to specializing. Each should do what he is best at. Similarly, when countries trade, each country can specialize in what it does best, and both can be better off.

In the previous example one party was absolutely better at cleaning and the other at cooking. What would happen if, as in the following example, Bill was better at both cooking and cleaning?

Table 10   Comparative Advantage

	Jane	Bill
Time it takes to cook	5 hours	1 hours
Time it takes to clean	3 hours	2 hours

Could the parties still benefit from trading their services? After all, since Bill is now better at both cooking and cleaning, does he have anything to gain by working with Jane? Actually, yes. If the parties work alone, it takes Jane eight hours to complete her chores and Bill three hours to complete his. But, if Bill does all the cooking and Jane does all the cleaning, it takes Jane six hours and Bill only two. Both parties can still benefit by trading services.

What is going on here is that Bill is comparatively better at cleaning than Jane is. True, in an absolute sense Bill can complete both tasks faster than Jane can. It takes Bill twice as long to clean as it does for him to cook. Jane, however, is better at cleaning than cooking. Thus the two parties can still benefit from trade.

This example shows that even when one person is better at everything than another, the two can still benefit from trade if each specializes in what he does best. The strength of this simple argument is why virtually all economists support free trade. Even when a productive country like the United States trades with a third-world nation, both can benefit from trade even if the United States is better at doing everything.

Consider the benefits of trade for a company. Assume that your company produces both widgets and sprockets, and the following holds:

In one day Jane can make either one widget or one sprocket.
In one day Bill can make either two widgets or seven sprockets.

Again, Bill is better at everything. Bill is clearly a more valuable worker than Jane is. Imagine that you are considering firing Jane. You should first determine her exact value to you. Consider this: *What can Jane produce over a two-day period?* The answer seems simple. It seems that over two days she could produce either two widgets, two sprockets, or one of each. Actually, Jane could do better. Through the magic of trade Jane could also produce seven sprockets over a two-day period.

Seven sprockets: how is this possible? Imagine your company has only Bill, and you develop an urgent need for two widgets. Obviously Bill would need to spend one day making them. This would mean that Bill does not spend that day making sprockets. Thus, the cost to your company of producing two widgets is seven sprockets. Now, assume that you hire Jane. Jane could spend these two days making two widgets. This would free up Bill to make seven sprockets. Two days of Jane's time allows your company to produce an extra seven sprockets, so this is what she is worth to your company.

The lesson from this example is that when considering what an employee can do, you should look at not only what she can accomplish, but also at what she can help other people accomplish by freeing up their time.

EMPLOYEE MANAGEMENT

What should one of my employees do to maximize his own welfare? What should one of my employees do to maximize the welfare of my company?

These are the two questions you must ask when considering whether you have created appropriate incentives for your employees.

The answers to these two questions will always differ at least slightly, but the more you can do to align your employee's interests with your needs, the better workers you will have.

NEGOTIATIONS

You can set the terms of trade with your own employees. In Chapter 14 we will consider how you can negotiate and trade with people who don't work for you.

LESSONS LEARNED

- Employees will always strive to maximize their own welfare, not yours.
- Paying employees based on their achievements maximizes their incentive to work but forces employees to take on lots of risk.
- Ideally you should compensate employees based on effort, not outcome; but effort is much harder to measure than achievement.
- Paying employees based on the performance of a large group creates incentives for workers to free ride on the efforts of others.
- Two people, or countries, can benefit from trade even if one is better at everything than the other.

14

NEGOTIATIONS

In a negotiation, he who cares less, wins.[1]

THE TWO OF YOU CAN SHARE A PIE but only after agreeing on how to divide it. Often it's clear that players would benefit from collaborating, but it's not obvious how the fruits of this collaboration should be shared.

Consider a simple game where a seller owns a good that is worth $1000 to him but $1300 to a buyer.

Value of Good to the Buyer = $1300
Value of Good to the Seller = $1000

We can make two inferences about negotiations between these parties:

- Both parties have the potential to benefit from trade.
- If the buyer acquires the good, he will pay between $1000 and $1300.

Parties can always benefit from trade when a potential buyer values the good more than the potential seller does. Whenever you consider bargaining with someone, you should first identify whether there are any possible gains from trade. If the good in our example was worth less than $1000 to the buyer, then the parties should not bother negotiating.

Given that the buyer values the good more than the seller does, how much will it be traded for? We can't tell without more information. We can, however, use the values the parties place on the good to determine its potential sale price range.

Since neither party will agree to an arrangement that makes him worse off, the seller will never accept less than $1000, and the buyer won't ever pay more than $1300. The amounts of $1300 and $1000 represent the buyer's and seller's respective walking away prices. Assuming that the two parties come to a deal, neither party will ever have to walk away. What would have happened if a party had walked away, however, is critical in determining the parties' negotiating strength. Consequently, the party who cares least about the negotiations succeeding has an advantage, for he would be hurt less by walking away.

Armies frequently launch attacks just before starting peace talks.[2] Even if both sides expect the peace talks to succeed, they still have massive incentives to carry out a successful strike before the talks to increase their negotiating strength. Similarly, even if you are certain you can negotiate some deal, you still should establish that you would do well if the deal fell through.

TAKE-IT-OR-LEAVE-IT OFFERS

What would happen in our example if the seller could make a take-it-or-leave-it offer to the buyer? If a take-it-or-leave-it offer is rejected, the game ends and the good isn't traded. If the seller could make such an offer, he should offer to sell the product for just under $1300. Since the buyer values the good at $1300, he would be better off accepting any offer less than $1300. As this example shows, a party who can make a take-it-or-leave-it offer gets all the benefits of the trade.

To make an effective take-it-or-leave-it offer, you must make credible your threat to walk away from negotiations if your initial offer is rejected. The threat to walk away, however, often lacks credibility because both parties will still benefit from further negotiations if the first offer is rejected. The best way to make credible take-it-or-leave-it offers is to establish a record of having walked away from past negotiations.

"Boulwarism"is making a reasonable offer and then refusing to negotiate further.[3] The term refers to Lemuel R. Boulware, a vice president at General Electric who developed a strategy of never negotiating with unions. Boulware would make a single take-it-or-leave-it offer to workers. By developing a pattern of making such offers, Boulware's stance gained credibility.

Imagine you're negotiating a business deal that must be concluded within the next 24 hours, and you would like to propose a take-it-or-leave-it offer. You are certain that if your prospective partner was forced to either (1) accept the offer or (2) walk away from the deal, then she would accept. Unfortunately, you suspect that your prospective partner will respond to your offer with a somewhat less favorable counteroffer. You can make a take-it-or-leave-it offer only if you can credibly threaten never to consider any other offers if yours is rejected. If your prospective partner believes that you really want the deal to succeed, then she will also know that you would be unwilling to walk away from her counteroffer. You could greatly improve your negotiating position by eliminating the possibility of your ever hearing her counterproposal. You could, for example, mail her an offer and then leave town for a vacation. By reducing your options. you would be reducing hers. If you could not respond to a counteroffer, then your potential partner would either have to either accept your offer or walk away.

BRING ANOTHER PARTY TO THE NEGOTIATIONS

Let's go back to our simple negotiating game between the buyer and seller. Assume that now, however, there exists a second buyer who also values the good at $1300. Further assume that the two buyers won't collude but rather will compete to buy the good from the seller.

Value of the Good to Buyer 1 = $1300
Value of the Good to Buyer 2 = $1300
Value of the Good to the Seller = $1000

When we add a second seller, we can determine the exact sale price. Would it be reasonable for buyer 1 to acquire the good for $1200? No, because this outcome is not stable since buyer 2 would be willing to pay more than $1200 for the item. Thus, if the two buyers compete, buyer 2 would never allow buyer 1 to acquire the good for only $1200. Imagine that the three people are in a room negotiating. The negotiations couldn't end with the seller agreeing to give the good to buyer 1 for $1200 because buyer 2 would offer to pay $1201 before he would ever leave the room empty-handed.

The only stable outcome in our three-person game is for the good to be sold for $1300. The existence of the second buyer gives the seller all the potential profits from trade. Both sellers need the buyer, whereas the buyer needs only one seller. Consequently, if the seller can get the buyers to compete against each other, he can drive down their profits to zero. Of course, if the buyers don't compete, then they would do much better.

Let's slightly change the game and assume that buyer 2 values the good at only $1250.

Value of the Good to Buyer 1 = $1300
Value of the Good to Buyer 2 = $1250
Value of the Good to the Seller = $1000

In this game buyer 1 will end up with the good because she would always outbid buyer 2. The sale price will fall between $1250 and $1300. It's not a stable outcome for the good to be sold for, say, $1230 because the buyer who didn't get the product would have been willing to outbid her rival. It is stable for the good to be sold for somewhere between $1250 and $1300 to buyer 1 because then buyer 2 wouldn't benefit from making a higher counteroffer.

Imagine that you are the seller and you get a call from buyer 2 just a day before the start of negotiations. Buyer 2 says that he isn't going to bother showing up since he knows he will eventually be outbid by buyer 1. It's entirely rational for buyer 2 to stay home and not waste his time in fruitless negotiations he is destined to lose. As the seller, however, you should be horrified by the prospect of buyer 2 staying home. Without buyer 2, the price will be somewhere between $1000 and $1300. With him, the range contracts to between $1250 and $1300. Consequently, the seller should beg buyer 2 to show up, bribing him if necessary.[4] Of course, buyer 1 should also be willing to bribe buyer 2 not to show. Therefore, even though buyer 2 won't end up purchasing the good, he could still profit from the negotiations.

In his negotiations with CBS, David Letterman exploited the tactic of increasing the number of buyers. David Letterman hosts a late night comedy show for CBS, and his contract was about to expire. CBS, reportedly, told the talk show host that he had no other place to take his show if he didn't renew with CBS. David Letterman's show plays best from about 11:30 to 12:30 P.M., during which time NBC runs the popular *Tonight Show* and ABC runs the highly respected *Nightline*. ABC, however, indicated that it would consider dumping *Nightline* and running Letterman's show instead. Although Letterman ultimately renewed his contract with CBS, getting ABC to express interest in him no doubt strengthened his bargaining position.

GIVING UP CONTROL

Giving up control can also increase your negotiating strength.[5] If you prove that you are not authorized to pay more than a certain amount, you may favorably contract the sale price range. In our first example,

Value of Good to the Buyer = $1300
Value of Good to the Seller = $1000

The seller would benefit by, say, convincing the buyer that she couldn't sell the item for less than $1250. Of course, the buyer might suspect that the seller is lying to increase her negotiating strength.

Giving up control to an agent who has a different objective than you can often enhance your negotiating position.[6] Imagine that in the above game the buyer hires a professional negotiator who has a reputation for either getting a great deal or walking away from the negotiations. Although the buyer would be better off paying $1250 than not getting the good, the agent would prefer to terminate negotiations than ruin his reputation by getting a poor deal. If the seller knows about the agent's reputation, then the possible price range should shift in the buyer's favor.

BRINKSMANSHIP[7]

A willingness to go to the brink may also strengthen your negotiating position. Brinksmanship is best understood in the context of war.

India and Pakistan have long been enemies. India is much larger than Pakistan and has a superior conventional army. In a conventional war between these rivals, India would almost certainly win. A war between these nations might not stay conventional, however, for Pakistan and India each have atomic weapons. Since both India and Pakistan would be devastated by an atomic war, how much protection does Pakistan get from its own atomic weapons?

A threat by Pakistan to attack India with atomic weapons if India invaded would not be credible because India would surely respond in kind to any atomic aggression. Pakistan would clearly be better off conquered by India's army than decimated by its atomic weapons. Consequently, a rational Pakistan would never deliberately use atomic weapons if it thought that India wasn't going to use them. Therefore, India would not believe that Pakistan would deliberately use atomic weapons in response to a purely conventional attack. So, how can Pakistan make its threat to use atomic weapons more credible?

Perhaps it could have loose control over its weapons. Pakistan could give control of each nuclear missile to a different general and put the missiles near the Indian border. Now, imagine that India attacks and its troops fire directly on a general who has control of an atomic weapon. Even if his leaders didn't want him to push the button, the general, who might be facing imminent death, would be tempted to use the atomics anyway.

By having weak control over its nuclear missiles, Pakistan would be employing brinksmanship. *Brinksmanship* means deliberately taking a crisis to the brink of disaster. If Pakistan had limited control over its nuclear missiles, then any conventional war between Pakistan and India would risk becoming an atomic catastrophe. Brinksmanship makes a threat far more credible, because when you are at the brink mistakes might occur. By practicing nuclear brinksmanship, Pakistan could use its atomic weapons to effectively deter India's conventional army even if India assumes that Pakistan would never deliberately use atomics.

Businesspeople, as well as military planners, can benefit from using brinksmanship. For example, a party to a labor negotiation might create the risk of an "unwanted" strike to increase his bargaining position.[8] Imagine that a union contract is about to expire, and it would be devastating to both the company and union to not have a new contract. The union, however, wants to threaten the company with a work stoppage. This threat normally would lack credibility because a strike would harm the union. The union could, however, use brinksmanship to enhance the threat's credibility. For example, the union could wait until the last minute to negotiate the contract so that failure might automatically result in a strike.

The union could also openly condemn management so that its workers might vote against an unfavorable contract even if the union's leadership wanted to avoid a strike.[9] This tactic would combine giving up control with brinksmanship. By deliberately making it difficult to accept a new contract, the union could enhance its negotiating position by credibly signaling that it couldn't accept a new agreement that didn't significantly increase employees' salaries.

GOALS OF NEGOTIATIONS

When you are about to commence negotiations, always determine what you and your potential partner would get if negotiations fail, for this determines the possible range of settlement. During negotiations, consider what credible threats you could execute to improve this range in your favor.

AUCTIONS

In this chapter buyers and sellers engaged in unstructured negotiations. Chapter 15 explores a highly formal method by which to sell goods: auctions.

LESSONS LEARNED

- What you would get if negotiations fail often determines what you do get if negotiations succeed.
- A party who can make a take-it-or-leave-it offer can get the entire surplus from a transaction.

- Bringing other parties to your negotiations can radically alter the bargaining environment.
- Giving up control can enhance your negotiating position.
- Taking negotiations to the brink of failure can make credible a threat to do something that is not in your self-interest.

15

AUCTIONS

Be not too hasty to outbid another.

Proverb[1]

WHILE AUCTIONS have always interested game theorists, the Internet has recently made them relevant to more ordinary mortals. Indeed, the on-line auction provider eBay has become one of the few profitable pure Internet companies.

Auctions reduce the cost of ignorance. A seller unaware of how much customers value his good normally faces a dilemma: He can set a high price and risk his good going unpurchased, or set a low price and, alas, get low prices. When auctioning goods, however, the seller need not determine the optimal price, because in auctions the price of goods automatically changes in response to buyer demand. Auctions are especially valuable to sellers of time-limited products like airline seats and hotel rooms. If you sell durable goods and set too high a price, you always have time to resell the items. If, instead, you sell a time-limited product but find no buyers, then the item is forever lost. Since auction prices will automatically be reduced until the market clears, auctions almost never leave you with unsold merchandise. The two most common types of auctions are first price sealed-bid auctions and second price sealed-bid auctions.

FIRST PRICE SEALED-BID AUCTIONS

In a *first price sealed-bid auction*, the buyers simultaneously submit bids for the good being sold. The person who bids the most wins and gets the good at the amount he bid. All bids are made simultaneously and secretly. For example, assume that the following amounts are bid:

Table 11

Bidder	Amount Bid
Tom	$100
Jane	$90
Sue	$30

Tom wins the auction and pays $100.

In a first price sealed-bid auction, you should always bid less than what the good is worth to you. If you bid more and win, you are worse off. If you bid what the good is worth to you and win, you really get nothing, because what you paid was exactly equal to what you got. In first price sealed-bid auctions, you need to decide how much to risk. The lower you bid, the greater the benefit of winning, but the lower the chance that you will actually win. Ideally, you should attempt to estimate what other people will bid when formulating your own bidding strategy.

SECOND PRICE SEALED-BID AUCTIONS (SLIGHTLY TECHNICAL)

Second price sealed-bid auctions include the type of auction effectively used on eBay. In these auctions each player secretly makes a bid, the person who bids the most wins. The winner, however, pays what the second highest person bid. For example, assume that the following bids are made:

Table 12

Bidder	Amount Bid
Tom	$100
Jane	$90
Sue	$30

Tom wins the auction, but he pays only $90. Neither Jane nor Sue pays anything. Had Jane not bid, Tom would still have won the auction but would have paid only $30. The surprising strategy in a second price sealed-bid auction is that you should bid exactly what the good is worth to you.

Imagine that the item being bid on is worth $100 to you. Let's first examine why bidding $100 is always better than bidding some amount less than $100, such as $99. If the highest bid exceeds $100, it doesn't matter whether you bid $99 or $100 because you lose the auction either way. If the highest bid other than yours is below $99, it again doesn't matter whether you bid $99 or $100. In both cases you win the auction and pay the amount of the second highest bid. (If the second highest bid is $88, you win and pay $88 regardless of whether you had bid $99 or $100.) The only time there is a substantive difference between bidding $99 or $100 occurs when the highest bid made by someone else is between $99 and $100. If the highest bid made by someone else is $99.50, you lose the auction if you bid $99 and win the auction if you bid $100. If you bid $100, you would get the good for $99.50, which is beneficial since the item is worth $100 to you. Consequently, if the highest bid other than yours falls between $100 and $99, you are always better off bidding $100 if the good is worth $100 to you. Thus, bidding $100 is either the same or better than bidding $99 or any other amount below $100.

Similar logic shows you should always bid $100 rather than some amount more than $100, such as $105. If someone else bids over $105, then bidding $100 or $105 both result in your losing the auction and paying nothing. If the highest bid other than yours is lower than $100, then bidding $100 or $105 is identical; in both cases you win, paying the second highest bid. The difference between bidding $100 and $105 manifests itself if the highest bid someone else makes is between $100 and $105. If the highest bid is $104, you lose the auction if you bid

$100 and win it if you bid $105. If you bid $105, however, you have to pay $104 for the item, which is more than its worth to you. Thus, bidding $100 is always better or equivalent to bidding over $100.

In a second price sealed-bid auction, the amount you bid determines whether you win; it does not determine how much you pay if you win. In these auctions you want to bid only when the amount you would have to pay if you won is less than the item's value. If you bid what the item is worth to you, you will win if and only if the second highest bid (the amount you pay if victorious) is less than what the item is worth.

The auctions on eBay are essentially second price sealed-bid auctions. In eBay the winner is always the person who bids the most, and the winner pays what the second highest person bid.[2]

If you know the value of the good, and believe the auction to be honest, the optimal strategy on eBay is to bid what the good is worth to you and never raise your price. If you bid what the item is worth, and someone bids more, you should never outbid her because then if you win, you will necessarily pay more than the item's value. Many people on eBay seem to follow the strategy of bidding small amounts and then raising their bid amount if outbid. This strategy wastes time, because your bid determines when you win, not how much you pay. To see this, assume again that the good is worth $100 to you. Imagine that there will be many other bids, and the highest is X. If you just bid $100 from the beginning, you will win the auction when X < $100 and will pay X if you win. If you initially bid $20, keep raising your bid when someone else outbids you, but never bid more than $100, then you get the same result as if you just bid $100 from the beginning. You win whenever X < $100, and when you win, you pay X.

If eBay were a first price auction, where the winner always paid what he bid, then you would always want to just barely outbid the second highest bidder. In a first price eBay auction, you would want to visit the auction just before it ended and bid just a little bit more than the second highest bidder. In fact, if everyone were rational, in a first price eBay auction, everyone would wait until the end of the auction to bid. It would be stupid to bid before the end; doing so would give you no advantage and might even hurt you because you could end up bidding far more than everyone else. Remember, in a second price auction it doesn't matter by how much you outbid everyone, since if you win, you always pay the second highest bid. In a first price auction, by contrast, the winner always wants to just barely outbid the second highest bidder, because the winner pays what he bids. Thus, in first price auctions, you want to wait until the end, when you have as much information as possible about the other bids.

CHEATING WITH FALSE BIDS

A dishonest seller could use false bids to increase the amount he receives in a second price auction. To see this, assume again that the following bids are made:

Table 13

Bidder	Amount Bid
Tom	$100
Jane	$90
Sue	$30

As before, Tom will win the auction and pay $90. If the seller knew the bid amounts, however, she should bid $99 herself. Such a bid would not prevent Tom from winning, but it would cause Tom to pay the seller $99 rather than $90. The seller, of course, would not want to bid more than $100, for this would cause the seller to win her own auction.

On eBay a seller would not know all the amounts bid. If the above three bids were made, eBay would show that Tom was the high bidder but would indicate that the current price was $90. Consequently, a new bidder wouldn't know how much he would have to bid to become the high bidder. Thus, a seller making false bids would be taking a chance if he bid more than $90. He might get lucky and bid less than Tom, but he also could bid too much and win the auction himself. If the seller won, he could auction off his good again or withdraw his bid. Both strategies have some drawbacks since sellers must pay eBay a fee for every completed auction and eBay imposes limitations on when a buyer can withdraw a bid.

If eBay allowed it, however, a seller could greatly benefit from making false bids and then withdrawing them if they were too high. A seller could keep raising her false bid by $1 until she won. She could then withdraw her final bid and thus get the maximum possible amount for her product. Making false bids constitutes criminal fraud, however, so a seller engaged in such a scheme would have to be careful about withdrawing too many bids, or eBay might catch on. Presumably eBay understands how sellers could use false bids to fraudulently increase their take, so eBay probably investigates at least some withdrawn bids. If you won an auction in which a bid was withdrawn, however, you should beware that a seller might have been trying to illegally increase the amount you had to pay.

If you fear that a seller might make false bids to increase his price, you should consider bidding only at the conclusion of an auction. This way a seller won't have the opportunity to test you with false bids.

WINNER'S CURSE

Sometimes winning an auction signals that you lost. Although in the previous sections it was assumed that you knew how much the good was worth to you, sometimes you don't have full information about the good's quality. For example, imagine that several oil companies are bidding for the mineral rights to some land. Each oil company sends a team of geologists to determine the likelihood of the land having oil. No company knows everything, and all companies unearth some slightly different information. Let's say 10 companies bid, including yours. You win, and it turns out you bid far more than most people. This means that your geologists thought that the land was more valuable than the geologists at the other companies did. There are now two possibilities: Everyone else is wrong and your geologists correctly determined the value of the land, or everyone else is correct and you overbid. While your geologists might be the best, the odds favor your having made a mistake.

Consider a simple analogy. You are in a room with 10 other people. You ask each person to guess your weight. Chances are that the person who guesses the highest overestimated your weight. The winner of an auction is the person who guessed that the good being sold has the highest value, and so odds are that he overestimated the good's value.

Winner's curse applies only when you are uncertain of the good's value. Imagine that you are determined to buy my book, which is being sold for, say, $30 at your local store. Before purchasing it, you decide to check for a copy on eBay. If you are definitely going to buy my book, you know it's worth paying up to $30 because that's how much getting the book on eBay would save you. There can be no winner's curse in this example because if you pay less than $30 (including shipping), you are better off.

Now imagine that you first encounter my book on eBay. Many people place bids, but you win. You must have a higher estimate of my book's value than any other seller does. Maybe you have insight into my brilliance that others lack. But perhaps you have overestimated my literary worth.

When you are uncertain of a good's value, then you learn something from everyone else's bid. High bids signal that others greatly value the good, while low bids show that your fellow bidders don't think the item has much worth. If the other bidders might know something about the auction item that you don't, then their bids should influence how much you are willing to pay.

Winner's curse afflicts sellers as well as buyers. When buyers are uncertain of a good's value, then they fear paying too much. Winner's curse will cause all buyers to bid less and will consequently reduce the seller's take. To combat winner's curse, sellers need to provide information about their goods so that buyers will realize the good's value and won't fear the winner's curse.

INTERNAL AUCTIONS

You can use auctions to reward and motivate employees. We have previously discussed the difficulty of determining quotas for salespeople when you don't have enough information to figure out how much each should sell. You could use auctions rather than quotas to assign sales areas. For example, if a new area opens up, you could auction it off to all your salespeople, with the person willing to pay the most getting the area. The auction would not only bring in money but would also result in the area going to the most confident salespeople.

NEGATIVE AUCTIONS

You can use negative auctions to dispose of goods that no one wants. Imagine that you need to send some employee to Buffalo, New York, for a week, but no one wants to go, You're unwilling to force someone to attend. You could hold a negative auction, where each employee bids for the minimum amount you would have to pay him to attend. The person bidding the least gets the money and the trip.

BENEFIT OF AUCTIONS

Consider if your business would benefit from using (more) auctions. Auctions are an informationally cheap means of selling goods to consumers or of allocating tasks among employees. The results of consumer auctions also provide you with valuable data about the demand for your goods.

THE STOCK MARKET

The most important auctions occur not on eBay but in financial markets. Chapter 16 will explore several topics in stock market economics.

LESSONS LEARNED

- Auctions are useful for sellers because they automatically adjust the price based upon buyer interest.
- Auctions are most advantageous to those selling time-limited goods or services.
- In first price sealed-bid auctions, you should always bid less than what the good is worth to you.
- In honest second price sealed-bid auctions, if you know exactly how much the good is worth to you, then you should bid this amount.
- If you are not sure of the good's value, you should beware of the winner's curse, which holds that the winning buyer is often the buyer who most overvalued the good.
- Auctions can be used to allocate tasks among employees.

16

THE STOCK MARKET

> He that could know what would be dear need be a merchant but one year.
>
> *Proverb*[1]

YOUR STOCK MARKET SCORE could well determine the quality of your retirement. This chapter does not attempt to provide an overview of the stock market, but rather it covers some topics in finance that have game-theory–like qualities.

STOCK MARKET COMMENTATORS

How seriously should we take commentators who predict future stock price movements? To figure this out, we first have to examine why anyone would widely disseminate his stock picks.

Pretend a pirate claims to know the location of a buried treasure. You figure there's a 1 percent chance that he is both sane and honest. The pirate then gives you a usable map that seems to show the exact location of the treasure. Do you still believe the pirate? Since it's unlikely that a sane pirate will reveal the location of treasure, the fact that the pirate freely tells you where his treasure is buried reduces the chance that he actually has any useful information.

Now imagine that instead of a pirate revealing the whereabouts of a treasure, a financial analyst reveals the name of a stock she claims will rapidly increase in value. The analyst's willingness to part freely with this information should itself eviscerate the credibility of that information. Knowledge about what stock will increase is valuable. If the analyst were someone whom many people believed and trusted. then the analyst would never just give away this information; she would sell it. Might not the analyst, however, both sell this information and freely reveal it? No. Those who paid would be upset that they had to pay for something others got for free. Consequently, the fact that the analyst willingly disseminates this knowledge shows that either the analyst does not believe her own predictions or lacks the credibility to actually get paid for this information.

What if the analyst works for a business publication, writing articles concerning which stocks will increase? If the owners of the magazine really believed in the analysis, they would not disclose the predictions but would trade on them themselves. No sane magazine owners would publish a map to a buried treasure if they believed the map to be accurate and the treasure to be precious. Similarly, sane magazine owners would sell the predictions for the price of their magazine only if they didn't believe that the predictions were valuable.

It's possible that the analyst is reliable, but no one believes her, and so the analyst can't sell this valuable information. If you do choose to follow this analyst's advice, however, you should at least acknowledge that the market doesn't value her opinion. People in the financial industry don't think this information has much value, or the analyst wouldn't freely part with her predictions.

Not all financial advice should be suspect. You shouldn't trust a pirate who gives you his map, because the pirate himself would be hurt by your taking his treasure. There are some types of financial "treasure," however, that everyone can enjoy. Consider two pieces of information:

1. Acme stock is undervalued.
2. Investors should diversify their portfolios.

Since only a few people can benefit from purchasing an "under-valued" stock, telling many people about (1) decreases the value of this information. In contrast, the idea that investors should diversify doesn't decrease the value of anything when many people act on it. You should consequently trust financial advice when the advisor wouldn't personally benefit from hoarding this information.

THE FUTURE IS NOW

As the following game illustrates, stock prices respond very quickly to new information. Pretend you have an asset that is useless to anyone but me. Next week I will be willing to pay $60 for this asset. How much is this asset worth today? Obviously, it's worth $60, yet many investors seem not to understand this game.

Imagine investors believe that the Federal Reserve Board will cut interest rates next week. For reasons I won't detail, interest rate cuts help stocks. Does this mean that next week stock prices will rise when interest rates fall? Of course not. Say a stock is worth $58 if interest rates are not cut and $60 if they are. If it is known that interest rates will be cut next week, then the value of the stock will increase to $60 today; the market won't wait for next week. Next week, when interest rates do change, they will not influence stock prices. Interest rate cuts increase stock prices only when first anticipated.

Just as expected interest rate cuts don't move the stock market, anticipated corporate developments don't change stock prices. Consider, for example, when the expiration of a patent will hurt a pharmaceutical company's stock price. When a drug company discovers some useful new compound, they obtain a patent on it. The patent gives the pharmaceutical company the sole right to sell the discovered drug for some limited period of time. After the patent expires, anyone can make and sell the drug. The pharmaceutical company obviously loses lots of money when a patent expires, because it loses its right to be the exclusive provider of the drug.

If a pharmaceutical company's patent will expire next week, will its stock price fall next week? No, since everybody knows that the patent will expire next week. It can't be that this week the stock is trading at $50, but everyone knows that next week the stock will trade at only $40. If this were the case, everyone would sell the stock this week, causing its price to fall immediately. If everyone knows the patent will expire next week, then next week's expiration will have no effect on the stock price. Recall, it's the *announcement* of the rate cut that affects the stock market, not the actual rate cut. Similarly, the expiration will affect the stock market when people first learn that a patent will expire. The time at which a patent will expire is known when the government initially issues the patent, so the expiration of the patent affects the stock price when the patent is first given.

For example, imagine that a pharmaceutical company's stock sold for $50 yesterday, but today the company unexpectedly discovers a wonder drug. Assume that if the company were given an infinite patent on this drug, then the company's stock would jump to $60. If, however, the company is granted only a 14-year patent, then the discovery will cause the company's stock price to jump to only $58. Today the stock will trade for $58 since the effect of the patent's expiration is factored into the stock price when the patent is first issued, not when the patent actually expires.

SHORT-RUN HOLDERS SHOULD CARE ABOUT THE LONG TERM TOO[2]

A firm announces its one-year plan, but you don't care because you're planning on selling the stock in one day. Actually, because anticipated future events affect today's stock price, even short-term day traders should worry about their investments' long-run prospects.

You consider buying a stock on Monday and selling it Tuesday. Should you be concerned about what could happen to the stock on Friday? Yes, because it will affect the price received on Tuesday.

If the person you sell the stock to is one of those boring buy-and-hold people, then obviously he will care about what happens on Friday. What he is willing to pay on Tuesday will be influenced by what he suspects will occur on Friday. But let's say that you sell the stock to another short-term trader who plans to sell it on Wednesday. Even if this buyer intends to sell to another person with a short time horizon, either that next buyer will care about Friday, or she will sell to someone who does. What she is willing to pay will be affected by what is supposed to happen on Friday. When a trader sells a stock, the price he gets is determined by what the next buyer will pay, which is affected by what the next buyer will pay, and so on. Consequently, not wanting to hold your stock for the long run does not mean that the long run doesn't have a hold on you.

Short-term traders should care about the future exactly as much as long-run investors do. If this were not true, short- and long-term traders would place different values on the same stock. If the short-run people valued the stock less, they would never buy the stock, and the market would rightly ignore their preferences. Market prices would then reflect long-run evaluations. If short-term traders valued it more, then they would be in trouble because if the short-term investors paid more than the long-run investors thought the stock was worth, then the short-term investors would be able to profitably sell the stock only to other short-run investors. But since short terms become long runs, these traders would eventually have to sell for a loss.

What if, however, it's known that a stock's price will go up to $90 today and go back to $80 tomorrow? If this kind of situation arose, then short- and long-run investors would indeed have different perspectives. This situation, however, should never manifest itself. A stock's value is determined by what someone would pay for it. Why would anyone pay $90 today for something that is going to be worth only $80 tomorrow? Perhaps because they will sell it to someone before the price goes down. But then why would this second buyer pay more than $80?

RISK VERSUS RETURN

The basic lesson of the stock market is that investors get greater average returns for taking on higher risk. What would you rather have:

1. $100,000 or
2. a 50 percent chance of getting $200,000 and a 50 percent chance of getting nothing?

Both choices give you on average $100,000. The majority of investors, however, would prefer the first choice: the sure thing. Most people dislike risk, which is why so many of us buy insurance. True, many people also enjoy gambling, but for most gambling is a form of entertainment, not an investment strategy. When most people invest, they want to avoid risk. People's desire to avoid risk ensures that stocks pay higher returns because they are risky.

Investors can either put their money in U.S. government bonds where they are guaranteed a certain rate of return, or they can buy stocks. Stocks are much riskier than government bonds. Would it make sense to live in a world where on average stocks and government bonds gave the same return? If they did offer the same return, everyone would buy the government bonds. The only reason anyone willingly takes a chance on stocks is because on average they yield a higher return. For our economy to survive, people need to buy both stocks and government bonds. Market forces ensure that the prices of stocks adjust until investors are willing to buy both stocks and government bonds. The market induces investors to buy both financial products by giving stock investors on average higher returns.

THE RETURN ON ART

Should you invest in art? Only if you're willing to sacrifice profits for artistic pleasure. On average, art appreciates less than stocks. To see this, imagine living in a world where on average a piece of artwork goes up as much as stocks do. If this were the case, most everyone would rather have a nice painting than a stock certificate. Consequently, if on average stocks and art performed equally well, no one would buy stocks. Since capitalism requires that people invest in stocks, the market automatically adjusts the return on stocks so that they do financially better on average than art does. Stocks' superior performance doesn't mean you should never invest in art; rather, you should accept that on average your artistic investments will earn a lower return than your stock market investments.

SURVIVORSHIP BIAS IN MUTUAL FUND REPORTS

Mutual funds remain one of the most important investment vehicles for the middle class. Mutual funds compete intensely for investors. They often tout superior past performance as proof that they will continue to yield a good return. How reliable, however, are reports of past performance? The SEC closely regulates how mutual funds' managers calculate and describe past returns, so these reports are factually accurate; but performance reports can, however, be both accurate and misleading. Mutual fund performance reports can be skewed by *survivorship bias*. To understand survivorship bias, consider the following fraudulent scheme used to cheat sports bettors:

First, find the mailing addresses of 1,600 people who place heavy bets on sports. Write to each of them and say that you will predict the outcome of three football games. Then, for $100, you will sell them your prediction for who will win the Super Bowl. If your prediction on the Super Bowl proves incorrect, you will refund their money. For the first game, you should send to 800 people a letter predicting that one team will win, and to the other 800, a letter predicting that the other team will be victorious. Next, forget about the people to whom you made the false prediction. For the 800 people for whom you correctly picked the outcome, send half of them a letter claiming that one team will win the next game, and send the other half a letter claiming the opposite team will win. After the second game you will now have 400 people to whom you have correctly predicted the outcome of two games. You repeat the same process for these 400 people. At the end of the third game you now have 200 people to whom you have correctly predicted the outcome of three football games. You mail each of these 200 people a letter saying that you will correctly predict the outcome of the Super Bowl for $100. You also promise to return their money if you incorrectly predict the outcome. For the people who send you the $100, you tell half of them that one team will win and the second half that the other team will be victorious. You then return the money to the people for whom you incorrectly predicted the Super Bowl outcome. Assuming that all 200 people paid you for your super bowl prediction you have now made a profit of $10,000 minus postal costs. Furthermore, all the people whose money you have kept are satisfied since they got what they paid for.

Now, imagine that instead of playing this game with sports bettors, you play it with investors. You start with a large number of mutual funds. They all make different investments. You close down the ones that do badly and keep the ones that do well. You only advertise the funds that do well, saying they have a successful track record and thus you must be good at investing.

The managers of mutual funds don't exactly play this game. Poorly performing mutual funds, however, are often closed down, making the ones that are kept operating seem better than they really are. For example, imagine that this year 100 new mutual funds are started. Further imagine that each fund manager makes his investment decisions by throwing darts at a newspaper listing of stocks. After a year the funds that do poorly are closed down. On average, the surviving funds' performances will be well above average. This doesn't mean that these funds' managers have any skill at picking investments, but rather that survivorship bias makes past performance misleadingly attractive.

CONCLUSION

For reasons that this book hasn't gone into, economists believe that stock price movements are mostly random, so attempts at market predictions are folly. The wisest investment strategy you can follow is to buy a diversified portfolio (or invest in an index fund), continually add to the portfolio over your working life, and sell only when you need the funds for retirement.

LESSONS LEARNED

- If someone freely gives you stock advice, ask why she can't get anyone to pay them for the information.
- Events affect stock prices when they are anticipated, not when they actually occur.
- Even short-term traders need to be concerned with the long-term prospects of stocks.
- To compensate investors for taking on risk, market forces cause stocks on average to pay higher returns than safe government bonds.
- Survivorship bias makes mutual funds' past performances seem misleadingly impressive.

17
C H A P T E R

FURTHER READINGS AND REFERENCES

I HOPE THAT AFTER READING *Game Theory at Work* you are motivated to learn more about game theory and economics. I have not been paid, unfortunately, for recommending any of the following books.

FURTHER READINGS IN GAME THEORY

Games of Strategy by Avinash K. Dixit and Susan Skeath is an excellent undergraduate textbook. The book requires no knowledge of economics but does require some understanding of calculus. It would make an excellent second book for a reader who has completed *Game Theory at Work* and wants to undertake a rigorous study of game theory.

Co-opetition by Adam M. Brandenburger and Barry J. Nalebuff is a nontechnical business book on how to negotiate, cooperate, and compete.

Thinking Strategically by Avinash K. Dixit and Barry J. Nalebuff is a nontechnical game theory book for a general audience, although it is less focused on business.

Games, Strategies, and Managers by John McMillan provides a very nontechnical introduction to game theory.

The Evolution of Cooperation by Robert Axelrod is a nontechnical explanation of cooperation in repeated prisoners' dilemma games.

Prisoner's Dilemma by William Poundstone is a nontechnical book devoted to the history, philosophy, and application of prisoner's dilemma.

A Beautiful Mind by Sylvia Nasar is a biography of John Nash.

Game Theory for Applied Economists by Robert Gibbons is a more advanced game theory book than *Games of Strategy*. As the title implies, it assumes that the reader has some knowledge of economics.

Strategy: An Introduction to Game Theory by Joel Watson is an advanced game theory textbook for undergraduates that incorporates contract theory.

http://www.gametheory.net is an excellent web resource for game theory.

FURTHER READINGS IN ECONOMICS

The Economics of Life by Gary S. Becker and Guity Nashat Becker is a collection of Becker and Becker's *Business Week* columns. The articles don't use much game theory, but rather apply economics to well-known public policy issues. The articles are written for a general audience. (Gary Becker, a Nobel Prize-winning economist, was one of my Ph.D. dissertation advisers.) *Sex and Reason* by Richard A. Posner applies economic reasoning to sex and is accessible to a general audience. (Judge Posner, probably the most influential living legal scholar, was also one of my Ph.D. dissertation advisers.)

Information Rules by Carl Shapiro and Hal R. Varian applies economic theory to high technology and information, providing many in-depth examples of network externalities. This book is accessible to a general audience. I highly recommend it to anyone seeking to understand the economics underlying the Internet and the computer industry. *Principles of Microeconomics* by N. Gregory Mankiw is an undergraduate textbook on microeconomics. Although a textbook, it is accessible to a general audience. Anyone who is serious about learning economics should read a microeconomics textbook, because microeconomics is the most successful nonreligious philosophy the world has ever known. It's not possible to understand politics, history, or business without knowing microeconomics.

A Random Walk down Wall Street by Burton G. Malkiel is a readable guide to how economists think the stock market works. Most of what is written about the stock market for general audiences has the validity and intellectual rigor of astrology, so many investors would benefit from this book.

References

Akerlof, G., "The Market for Lemons: Quality Uncertainty and the Market Mechanism," Quarterly Journal of Economics, *89: 488–500, 1970.*

Axelrod, Robert, The Evolution of Cooperation, *Basic Books, New York, 1984.*

Baird, Douglas G., Gertner, Robert H., and Randal, Picker C., Game Theory and the Law, *Harvard University Press, Cambridge, MA, 1994.*

Becker, Gary S., and Becker, Guity Nashat, The Economics of Life, *McGraw-Hill, New York, 1997.*

Boone, Louis E., Quotable Business, *second edition, Random House, New York, 1999.*

Brandenburger, Adam M., and Nalebuf, Barry J., Co-operation, *Doubleday, New York, 1996.*

Browning, D. C., Dictionary of Quotations and Proverbs, *Cathay Books, London, 1989.*

Carter, Stephen L., The Emperor of Ocean Park, *Alfred A. Knopf, New York, 2002.*

Clotfelter, Charles T., and Cook, Philip J., Selling Hope, *Harvard University Press, Cambridge, MA, 1989.*

Davis, Morton D., Game Theory: A Nontechnical Introduction, *Dover Publications, Mineola, NY, 1970.*

Dixit, Avinash K., and Nalebuff, Barry J., Thinking Strategically, *W. W. Norton & Company, New York, 1991.*

Dixit, Avinash, & Skeath, Susan, Games of Strategy, *W. W. Norton & Company, New York, 1999.*

Felton, Debbie, and Miller, James D., "Truth Inducement in Greek Myth," Syllecta Classica, *13: 104–125, 2002.*

Gibbons, Robert, Game Theory for Applied Economists, *Princeton University Press, Princeton, NJ, 1992.*

Gintis, Herbert, Game Theory Evolving, *Princeton University Press, Princeton, NJ, 2000.*

Harvard Business School, "Microsoft, 1995" (Abridged), Case No. 799–003, *Harvard University Press, Cambridge, MA, 1996.*

Hills, J. D., The Fifth Leicestershire: 1914–1918, *Echo Press, Loughborough, U.K., 1919.*

Klein, Benjamin, Crawford, Robert, and Alchian, Armen, "Vertical Integration, Appropriable Rents, and the Competitive Contracting Process," Journal of Law and Economics, *21 (October): 297–326, 1978.*

Lee, Kuan Yew, From Third World to First, *HarperCollins, New York, 2000.*

Lessig, Lawrence, The Future of Ideas, *Random House, New York, 2001.*

Machiavelli, Niccolo, The Prince, *1514.*

Malkiel, Burton G., Random Walk down Wall Street, *W. W. Norton, New York, 1973.*

Mankiw, N. Gregory, Principles of Microeconomics, *second edition, Harcourt College Publishers, Fort Worth, TX, 2001.*

McArdle, Megan, "The Agency Problem," posted on *www.JaneGalt.net, April 12, 2002.*

McMillan, John, Games, Strategies, and Managers, *Oxford University Press, New York, 1992.*

Milgrom, Paul, and Roberts, John, The Economics, Organization, and Management, *Prentice Hall, Englewood Cliffs, NJ, 1992.*

Miller, James D., & Felton, Debbie, "Using Greek Mythology to Teach Game Theory," The American Economist, *forthcoming.*

Nasar, Sylvia, A Beautiful Mind: A Biography of John Forbes Nash, Jr., Winner of the Nobel Prize in Economics, *Simon & Schuster, New York, 1998.*

Posner, Richard A., Economic Analysis of Law, *5th edition, Aspen Law & Business, New York, 1998.*

Posner, Richard A., Sex and Reason, *Harvard University Press, Cambridge, MA, 1992.*

Poundstone, William, Prisoner's Dilemma, *Anchor Books, Doubleday, New York, 1992.*

Rose, H. I., Hygini Fabulae, *A.W. Sythoff, Lyden, 1933.*

Schelling, Thomas C., The Strategy of Conflict, *Harvard University Press, Cambridge, MA, 1999.*

Shapiro, Carl, and Varian, Hal R., Information Rules, *Harvard Business School Press, Boston, 1999.*

Smith, John Maynard, Evolution and the Theory of Games, *Cambridge University Press, Cambridge, 1982.*

Spence, M., "Job Market Signaling," Quarterly Journal of Economics, *87:355–374, 1973.*

The Sveriges Riksbank (Bank of Sweden) Prize in Economic Sciences in Memory of Alfred Nobel, press release, October 11, 1994.

Watson, Joel, Strategy: An Introduction to Game Theory, *W.W. Norton & Company, New York, 2002.*

Magazine Article References

Campaign for America, *Warren E. Buffett, "The Billionaire's Buyout Plan," September 10, 2000.*

CNBC.com, James Miller, "Bundling Doesn't Always Boost Profits," February 15, 2000.

CNBC.com, James Miller, "Long View Affects Day Traders, too" April 25, 2000.

CNET News.com, Larry Dignan, "Blunders Aplenty in AT&T, @Home talks," December 4, 2001.

Dismal.com, James Miller, "Genetic Testing and Health Insurance," August 17, 2000.

Forbes.com, Dick Teresi, "The Wild One," May 3, 1999.

MSNBC.com, Margaret Kane, "AT&T to Offer Flat-Rate Long Distance," February 6, 2002.

New York Times, *Roger Lowenstein, "Into Thin Air," February 17, 2002.*

Red Herring, *J. P. Vicente, "Toxic Treatment," May 31, 2001.*

Salon.com, Charles Taylor, book review of Koba the Dread, *July 16, 2002.*

Slate.com, Jennifer Howard, "The Relentless March Upward of the American Shoe Size," May 10, 2002.

Slate.com, Steven E. Landsburg, "Sell Me a Story," September 6, 2001.

Slate.com, Chris Mohney, "Changing Lines," July 3, 2002.

The Wall Street Journal, *Aaron Lucchetti, "Fidelity Uses Voting Threats to Fight Excessive CEO Pay," July 12, 2002.*

The Wall Street Journal, *Sholnn Freeman, "GM, Ford to Offer Discounts Amid Signs of Softening Sales," July 2, 2002.*

The Wall Street Journal, *Jennifer Ordonez, "Pop Singer Fails to Strike a Chord Despite the Millions Spent by MCA," February 26, 2002.*

The Wall Street Journal, *Scott McCartney, "We'll Be Landing in Kansas So the Crew Can Grab a Steak," September 9, 1998.*

STUDY QUESTIONS

It signifies nothing to play well if you lose.

CHAPTER 2. THREATS, PROMISES, AND SEQUENTIAL GAMES

1. What is the likely outcome to the game in Figure 47?

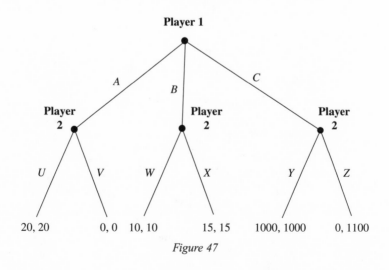

Figure 47

2. What is the likely outcome to the centipede game in Figure 48?

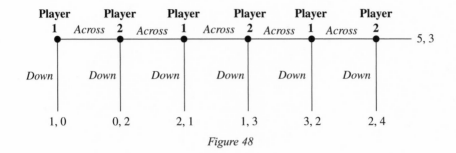

Figure 48

3. In the games in Figures 49, 50, and 51, Player Two threatens to be mean to Player One if Player One is first mean to Player Two. In which games is Player Two's threat to retaliate credible?

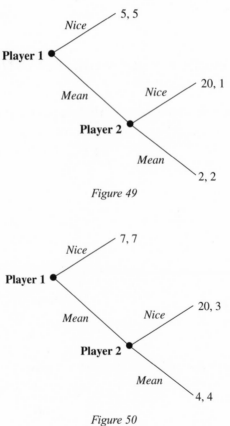

Figure 49

Figure 50

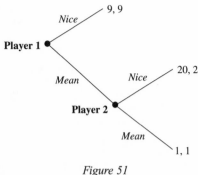

Figure 51

4. Yesterday you bought a movie ticket for $8. When you arrive at the theater today you realize the ticket is lost. Should you buy another ticket?[2]

CHAPTER 3. THE DANGERS OF PRICE COMPETITION

5. Assume that three people *secretly* write down a dollar amount on a piece of paper. They must pick a whole dollar amount between $0 and $100. The person who writes down the lowest number wins the amount she wrote down. If there is a tie, the winners split the total. Thus if:

Person one writes down $53 and

Person two writes down $22 and

Person three writes down $30,

then person two wins $22. If person three had also written down $22 rather than $30, then persons two and three would have each received $11 because they would have split the $22. Find the reasonable outcome in this game when all players are rational.

CHAPTER 4. SIMULTANEOUS GAMES

6. For the games in Figures 52, 53, 54 identify which is a coordination game, an outguessing game, and a chicken game.

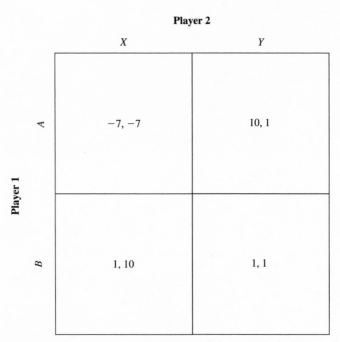

Figure 52

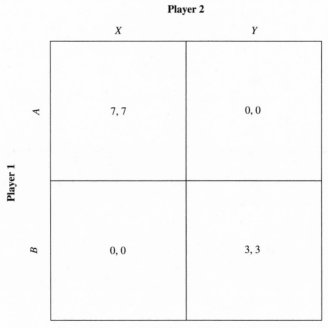

Figure 53

Player 2

		X	Y
Player 1	A	7, −3	0, 5
	B	0, 5	7, −3

Figure 54

7. Solve the game in Figure 55 by eliminating the strictly stupid strategies.

Player 2

		W	X	Y
Player 1	A	10, 1	30, 0	5, 4
	B	0, 5	100, 0	0, 1
	C	2, 2	100, 0	4, 8

Figure 55

8. Assume that you are Player Two in the games in Figures 56, 57, and 58. In each of the games first you make your move, then you have the option of letting Player One see how you move. Finally Player One gets to move. In which of the three games would you want Player One to see how you moved?

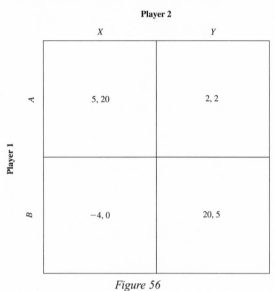

Figure 56

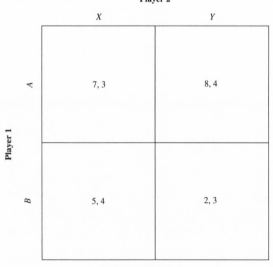

Figure 57

Player 2

	W	X	Y
A	5, 1	1, 4	0, 2
B	3, 0	4, 4	1, 3
C	4, 0	0, 1	4, 4

Figure 58

CHAPTER 5. MASSIVE COORDINATION GAMES

9. How does QWERT relate to massive coordination games and network externalities?

CHAPTER 6. NASH EQUILIBRIA

10. Identify all the Nash equilibria in the games in Figures 59, 60, and 61.

11. Two firms can produce widgets. It costs firm one $10 to produce each widget, and it costs firm two $13 to produce each widget. Both firms choose the selling price of their widgets. The customers will buy their widgets from whomever charges the least. If the firms set the same price, all customers, for some reason, go to firm one. What is the Nash equilibrium of this game?

Player 2

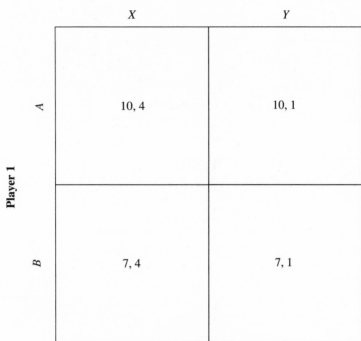

Figure 59

Player 2

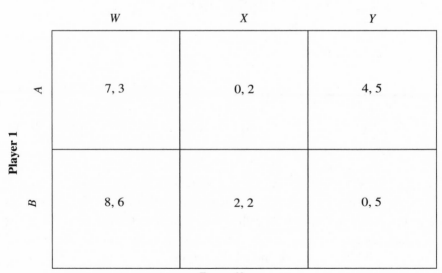

Figure 60

Player 2

	X	Y
A	1, −1	−1, 1
B	−1, 1	1, −1

Figure 61

CHAPTER 7. PRISONERS' DILEMMA

12. Identify which of the games in Figures 62–65 are prisoners' dilemma games.

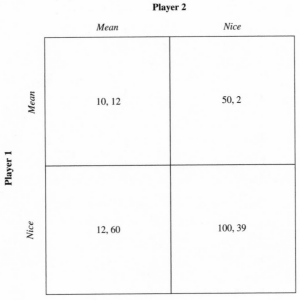

Player 2

	Mean	Nice
Mean	10, 12	50, 2
Nice	12, 60	100, 39

Figure 62

Player 2

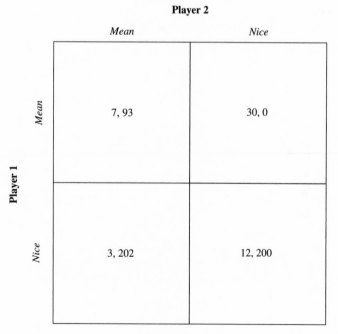

Figure 63

Player 2

Figure 64

Player 2

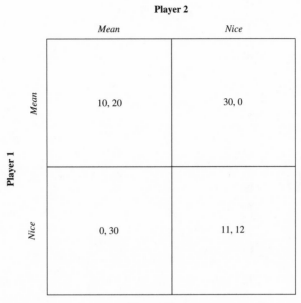

Figure 65

13. Both prisoners' dilemma games in Figures 66 and 67 are played repeatedly with no definite last period. In which game are the players more likely to betray each other?

Player 2

Figure 66

Player 2

	Nice	Mean
Nice	20, 20	0, 35
Mean	35, 0	5, 5

Figure 67

14. Both prisoners' dilemma games in Figures 68 and 69 are played repeatedly with no definite last period. In which game are the players more likely to betray each other?

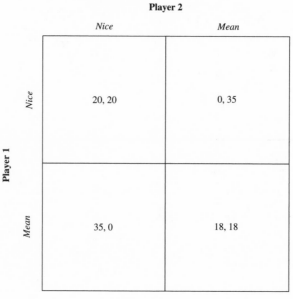

Player 2

	Nice	Mean
Nice	20, 20	0, 35
Mean	35, 0	18, 18

Figure 68

Player 2

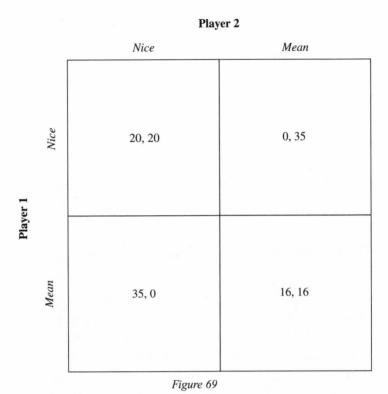

Figure 69

CHAPTER 8. ADVERSE SELECTION

15. After moving, you try to find a new dentist. Why might you want to make an appointment only with a dentist who couldn't schedule you in for at least several months?

16. You put $100 in nine envelopes and nothing in the 10th envelope. The envelopes are shuffled. Debbie picks one envelope at random and examines its contents. Jim offers to buy the envelope Debbie picked for some amount of money that Jim chooses. When Jim makes his offer, he does not know what is in Debbie's envelope. Debbie either accepts Jim's offer or rejects the offer and keeps the envelope. How much should Jim offer to buy Debbie's envelope for?

17. You want to buy a car, but you are unsure of its value. You estimate that it is equally likely that the car is of high quality or it's junk.

The seller knows the car's quality. The following gives the value of the car to both you and the seller.

Car's Quality	Value To You	Value to Seller
High	$10,000	$6,000
Junk	$0	

In the game you make an offer to buy the car. If the offer is rejected, the game ends. Even though there is a 50 percent chance that the car is of high quality, you should still not offer to pay anything for it. Why?

CHAPTER 9. SURVIVING WITH LIMITED INFORMATION

18. Let's Make a Deal

You are on a game show and are offered a choice of three closed boxes. Two boxes are empty, but the third contains an expensive prize. You don't know which box has the prize, but the host does. You are first told to choose one of the boxes. Next, the game show host will pick an empty box that you didn't choose and open it, showing that it's empty. Finally, the host gives you the option to change boxes. You can switch from the box you picked to the other unopened box. Is there any advantage in switching boxes?

19. The 99 Percent Accurate AIDS Test

You have just taken an AIDS test. You know a lot about how AIDS is transmitted, and, thankfully, you are almost certain that you don't have the disease. Anything is possible, however, and you estimate that there is a 1/100,000 chance that you have AIDS.

The AIDS test you took is good but not perfect. The test is 99 percent accurate. This means that if you do have AIDS, the test is 99 percent likely to give you a positive result, while if you don't have AIDS, there will be a 99 percent chance that the test results will come back negative.

You get back your test results, and they are positive. How concerned should you be?

20. Newcomb's Problem

A super-intelligent being places two closed boxes in front of you. Box A always contains $1,000. Box B contains either $1 million or nothing. You are given a choice of either taking only box A, or taking both boxes A and B.

Your choice might seem simple, but this super-intelligent being is very good at making predictions. If he thinks you are going to pick only box B, he will put $1 million in that box. If he thinks you are going to be greedy and pick both boxes, he will leave box B empty. Which box(es) should you pick? Remember that the being makes his choice before you make yours. This question is known as Newcomb's Problem.

21. John and Kim negotiate over the sale of Kim's car. The car is worth $5,000 to John and $3,000 to Kim. Both people know everything about the car, so there is no concern about adverse selection. John makes an offer to buy the car. If the offer is rejected, the game ends. What offer should John make?

22. Abe owns an antique that Bill wants. Abe values the antique at $3,000, and Bill values it at $5,000. Without knowing anything about how the negotiations will be conducted, what can we guess might happen?

23. Use the same facts as in question 22, but now consider that Cindy also wants to buy the antique. Cindy is willing to pay $5,000 for it. Without knowing anything about how the negotiations will be conducted except that Bill and Cindy won't collude, what can we guess might happen?

ANSWERS TO STUDY QUESTIONS

1. Player One picks A, and Player Two chooses U. This outcome gives each player a payoff of 20. Player One will not choose C because if he did, Player Two would maximize her payoff by picking Z, which would give Player One a payoff of zero. Player Two would like to be able to credibly promise Player One that if Player One picks C, she will pick Y. Such a promise, however, lacks credibility because given that Player One picks C, Player Two gets a higher payoff by choosing Z over Y.

2. Player One should immediately move down ending the game. If the game were to reach the final node, Player Two would move down to get a payoff of 4, rather than move across and get only 3. Consequently, at the second to last node Player One should move down to get

3 rather than move across and get only 2 when Player Two moves down. You can similarly show that each player is always better off moving down than across. This outcome seems very wasteful because had the parties worked together and made it to the last node, they both would have done much better. Unfortunately, as in much of game theory, rational mistrust dooms the players to low payoffs.

3. This threat is credible only in Figures 49 and 50. Player Two's threat to be mean is only credible if (given that Player One is mean) Player Two is better off being mean than nice.

4. You should buy another ticket. The lost $8 is an irrelevant sunk cost that you should ignore. Unless you have acquired new information about the movie, if it was worth $8 yesterday to attend it should still be worth $8 today.

5. Answer: All three people choose $1.

First, note that no one should ever write down $100. If you choose $100, the best possible result for you is if your two opponents also write down $100. (If either one of them wrote down any other number, you would get nothing.) In this case you would win $33.33. If everyone else wrote down $100, however, you would be better off writing down $99 because if your two opponents wrote down $100, you would win $99. Thus, in the only circumstance where writing down $100 wins you money, you would have been better off writing down $99. Consequently, writing down $99 always gives you a better or equal payoff than writing down $100. Thus, you should never choose $100, and you should assume that no one else will ever pick $100.

Since $100 will never be chosen, no player should write down $99. If you were to choose $99, your only hope to win would be if both of your opponents also wrote down $99 (since neither of your foes will pick $100). In this case, however, you would only win $33. If both of your opponents wrote down $99, you would have been better off writing down $98 because then you wouldn't have to split the money. Thus, in the only possible circumstance when you could win with $99, you're better off writing down $98. Consequently, you should never write down $99. Can you see the pattern emerging?

Should you ever write down $98? Well, since no one is going to pick $99 or $100, the only chance to win with $98 is if both of the others also choose $98. In this case, however, you would have been better off writing down $97. Thus, $98 is out. This process continues all the way down to $1. You don't want to pick $0 because then you would always get nothing. You would rather split $1 than get zero. Therefore, the only reasonable outcome in this game is where everyone chooses $1. It seems very wasteful that all of you split $1 when you could all have split $100. The logic of game theory, however, compels the players of this game to bid against each other and throw away almost all of the available money.

6. Figure 52 is a chicken game, Figure 53 is a coordination game, and Figure 54 is an outguessing game. In Figure 52 the macho strategies are A for Player One and X for Player Two. If one player chooses the macho strategy, and the other, the wimpy strategy, the player who takes the macho course will do much better than his opponent.

Figure 53 is a coordination game because the parties want to work with each other to get either A,X or B,Y. The players should be open with each other about their moves. If Player One is going to play A, she wants Player Two to know this so that Player Two will play X. Similarly, if Player One is going to play B, she also wants Player Two to be aware of his move so that Player Two will pick Y rather than X.

Figure 54 is an outguessing game because both players want to keep their strategy secret. Thus, Player One would want to keep his move secret and force Player Two to try to outguess him. Player Two would want to adopt a similar outguessing strategy.

7. A,Y; First eliminate strategy X for Player Two (draw a line through it.) When strategy X is eliminated, you can eliminate strategy B for Player One (draw a line through this), because Player One would only consider playing B if Player Two would play X. Now you can eliminate choice W for Player Two. Finally, you can eliminate strategy C for Player One. This results in Player One picking A and Player Two picking Y.

8. Figure 56 is a chicken game with B and X as the macho strategies. Player Two would want to play X and then reveal to Player One what she did so it would be in Player One's interest to play A.

In Figure 57 Player One has a dominant strategy of A that he will always play. Thus, it does not matter whether Player One sees Player Two's move since Player One will always make the same choice.

For Figure 58 note that strategy W for Player Two is a strictly stupid strategy and will never be played (draw a line through it). After strategy W is eliminated, strategy A for Player One becomes a strictly stupid strategy, and it too should be eliminated. The resulting game is a coordination game where the players want to play either B and X or play X and Y. As in all coordination games, Player Two wants Player One to know how she is going to move.

9. QWERT is the first five letters on the top left of almost all English language keyboards. It's practical for everyone to use the same keyboard, so it's easy for people to switch from using one keyboard to another. As a result, most keyboard users have coordinated on this same type of keyboard arrangement.

10. In Figure 59 A,X is the only Nash equilibrium. A is a dominant strategy for Player One, and X is a dominant strategy for Player Two. Since a dominant strategy gives a player the highest payoff no matter what, a player would always regret not playing a dominant strategy. Thus, if a dominant strategy exists, a player must play it in any Nash equilibrium.

In Figure 60 A,Y and B,W are the Nash equilibria. If Player One plays A, Player Two cannot do any better than playing Y, so Player Two would be happy playing Y in response to A. Similarly, if Player Two chooses Y, Player One cannot do any better than playing A. Thus A,Y is a Nash equilibrium. By similar logic one can show that B,W is also a Nash equilibrium. X is a strictly stupid strategy for Player Two, so it will never be part of any Nash equilibrium since Player Two will always be unhappy playing X. A,W is not a Nash equilibrium because if Player Two Plays W, Player One would be unhappy playing A because he would get a higher payoff picking B. B,Y is not a Nash equilibrium because if Player One picks B, Player Two would regret playing Y since he would have gotten a higher payoff playing W in response to B.

Figure 61 is the matching pennies game we have previously seen, and it is also an outguessing game. Recall that in an outguessing game the players always randomize. In this game there is no Nash equilibrium where either player always plays one strategy. For example, if Player One played A and Player Two played X, then Player Two would regret not playing Y in response to Player One choosing A. For any of the four possible combinations (A,X; A,Y; B,X; and B,Y) one of the players would always regret his choice. Although this book hasn't fully motivated this result, there is a Nash equilibrium where each player randomizes and picks each strategy half the time.

11. There is a Nash equilibrium where both firms charge $13. This outcome is a Nash equilibrium because if firm two charges $13, firm one gets no customers if it charges more than $13, and all the customers if it charges $13 or less. Thus, firm one's optimal response to firm two's charging $13 is for it to charge $13, too. If firm one charges $13, then there is no possible way for firm two ever to make a profit. If it charges less than $13 (which is firm two's cost of production), then firm two would actually lose money on every sale. If firm two charges $13 or more, then it would get no customers. Thus, if firm one charges $13, firm two would not regret charging $13 because it could not possibly do better.

There does not exist a Nash equilibrium where either firm charges more than $13. If this occurred, each firm would want to slightly undercut the other and take all the customers. There can't be a Nash equilibrium where a firm charges an amount below its cost and loses money, because such a firm would rather charge a very high amount and get no customers.

There are, however, many other Nash equilibria besides the one where both firms charge $13. It's a Nash equilibrium for both firms to charge the same price if that price is between $10 and $13. In these equilibria all the customers will, by assumption, go to firm one, so firm two will make zero profit. Recall, however, that if firm one charges less than $13, it's impossible for firm two to make money anyway. Thus, if firm one charges less than $13, firm two does not regret a strategy that gives it zero (as opposed to a negative) profit. Furthermore, if firm two is charging between $10 and $13, firm one can still make a profit on each customer, so it wants to charge the highest possible price and still take all the customers. Thus, if firm two charges between $10 and $13, firm one's optimal response is to charge the same price.

12. The games in Figures 63 and 64 are prisoners' dilemmas. To be a prisoners' dilemma game, a dominant strategy for both players is to be mean, and both players must be better off at the nice, nice outcome than the mean, mean one. Figure 62 is not a prisoners' dilemma game because Player One has a dominant strategy of being nice. Figure 65 is not a prisoners' dilemma game because Player Two is better off at the mean, mean outcome than the nice, nice outcome.

13. If your opponent is being nice, you get an extra 2 from being mean in Figure 66 and an extra 15 from being mean in Figure 67. Con-

sequently, betrayal is more profitable (and thus more likely) in Figure 67.

14. Once you betray your opponent, you are likely to end up at the mean, mean outcome. The worse this outcome is, the less benefit there is to treachery. Consequently, betrayal is more costly (and thus less likely) in Figure 69.

15. A patient should most want to see a dentist who pleases his current patients and as a result continually gets repeat and new customers. Such a dentist would necessarily have a long waiting list for new patients. A bad dentist who quickly lost customers would have a lot of free time available. The type of dentist who could schedule you for the earliest appointment might be the type whom you should least trust to put sharp instruments in your mouth.

16. Jim should offer to buy the envelope for $0. If Jim offered to buy the envelope for any positive amount less than $100, Debbie would accept only if the envelope was empty. For example, if Jim offered to buy the envelope for $5, Debbie would take the $5 if the envelope was empty and reject the money if it had $100. Thus, Jim is better off offering $0 than $5.

17. If you offer to buy the car for less than $6,000 the seller will always reject your offer if the car is of high quality. So, for example, if you offer to buy the car for $200, 50 percent of the time your offer will be rejected, and 50 percent of the time it will be accepted, but you will have paid $200 for worthless junk. Consequently, you never want to offer a positive amount less than $6,000. If you pay $6,000 or more, then you will get a high-quality car only one-half of the time. Thus, one-half of the time you get something worth $10,000, and one-half of the time you get junk, giving you on average something worth $5,000. You shouldn't pay $6,000 or more for something worth on average only $5,000.

18. Answer: Let's Make a Deal

You should definitely change boxes. Let's label the three boxes as A, B, and C and assume that you picked box A. Obviously there is a 1/3 probability that the prize is in box A and a 2/3 probability that the prize is in either box B or C. Either or both boxes B or C are empty. Thus, after you pick box A, it will always be possible for the host to open either box B and C to reveal an empty box. Consequently, the host's actions do not affect the probability of the prize being in box A.

Before the host opened one of the two other boxes, there was a 1/3 chance of the prize being in box A, and after he opened one of the other boxes, there is still a 1/3 chance of the prize being in box A. Let's say that the host opened box B and showed you that it was empty. Now, since there is a 1/3 chance that box A has the prize, and a zero chance that box B has the prize, there must be a 2/3 chance that box C has the prize. Consequently, you should switch to box C because it will double your chance of winning.

19. Answer: The 99 percent Accurate AIDS Test

You actually shouldn't be that worried since you almost certainly don't have AIDS. To see this, imagine that 1,000,000 people, who are just like you, take the test. Each of these people has a 1/100,000 chance of having AIDS. Thus, of these 1,000,000 people, 10 have the disease and 999,990 are free of it. When these people get tested, probably nine or ten of the people with AIDS will get back positive results. Of the 999,990 who don't have the disease 1 percent will get false positives. This means that there will be about 10,000 false positives. Consequently the vast majority of people who get positive results got false positives. Your chance of actually having AIDS after getting the positive test results are only about 1/1,000.

This result seems very paradoxical since the test is 99 percent accurate. After getting your tests results, however, you have two pieces of information: the tests results and your initial belief that you almost certainly didn't have AIDS. You don't lose the second piece of information just because of the positive test results; rather the test results should be used to update your beliefs. These two pieces of information need to be combined. When you (sort of) average the 1/100,000 chance of having AIDS with the 99 percent chance of not having AIDS, you get an approximate 1/1,000 chance of having the disease.

20. Answer: Newcomb's Problem

There is no generally accepted answer to Newcomb's problem. Since the super-intelligent being has already made his decision before you decided what box to pick, it would seem reasonable always to take both boxes. After all, regardless of whether he put any money in box B, you're always better off taking both boxes. Of course, if the being really is able to predict your move, and you pick both boxes, you will get only $1,000; whereas if you took only box B, you would get $1 million.

21. John should offer to buy the car for just over $3,000. Since Kim must either accept the offer or allow negotiations to end, if she is rational, she will accept any offer over $3,000.

22. Abe will sell the antique for some price between $3,000 and $5,000.

23. Abe will sell the antique to either Bill or Cindy for $5,000. There is no other reasonable outcome. It would be unreasonable, for example, to assume that Abe would sell the good to Bill for $4,800, because Cindy would be willing to offer Bill more than this. As long as the price is below $5,000, we don't have a stable outcome, because the buyer who didn't get the good would be willing to pay more.

NOTES

CHAPTER 1

1 Browning (1989), 384.

CHAPTER 2

1 *The Prince* (1514), Chap. 18.

2 Dixit and Nalebuff (1991), 152–153.

3 Schelling (1960), 19.

4 Davis (1970), 107–108.

5 Ibid.

6 *Red Herring* (May 31, 2001).

7 *Wall Street Journal* (June 12, 2002).

8 Dixit and Nalebuff (1991), 16–19.

9 Schelling (1960), 17.

CHAPTER 3

1 Boone (1999), 114.

2 See also Brandenburger and Nalebuff (1996), 222–228.

3 Ibid., 225.

4 Ibid., 134–138.

CHAPTER 4

1 Browning (1989), 389.

2 *Wall Street Journal* (July 2, 2002).

3 Game theorists use the phrase "dominated strategies," but this phrase can be confusing since it looks and sounds like "dominant strategies." Consequently I have decided to substitute the more scientific sounding "strictly stupid" for the term "dominated."

4 Campaign for America (September 12, 2000).

5 Shouldn't a rational taxpayer realize the benefits his government provides him and thus gladly pay his taxes? No! If you alone didn't pay taxes then the total tax revenue the government receives would be only trivially smaller. Consequently, by not paying taxes you would save a lot of money but not notice any reduction in governmental services. Shouldn't a potential taxpayer worry that if many people didn't pay their taxes then the government would have to cut back on services? Again, no! Your not paying taxes is certainly not going to cause many other people to not pay their taxes. (Especially because if you become a tax cheat you will probably not advertise your activities.) Furthermore, if many other people are not planning on paying their taxes there is probably nothing that you can do about it. Consequently, it is best for you to ignore whether other people will pay their taxes and just concentrate on how you can minimize your tax burden.

6 Actually, most sensible people would be better off never playing the classic game of chicken. If a sensible person somehow found herself in such a game the optimal strategy would simply be to turn at the earliest possible moment. The classic chicken game assumes, however, that both players desperately want to be perceived as macho.

7 CNET News.com (December 4, 2001).

8 See Dixit and Skeath (1999), 110–112.

9 Dixit and Skeath (1999) provide an interesting and readable game theoretic analysis of the Cuban missile crises in Chapter 13 of their textbook.

10 See McMillan (1992), 73–74.

CHAPTER 5

1 "Microsoft, 1995 (Abridged)," Harvard Business School Case No. 799–1003, 1.

2 Lessig, 63.

3 Ibid.

4 Ibid., 51.

5 Watson (2002), 88.

6 MSNBC.com (February 6, 2002).

7 Clotfelter and Cook (1989), 9.

CHAPTER 6

1 The Sveriges Riksbank (Bank of Sweden) Prize in Economic Sciences in Memory of Alfred Nobel, press release, October 11, 1994.

2 In the movie, John Nash rushes out of the bar after formulating his strategy so we never see if it could have been successfully implemented.

3 See Dixit and Nalebuff (1991), 248–250.

4 *Slate* (May 10, 2002) provides a non-game theoretic analysis of this issue.

5 Ibid.

6 Ibid.

7 Ibid.

CHAPTER 7

1 Browning (1989), 364.

2 I am assuming that both criminals would rather receive a punishment of life in prison than be executed.

3 See McMillan (1992), 118–119.

4 If there were a smart pill that would give me a slight chance of getting cancer but also give me a reasonable shot of winning a Nobel Prize in economics, I would probably swallow it.

5 It's true that some professional basketball players can make large salaries through endorsements. But they are able to do this only because of their prior success in their sport. As a result, endorsement money can be seen as part of an athlete's basketball salary, although a part not paid by his team.

6 In economics such a phenomenon is called a "backward-bending supply curve." As people get richer they usually desire greater leisure time. Paying someone a higher salary makes a person richer and consequently could cause him to work less.

7 Carter (2002), 111.

8 McMillan (1992), 66 applies prisoners' dilemma to the oil extraction problem.

9 Ibid.

10 Gibbons (1992), 224–225.

11 See Axelrod (1984), 110–113.

12 Ibid., 77.

13 See Axelrod (1984), 86 who cites Hills (1919), 96.

14 See Axelrod (1984), 78–79.

15 See Axelrod (1984), Chapter 4.

16 Brandenburger and Nalebuff (1996), 161–169.

17 See Smith (1982).

CHAPTER 8

1 Akerlof (1970).

2 This example is taken from Milgrom (1992), 154.

3 Browning (1989), 359.

CHAPTER 9

1 Browning (1989), 353.

2 Lee (2000), 62.

3 Ibid.

4 Spence (1973).

5 See Gintis (2000), 307–308.

6 See Dixit and Skeath (1999), 404.

7 Many Smith College students have told me that it would indeed be embarrassing to be seen kissing a 13-, 14-, 15-, or 16-year-old boy.

8 See Baird, Gertner, and Picker (1994), 79–121.

9 Rose (1933), 96.

10 *Slate* (September 6, 2001).

CHAPTER 10

1 See Felton and Miller (2002), 104–125; and Miller and Felton (2002).

2 Slate.com (July 3, 2002).

3 Watson (2002), 155–156.

4 Based on CNBC.com (February 15, 2000).

CHAPTER 11

1 Browning (1989), 236.

2 117 F. 99 (9th Cir. 1902). See Posner (1998), 110–111 for a full discussion of this case.

3 Lessig (2001), 53.

4 Ibid.

5 Ibid. My emphasis.

6 This section is based upon the outstanding article "Into Thin Air" by Roger Lowenstein, *The New York Times Magazine,* 2/17/2002.

7 Ibid.

8 Ibid.

9 *The Wall Street Journal* (February 26, 2002).

10 See Lessig (2001), 214 for a brief discussion of this issue.

11 See Watson (2002), 201–205.

12 Facts and analysis based on Klein (1978).

CHAPTER 12

1 Boone (1999), 167.

2 *Wall Street Journal* (September 8, 1998).

3 Ibid.

4 Ibid.

5 Forbes.com (May 3, 1999).

6 Ibid.

7 Professors can still be fired for gross misconduct such as sexual harassment.

8 See Dismal.com (August 17, 2000).

CHAPTER 13

1 Browning (1989), 417.

2 See McMillan (1992), 95.

3 Ibid.

4 *Salon* (July 16, 2002).

5 Employee stock ownership also unnecessarily increases a worker's risk. If her company goes bankrupt, she would lose not only her job but also much of her savings. From the point of view of risk allocation, an employee would be far better off owning stock in her company's main competitor because if the competitor beats her company, she would (probably) have more limited short-term career options but greater financial wealth. Many employees at Enron learned this lesson when Enron's company's stock price plummeted after the employees had invested most of their retirement savings in Enron stock.

6 Posted on April 12, 2002, and printed here with her permission.

CHAPTER 14

1 Boone (1999), 113.

2 McMillan (1992), 49.

3 Ibid., 56.

4 Brandenburger and Nalebuff (1996), 83–85.

5 See McMillan (1992), 55.

6 Schelling (1960), 29.

7 See Dixit and Nalebuff (1991), 292–295.

8 Ibid., 293–294.

9 Schelling (1960), 27.

CHAPTER 15

1 Browning (1989), 360.

2 I'm assuming that at least two bids exceed the seller-specified reserve price.

CHAPTER 16

1 Browning (1989), 378.

2 CNBC.com (April 25, 2000).

INDEX

James D. Miller is an assistant professor of economics at Smith College. He has a Ph.D. in economics from the University of Chicago and a J.D. from Stanford Law School. He has written on game theory in Greek mythology, computer encryption, perjury law, e-commerce, investing, genetic testing, Internet piracy and lotteries. His work has appeared in popular and professional resources including the *Orlando Sentinel*, *The Weekly Standard*, *International Review of Law and Economics*, *Tech Central Station*, *Journal of Information*, *Law and Technology*, and the Internet sites for *National Review*, CNBC, and Fox News.